JOHN TOSHACK

FourFourTwo | *great footballers*

Chris Hughes

First published in Great Britain in 2002 by
Virgin Books Ltd
Thames Wharf Studios
Rainville Road
London W6 9HA

ISBN 0 7535 0667 X

Photography © Empics

Typeset by TW Typesetting, Plymouth, Devon

Printed and bound in Great Britain by
Mackays of Chatham PLC

Contents

Acknowledgements

First, thanks to Dave Cottrell, Jonathan Taylor and Cormac Bourne for asking me to do it. Respect to Phil Ball, Jeff King and Huw Richards for their magnificent assistance. Thanks to John Aldridge, Ian Callaghan, Pedro Estevao, Peter Jackson, Ronnie Moran, Kevin Richardson and Tommy Smith for their thoughts. And thanks to everybody on the *Liverpool Matchday Magazine*, truly the planet's greatest football magazine.

Neatly, Toshack was in the dugout during the first proper football match I ever saw, so thanks to my dad for standing with me in the cold that night, and for all those Anfield Reviews, and to mum, Christine and Matthew.

Chris Hughes
January 2002

Introduction

It's just before 9.30 on a Saturday night in Bilbao. It might be January but it's a mild evening in northern Spain, the temperature touching 60 degrees before kick-off. And John Toshack is giving his team talk ahead of one of the most important matches of Real Sociedad's entire season, the *derbi* against their fiercest rivals in the Basque country, Athletic Bilbao. Local pride's on the line tonight.

Toshack's final instructions to his players aren't complicated. Keep it tight. Real have one of the leakiest defences in *La Liga*, which goes a long way to explaining why they're firmly anchored in the relegation zone. Real's dressing room is a cosmopolitan place. Norwegian sits next to Yugoslav, Dutchman alongside Turk and Brazilian. But no Spaniards. Toshack has been talking about relaxing the club's ban on recruiting non-Basque Spaniards, but for now it's natives and imports only at Real Sociedad. Athletic, despite a long history of English coaches, remains a Basque stronghold.

In black tracksuit and white trainers, Toshack follows his players up the tunnel steps, into the heart of the Estadio San Mames, a pleasingly old-fashioned, tight sort of ground, known locally as *La Catedral*, the 40,000 unsegregated supporters forming a coalition of the red and white stripes of Athletic, and the blue and white of Real, studded here and there by the Basque flag, a red, green and white take on the Union Jack.

Throughout the match, the revolving advertising boards around the pitch will spool through adverts for Ericsson, Siemens and Vodafone. Not that Toshack would take much notice, for he refuses to own a mobile phone or a credit card. History is against him tonight. In the history of the fixture, Athletic have won 47 to Real's 36. Add to that the fact that Real are second from bottom in the standings, having made their worst ever start to the season, while Athletic are fifth from top, and the omens aren't good.

In their last meeting, Athletic won 3–1 in San Sebastian on the opening day of the season. Nobody had expected that Real would struggle again this season after being rescued last year by their prodigal coach, but for 17 of the 19 weeks of the campaign so far, Real have been in the bottom four. Three points this evening would move Real out of the relegation zone and Toshack out of the ulcer zone.

Heading for the dugout, Toshack stops for a word and an embrace with Athletic's coach Jupp Heynckes, the Dutchman he first encountered while playing for Liverpool against Borussia Moenchengladbach in the 1970s. More recently, both have coached arguably the planet's biggest football club, Real Madrid – and both picked up the gold Rolex after getting the sack.

In the opening minutes, Real look confident, passing the ball with a fluency that belies their League position, and Athletic are restricted to a couple of long shots. Six minutes in, Francisco De Pedro streaks down the left, before laying off the ball to Inaki Idiakez, who whips in an immaculate cross to striker Darko Kovacevic. But the Yugoslav misfires, putting his shot inches to the right of the far post. It's Real's first chance, but Kovacevic, back for his second shift in San Sebastian after an unhappy spell in *Serie A*, can be forgiven, his brother having died barely a week ago. On the bench, Toshack is starting to look pensive.

Athletic respond. From a corner, Ismael Urzaiz directs his header to the right of Real keeper Sander Westerveld's goal. The home side are starting to trouble Real down the left, and when the frustrated Aitor Lopez Rekarte fouls Santi Esquerro, he's forced to avoid a barrage of bottles from the Athletic fans.

In midfield, however, Real's Xabi Alonso is coping with an assurance far beyond his nineteen years. He's just the latest in the long line of prospects to be thrown in at the deep end by Toshack and perform like Mark Spitz. Back in the dugout, Toshack has started rubbing his hands together.

In comes another cross, this time from Rekarte, and Kovacevic, looking as if he's enjoyed a little too much *carbonara* during his time in Italy, is again just inches away. Toshack is now off the bench, prowling around the technical area. All week he's been off radar, maintaining a media silence, but he's making up for it now.

Athletic are getting on top, and he's now virtually on the touchline, and the fourth official has the unenviable job of ushering him back to his seat after Kovecevic is punished for a dubious foul on Jesus Maria Lacruz.

Seven minutes from the break, an Athletic throw is headed away by Real, but the ball comes back again, and following some beautiful one-touch play from Athletic, Roberto Tiko launches a spectacular right-footed shot from outside the box that arcs above the helpless Westerveld. The Athletic coaching staff are off the bench, as their fans swirl their scarves above their heads. 1–0.

Real step up their game. Right on half-time, Kovacevic again tangles with Lacruz, who's climbing all over him, and this time the referee's decision is in Real's favour. De Pedro hits a left-foot bullet into the bottom corner of the goal, swerving inside the foot of the near post. It's even more dramatic than Tiko's strike, but Toshack merely sits down calmly again. There's barely time to kick off again. One all at half-time.

Three minutes into the second half, the Turk Tayfun responds to the orders Toshack is now barking out on the touchline by missing a chance from seven yards out following a cross from Kovacevic. But De Pedro dances through the Athletic defence, and despite firing over the bar, Real are starting to get back on top.

Until the hour-mark. A long Real ball is intercepted by Athletic and played up to Tiko, who instinctively unleashes a thunderous angled rising shot from, well, miles out, past the shellshocked Westerveld and into the net. 2–1. It's starting to heat up, and there's a booking for Idiakez for his hack on Exteberria.

Twenty minutes from the end, however, Real get their equaliser. Luis Alberto ingeniously floats a ball over Athletic's flat-footed defence into the path of Kovacevic, who assuredly sticks it away. 2–2.

But the referee has disallowed it. Toshack is doing his nut on the touchline, and rightly so, too. Kovacevic definitely wasn't offside, and there was no sign of a foul. Arms outstretched, Toshack mouths his fury at Senor Cantalejo. In the bars after the match, however, during the multitude of television replays, the Real fans will see Athletic defender Murillo cynically fall over as the ball was played, fatally deceiving the referee.

Cantalejo melodramatically dashes to the touchline to punish Toshack for his remonstrations with a red card, banishing him from the bench. But he can't find anywhere in the stand to sit, and as the rain starts to hammer down, he has to strut around the pitchside area, ignoring the jeers of the Athletic fans, until he finally manages to find a spot at the back of the stand. Real are going all out now for a legitimate equaliser bearing down incessantly on the Athletic defence, but despite all the pressure, a De Pedro free-kick, and a header from Luis Alberto that misses the target, is the closest they come to beating Lafuente in the Athletic goal. It's 2–1 to Athletic. Real are still in trouble.

Reporters with microphones swarm on to the pitch, cajoling a quote for the cameras from everyone they can grab. Including Toshack. 'I've never been treated like that before,' he tells the cameras, before attempting to report that he'd been spat on. But thanks to his unique interpretation of the Spanish language, Toshack can't quite explain, so he has to resort to mime. 'Ah, they spat on you?' prompts the reporter. 'Yes,' replies Toshack, 'three times.'

'Medina Cantalejo's decisions were premeditated,' he adds. 'He disallowed the goal too quickly. This has happened to us before when he's been the ref – it's no coincidence. He's refereed us nine times and given us seven red cards. And he sent me off without even looking at me. He heard me say the decision was shameless and whipped the card out as quick as you like.

'Certain officials have a persecution mania against me. Referees know that if they send me off and there is controversy, they will become famous for a few days. I know coaches have no right to protest, but I could not contain myself at the way he refereed the game. I protested because I'm sure there was a goal. We have scored two goals and a draw would have been a fair result.'

Just another late night at the office for John Toshack, then. In close on two decades spent coaching across Europe, principally in Spain, he has attracted notoriety and success in equal measure, following an improbable managerial debut at Swansea City, taking the club from the basement of British football to the penthouse, an achievement which will never be repeated.

And before that was the celebrated playing career in the number ten shirts of Cardiff City and Liverpool. In the 1970s he engineered a form of goal-scoring alchemy with Kevin Keegan so profitable it was tested under laboratory conditions to determine whether it was telepathic. And he overcame a career-threatening injury to become an even better footballer. 'John Toshack was about skill and strength. He was a big man but he was quick and had a brilliant head,' applauded Bill Shankly. 'There were few in his class when I signed him. And we made him better.'

But at first glance, perhaps the most prominent aspect of Toshack's life in the dugout is his infamous aptitude for falling out with anyone and everyone. As a player he argued on occasion with both Bill Shankly and Bob Paisley, but his managerial CV is spiked with feuds with players from Ray Kennedy to Rivaldo, myriad chairmen and presidents, and even the entire Turkish military.

'One of the things which has brought him problems is that for a Spanish-based coach, he's very outspoken,' says Spanish football journalist Jeff King. 'He says what he thinks, slags off his players, and it's not part of Spanish football culture, so he's had lots of problems with name players.'

Toshack isn't alone in this, of course. Every manager has spats with his players and his directors. Toshack just does it more publicly than most. He has spent most of his managerial career, after all, in the aquarium that is Spanish football, under the scrutiny of a breathless sports press keeping the nation abreast on a daily basis on what the players had for breakfast, and with whom they had it.

Perhaps it's this reputation that has, despite ensuring he's had to hand in his club car keys on his way out on a regular basis, also meant he's never been out of work for long, either. 'He has never suffered fools easily,' says San Sebastian-based journalist Phil Ball. 'He has been involved in some astonishingly bitter episodes over the past fifteen years, but it has never put other directors off signing him.

'What you seem to get in the package now is a hard-bitten tactical nous, meticulous attention to detail and a don't-mess-with-me sort of stare that impresses a certain kind of president and player. What Toshack seems unable to resist is a challenge, and this fact, combined with this now famous tendency to ruffle feathers wherever he goes, has meant that he has moved around quite a bit since cutting his teeth at the Vetch Field all those years ago.'

He might have reportedly once described himself as *soy un cabron muy simpatico* – a very friendly asshole – but to cast Toshack as merely a stubborn sergeant major forever slating his players would be inaccurate. Ever since his teenage debut at Ninian Park in the 1960s Toshack seems to have known precisely where he wanted to be, and, blessed with a remarkable streak of self-belief, has spent the last thirty years just doing it his way. For instance, he's always ignored the footballing maxim that states: never go back. And it's impossible to imagine, say, Alan Shearer publishing an anthology of his own poetry. But Toshack did.

That inner confidence must have been invaluable during long months away from home, frequently being forced to adapt to new cultures apart from his family who have always remained in Wales, at the same time bearing the solitary stresses of football management. But even if the results haven't always gone his way, Toshack has become remarkably assimilated into Spanish football culture.

'I think he's considered a Spanish coach now,' says Jeff King, 'he's had spells elsewhere, but he's spent most of the last twenty years in Spain. There's been a sea change in attitudes towards coaches here, literally a couple of years ago, ten or fifteen of the top-flight coaches were foreigners, now it's the other way round. There's only a handful of foreign coaches, and most of them are people like Toshack who've been in Spain forever, so he's considered now almost an honorary Spanish coach.'

In fact, it's difficult to name another British footballer blessed with quite the same intense self-assurance and cosmopolitan philosophy. Graham Souness, perhaps, or Johan Cruyff, another worldly, wilful individual, who chain-smoked his way through a brilliant playing career before becoming an astute strategist, and for many years a *La Liga* rival at Barcelona. Tellingly, in 2000, Toshack was flown over by a Spanish radio station all the way from South Wales to Madrid, to provide analysis on Real's Champions League semi-final against Bayern Munich.

His success, where so many other British emissaries have failed through the years, has largely been down to his open-minded and innovative approach to the game. Even in the early 1980s at Swansea, Toshack was deploying wing backs and showing British football how the sweeper system – perennially associated in England with sterile football – could be a positive strategy, an attacking blueprint that's become known throughout Spain as *Sistema Toshack*.

He has frequently criticised the paucity of tactical thinking in the Premiership, but despite many overtures from English clubs, he has never returned to English club football, not even when he had the chance to manage his old club Liverpool. Toshack has made his home not in Wales or Merseyside but in San Sebastian, next door to his favourite golf course and restaurant (specialities of the house are Partridge Escabeche, Spanish Foie Gras with a Sherry-Vinegar Sauce and Hake Cheeks in Parsley Sauce).

'Something in his manner suggests he is both sympathetic and open to the cultures he often confronts,' says Phil

Ball. 'The Basques, not an easy people to win over, like him, and treat him almost as one of their own, even forgiving his two spells in Madrid. Toshack likes the Basques too, and makes no secret of it.'

It's impossible to imagine Toshack describing Europe, like certain other British exports, as being like a foreign country. In fact, it's possible to trace his affinity with a broader footballing culture back to his time at Cardiff City, when John Charles, perhaps British football's greatest ambassador of all time, regaled him with stories of life in *Serie A*. Throughout his grand tour of Europe, Toshack has always immersed himself in the local culture, even if his grasp of the language has frequently and sometimes fatally let him down.

'His Spanish is grammatically awful, but he communicates really well,' adds Ball, 'he's got this ability to get over what he means, and he's quite funny at times as well. I quite like the guy, there's a human side to him, he's got this King Lear side to him, at times he gets quite lyrical. He's obviously a quite emotional bloke. And he's got this ability at press conferences to say quite sharp things, he comes out with these one-liners, you can see that that sort of person is always going to be a good man-manager, it's the Shankly thing, it's that ability to wound verbally if necessary, but also to express himself.'

These days, Toshack is not quite the folk hero of San Sebastian he once was, however, as Real Sociedad continue to struggle at the bottom of *La Liga*. 'You could almost split his career in two halves,' says Jeff King. 'He was absolutely brilliant at Swansea, went to Sporting Lisbon, did really well there, went to Real Sociedad, did really well there, then went to Real Madrid and won the League in that first year. If you take that point, which is probably halfway through his managerial career, to now, it's been downhill since, and he's been living on past glories.'

But even if Toshack isn't quite the force he once was, you get the impression he's interested in the bigger picture, he seems to have the rare gift in football of being able to keep everything in perspective. 'I'm being paid to do what I'd do for nothing,' he said during his embattled second spell at Real Madrid. 'I've seen real pressure close up, being a miner, coming up and going to the pub and discovering the mine's to be closed.'

This is his story. Here's the mighty Toshack, to do it once again . . .

1 Local Boy in the Photograph

Steelworks and street after street of terraced houses flicker past as the train heads for Cardiff, back to where it all started for John Toshack. Stepping out of Central Station, the first thing you see is the Millennium Stadium. It might have been built for rugby but, towering above everything around it, it has rapidly acquired iconic status in football circles.

Just like Toshack, in fact. He might have been a useful outside half in his schooldays, and a contemporary of the golden generation that produced Gareth Edwards, J.P.R. Williams, Barry John and the rest, who ensured that Wales would dominate rugby throughout the 1970s, but Toshack's first love was always football.

Turn left, cross the River Taff and walk for a mile or so, and you'll find yourself in Canton, a working-class district of the city, where he was born in March 1949, and he has never quite shaken off his roots, barking out team orders in Spanish with a distinct 'Kairdiff' twang to this day.

But although Toshack dedicated himself to football, his ambitions came under threat once he'd passed the 11-plus exam to graduate to Canton Grammar School. It was a rugby-playing school and, as he would later recall, 'No soccer was allowed during the games period, and if you were seen playing soccer in the school yard, you were sure to get a nasty look from one of the games masters.' In fact, he captained Canton's first XV, and his teachers encouraged him to participate in trials for the Cardiff schools team.

He had nurtured his passion for the game behind his home in Northumberland Street, and it helped that his father George, a former airman, was useful with a hammer and a saw, especially when the ball crashed not through the set of portable goalposts he'd lovingly constructed for his son, but yet another neighbour's window.

His team-mate in those back-yard cup finals was his cousin John Mahoney, whose father Joe had played rugby league professionally with Oldham, and who would go on to enjoy a successful career himself with Stoke and Middlesbrough before signing for Toshack at Swansea City decades later.

Toshack's introduction to competitive football had come at Radnor Road Junior School, thanks to his PE teacher, Roy Sperry. Initially, Toshack, who would even forego his lunch to preserve more time for a kickabout, played inside forward for the school team, despite being a year younger than most of his team-mates and rivals, before graduating, like most tall schoolboys, to the centre of defence.

Prophetically, he and his Radnor Road team-mates wore an all-white strip in their matches on Llandaff Fields. 'Similar to Real Madrid,' he would later recall, 'but I remember the collars being strung together like the old Hungarian shirts.' Some pedigree. But it's unlikely that Di Stefano or Puskas ever had to carry their own goalposts from the changing rooms to the pitch, like Toshack and his Radnor Road Juniors team-mates.

But the football-mad Toshack neglected his schoolwork, as his school reports revealed. 'John can work much harder, he is able to produce good results when he puts his mind to it, but he seems far more concerned in channelling his efforts to the sports ground.'

If they were disappointed with John's academic prowess, the Toshacks didn't show it. 'To their eternal credit, they did everything to see I was properly kitted out,' he recalled, 'and they must have made many sacrifices to enable me to get where I did.'

Saturday mornings would see George Toshack transport John and his team-mates to the playing fields, stand and watch in all weathers, before dropping everybody off after the match. 'He saw to it that I got everything I needed, he got me wherever I had to go in good time, then just stayed quietly in the background and let me get on with it.'

During his grammar school years, Toshack's football career was restricted to Saturday morning run-outs for a local outfit called Pegasus, before playing rugby in the afternoons. But when he was fifteen, he was called up for Cardiff Schools' football trials, and following a couple of run-outs, he was chosen for the city team, finally finding his niche and starting to punch his height at centre forward.

In one season, he netted 47 goals in 22 appearances for Cardiff Boys, the kind of form that attracted the Welsh schoolboy selectors, and he scored a hat-trick on the first of his five appearances in a 3–1 victory over Ireland at Swansea. With that kind of reflected glory, it's not surprising Canton Grammar introduced football on to the curriculum for the first time. 'If I did nothing else in school, at least I helped to give those who followed me a chance to play the sport of their choice, something I am desperately in favour of. I love rugby as much as any Welshman but I don't think any one sport should be compulsory in school.'

Like most football-mad kids growing up in the 1950s, his idols were not those of Liverpool, still in the Second Division awaiting the Shankly revolution, but of Manchester United. The Munich air disaster of 1958 brought the sport and its fans into collective mourning. 'The Busby Babes were creating a tremendous following all over the country and it was a major disaster that stopped them from being a force in European football,' he recalled. 'I remember sitting down after the Munich air crash and writing a letter to Matt Busby wishing him a speedy recovery.'

But Toshack's main allegiance was for his home-town club. Cardiff City were and still are most famous for their FA Cup success of 1927, and if they weren't exactly a sleeping giant in the late 1950s, they were certainly putting the cat out and making the Horlicks.

In 1960, however, the Bluebirds returned to the top flight, and he was among the 55,000 fans at Ninian Park who watched Graham Moore secure promotion with the only goal against Aston Villa. As he watched from the

Grange end, he resolved that one day he'd play for his home-town club.

The following season, though, Toshack suffered a less happy experience at Ninian Park, watching Cardiff play host to Tottenham, then chasing the League and cup double. 'We had been standing behind the goal for over thirty minutes when a barrier broke and some of the crowd spilled over on to the track,' he recalled. 'Along with many other young boys I was sick and had to be escorted from the ground.'

It didn't have an effect on his goal-scoring prowess, however, and that near half-century of goals meant the name of John Toshack started to appear regularly in the notebooks of scouts across the country. In 1964 he was invited to Tottenham Hotspur for a week to train along-side the first team, featuring players he'd witnessed on that dramatic afternoon at Ninian Park, names like Jimmy Greaves, Dave Mackay and Danny Blanchflower.

'Returning home to Cardiff, I felt very impressed with Spurs and quite pleased with my week's work,' he recalled. Seven days later, an envelope postmarked N17 dropped through the Toshack letter box, and as he eagerly ripped open the letter and read it, it must have stung to discover that manager Bill Nicholson didn't believe he quite met the White Hart Lane standard. He threw the letter onto the fire. If Tottenham didn't want him, he'd just have to prove them wrong.

There were plenty of other clubs out there, after all. Recommended to Leeds United by the scout who had unearthed John Charles, manager Don Revie sent Toshack a sort of recruitment brochure, extolling the virtues of life at Elland Road, before offering him an apprenticeship. But he turned Revie down, as well as an approach from Wolves.

Instead, he stayed exactly where he was and signed for Cardiff City. Despite being relegated following that pro-motion in 1960, they were the team he'd watched as a boy, it seemed the natural starting point, and under the encouragement of his father, it meant John could stay on at school for a year and take his O-levels. And besides,

Leeds and Spurs might have been First Division giants, but they didn't have what Cardiff City had. John Charles.

Indisputably the greatest Welsh footballer of all time, Charles had been a legend at Leeds United in the 1950s before moving to Juventus, where he remains a hero of the *Bianconeri* to this day, having scored 93 goals in five seasons at the Stadio Comunale and inspiring Juve to the *Scudetto* three times and the final of the Coppa Italia twice. Sometimes he'd play the first half upfront, and having scored a couple of goals, revert to the centre of defence after the break to help Juve retain their lead. Perhaps the apex of his career came in 1958, guiding Wales to the last eight in their only appearance in the World Cup, and even Pele would later admit that Brazil's quarter-final victory over the Welsh might have been in doubt had Charles not been ruled out through injury.

Now he was winding down his career at Cardiff, but he hadn't quite lost it yet, scoring on one occasion from seventy yards against Norwich. The awestruck Toshack learned plenty from the man the Juve *tifosi* had christened *Il Buono Gigante*, the Gentle Giant, as Charles stayed behind in the afternoons to regale him with tales of life in *Serie A* and help coach Toshack. 'I can remember one afternoon when we spent over half an hour just standing heading a ball back and forward,' he recalled, 'before John decided to pack in before rigor mortis set in. I learned as much from John as I did from years playing the game.' Toshack's relish for the challenge offered by European football, and the ease with which he'd later slip into a new cosmopolitan lifestyle miles away from Ninian Park, must have been inspired, in part at least, by Charles's stories.

Toshack spent a season in Cardiff City's youth team, interspersed with run-outs for their reserve team. It proved an invaluable – and bruising – baptism for the teenager. He even managed to put one over on the club who'd rejected him, scoring against Tottenham Reserves, admittedly in a 5–1 defeat to a team including future Northern Ireland keeper Pat Jennings.

In the summer of 1965, Toshack left Canton Grammar and became a fully fledged apprentice at Ninian Park. He would later admit to disliking the typical apprentice's chores of sweeping terraces and tidying dressing rooms. But Toshack threw himself into training, determined to match the Ninian Park pros in the five-a-sides.

Now scoring regularly in the reserves, he must have impressed Jimmy Scoular, the kind of manager perennially described as a 'craggy Scot'. In his playing days at Portsmouth and Newcastle, Scoular had been one of the game's hardest hard men, but as a manager he liked his teams to play good football. However, he couldn't have been too pleased on a European trip in October 1965 when his teenage striker ended up behind bars.

City had been paired with Standard Liege in the first round, losing 2–1 in the first leg at Ninian Park. Cardiff's front line had been depleted by injuries, so Toshack travelled at the last minute with the squad to Belgium, after forging his father's signature to enable him to get a passport in time for the flight on Tuesday morning.

On his first evening abroad, the 16-year-old Toshack, accompanied by a couple of team-mates, wandered from the team hotel across the road to a riverside cafe. After a few drinks and sandwiches, an argument about the bill ensued, and the trio decided on a revenge mission. Their inspired plan was to throw a chair into the river. But as the chair hit the water, Toshack noticed a man on the phone. Ten minutes later the police arrived, carting the Cardiff Three off to Liege's police station. Scoular arrived soon after, and after what the papers described as 'frantic negotiations', the players were released from their cells at 3 a.m. on the morning of a crucial European tie. 'I don't think,' Toshack later recalled, 'I have ever been as frightened in my life as I was then.' That night Cardiff went down 1–0 and out of Europe at the first hurdle.

But the incident couldn't have left a black mark against Toshack's name, as on 13 November 1965, at the age of 16, he was selected for Cardiff City as substitute for their Division Two match against Leyton Orient. Just 25 minutes into the match, defender Graham Coldrick damaged his knee and Toshack was on. Whether it was nerves or just a teenager's natural inexperience, he felt decidedly weak, but soon adjusted to the pace. Incredibly, he found himself up against a 15-year-old centre half, Paul Went. Four minutes from time, Toshack scored City's final goal in a 3–1 victory, and toasted his first strike in the Ninian Park dressing room with a Coke.

Three days later, he was in the starting eleven for the first time, in a 2–0 League Cup victory over Ipswich Town, and rounded off the week with the first two goals in a 4–3 win at Middlesbrough. 'Jimmy Scoular was left with the problem of whether to continue with me in the side or to leave me out. I had scored three goals in three games, and even if I had done very little else, these were facts that were hard to argue with.'

Toshack was already beginning to exhibit signs of the brooding ambition that would spur him on throughout his career, recalls journalist Peter Jackson, then following Cardiff City for the South Wales Echo. 'Toshack was a bright bloke in every sense. He was different from the rest of the players in that he was always someone who gave you the impression that he knew where he was going, almost one-dimensional in that respect, he knew he was going to make something out of the game and sadly Cardiff in those days and subsequently, had such a chronic lack of ambition. He was ahead of his years as a young bloke at seventeen.'

But a month after making his debut, Toshack sustained a freak injury. Still on the ground staff at Ninian Park, he was helping to move a piano, which somehow ended up on his foot, breaking a bone. It put him out of action, and it also meant he had to stand up Sue, the department-store girl he'd asked out to the cinema to see Hayley Mills in *That Darned Cat*. Still, the next time she saw him, he was at home in plaster . . . playing the piano.

In March 1966 he signed his first professional contract, earning £20 a week, and quickly earned a call-up to the Wales U23 squad. Not bad for starters. But it wouldn't always be quite so easy. Toshack found himself in and out of the starting eleven for a couple of seasons. It was still the era of 2–3–5, with eight forwards on the books at Ninian Park vying for five places. To make matters worse, he got the impression some of Cardiff's older lags weren't exactly delighted to see a new boy trying to make a name for himself, and like most strikers on the fringes of first-team action, he admitted to finding it difficult to develop a thread of consistency. 'I was obviously feeling the strain, though, for centre halves like George Curtis at Coventry, John Coddington at Huddersfield and Jack Connor at Bristol Rovers were tough opponents for a sixteen-year-old.'

And, says Peter Jackson, not everybody at the club fully appreciated his blossoming talent. 'I don't think that they really rated Toshack very much. I can remember somebody at Ninian Park whose name I won't mention because I don't want to embarrass him, but towards the end of his Cardiff career, I'd been giving them a hard time in the paper about selling Toshack and going on about selling promotion down the river and all the rest of it. This bloke who was on the staff of Cardiff City, we were having a bit of an argument after a night match and he pointed to an empty beer bottle and said "That's got more talent than John Toshack."'

In Toshack's first season, with just two wins away from home, Cardiff finished just a point above the Division Two relegation zone, losing their penultimate game 9–0 at Preston and being knocked out of the FA Cup by Fourth Division Southport. The following season, they found themselves in exactly the same spot, avoiding the drop by just three points.

Eventually, under Scoular's guidance, the team began to settle down, finishing comfortably in mid-table in 1967/68. But that season City enjoyed an incredible run in Europe. Back then, Welsh teams playing in England were eligible for the European Cup Winners Cup, and Cardiff's monopoly on the Welsh Cup meant an almost annual passport to the continent.

Scoular, a veteran of cup battles from his playing days at Newcastle in the 1950s, had worked out a strategy for playing away in Europe with an extra defender – a system that would become a leitmotif of Toshack's own management style two decades later – with which they would embark on an unforgettable voyage to the semi-finals.

It began with a 3-1 first-round aggregate win over Shamrock Rovers, Toshack netting his first goal in Europe in the second leg at Ninian Park. In the second round the Welshmen faced Dutch side NAC Breda. Drawing 1-1 in Holland, City suffered a crisis prior to the second leg, when the boots of Toshack and his team-mates went missing after a League trip to Carlisle. The boots turned up in Bristol, and were returned in time for a thumping 4-1 win at Ninian Park, Toshack netting the third.

It was here that football began to take notice of the classic Toshack powerhouse style. 'I enjoyed the matches against foreign opposition,' he recalled. 'They were not good headers of the ball, and this was a weakness that I was able to exploit.'

In the quarter-finals, Cardiff were paired with Moscow Torpedo, and won the first leg at Ninian Park 1-0 against a side made up entirely of Soviet internationals. Two weeks later, City embarked on the 12,000-mile round trip for the return, played in Tashkent, as Moscow in springtime was deemed still too cold for football. But the Soviet capital still provided the training base for Toshack and his team-mates, where they worked out in the gym beneath the frozen Lenin Stadium pitch. Naturally, the players did all the things touring football teams should do while taking on 'crack' eastern European opposition – filing past Lenin's tomb in Red Square, and taking in the Moscow State Circus.

The team moved on to Uzbekistan for the match itself. Tashkent is just 200 miles from the Chinese border, and Toshack would later recall that living conditions were worse than he'd ever seen anywhere in the world. Typically for the era, Cardiff had chosen not to trust the local cuisine, and taken their own supplies. So Toshack and his team-mates prepared for Cardiff's biggest match since the 1927 Cup Final by queuing up outside Scoular's hotel room to obtain their daily rations of tinned meat and chocolate.

City, who deployed their sweeper system, lost 1-0 thanks to a first-half goal in front of a 70,000 crowd, and poised at 1-1 on aggregate, the match entered extra time.

The penalty shoot-out had yet to be devised, so two weeks later – having mislaid their boots again – Cardiff found themselves in Augsberg, West Germany for a decider, devastated by injuries.

Scoular, without five regulars, was forced to draft in reserves. First-choice centre half Don Murray was replaced by young reserve Richie Morgan, and despite being injured himself during the match, he kept Soviet Union striker Eduard Streltsov at bay all night. Cardiff finally saw off the Russians 1–0 with a goal by reserve centre forward Norman Dean, thanks to a nod-down from Toshack.

'Those three games against the Russians were of tremendous benefit to all the Cardiff players,' he recalled, 'and it was certainly a great experience for me personally. We were now beginning to fancy our chances a bit.'

Cardiff might have been third from bottom of Division Two, but they were in the semi-finals, where they were drawn against Hamburg, boasting West German internationals Uwe Seeler and Willie Schulz among their ranks. City returned from the first leg in the Volksparkstadion with a creditable 1–1 draw, having taken the lead after just four minutes.

But the second leg on May Day 1968 will never be forgotten by any Cardiff fan aged 40 or over. At 11 minutes, Dean gave Cardiff a 2–1 aggregate lead, but it was short-lived, as Hoenig levelled matters five minutes later. Seeler gave Hamburg the upper hand shortly after the break, but City weren't dead and buried. Brian Harris headed an equaliser 12 minutes from the end to restore hopes of another play-off and keep alive the dream of a place in the final in Rotterdam against Milan, Trapattoni, Schnellinger, Rivera and all. But three minutes into injury time Hoenig struck a speculative effort from 25 yards which squirmed heartbreakingly under the body of City goalkeeper Bob Wilson and into the net. The dream had died.

Still, Toshack had started to make waves across Europe. Helmut Schon, manager of West Germany, wrote that, 'Toshack is the first player of potential world class to come out of Wales since John Charles.'

Buoyed by that European excursion, Scoular's team spent the 1968/69 season making a concerted bid for promotion after a 4–0 opening-day thrashing at home to Crystal Palace, with Toshack topping the Division Two scoring charts with 23 goals after striking up a fruitful relationship with Brian Clark, like himself a big striker and an honest and productive footballer, if not quite as powerful in the air.

But Cardiff finished fifth after too many defeats in March and April. And their European run failed to hit the heights of the previous season. Cardiff could only draw 2–2 with Porto at Ninian Park after Toshack had opened the scoring and Ronnie Bird made it 2–0 from the spot in the second half, but substitute Pinto bagged two to level matters. Cardiff complained to UEFA about Porto's shirt-tugging, but the tactics were nothing compared to what they would experience in Portugal.

Toshack and his team-mates stormed out of their hotel in disgust after just a few hours, as they were greeted by bags of cement and noisy renovations. Before the game, each Cardiff player was presented with a bottle of port.

When the match kicked off, Djalma scored early on, and Cardiff were facing oblivion when Graham Coldrick was sent off just before the break. But Toshack put Cardiff back in the contest with a header after half-time, until Pinto scored thirteen minutes from the end. City were handed a lifeline when Pinto fouled Toshack in the box with four minutes left. He took the penalty himself, but Americo comfortably saved his shot and City were out.

But worse was to come. The Cardiff players were attacked by supporters as they left the field, while goalkeeper Bob Wilson was beaten up, blood pouring from a head wound. The police failed to act, and even lashed out at the City supporters with their truncheons. It was a night to forget in every respect.

Still, Cardiff did renew their cup-fighters reputation with a goalless draw at Arsenal in the FA Cup third round before going down 2–0 in the replay at Ninian Park. And Toshack made his full debut for the Welsh international team against West Germany.

In June 1969, he married Sue in Cardiff, and they set up home in a village called Wenvoe, soon joined by a baby son, Cameron, the following March.

The following season, Cardiff again fell short of promotion, finishing well back in seventh place, although Toshack did at least score his first hat-trick against leaders QPR. And Europe again proved a disappointment, the Welshmen losing 3–1 on aggregate to Goztepe of Turkey in the second round.

In November 1970, he completed a century of goals in a Cardiff shirt during a Cup Winners Cup victory in Nantes. City finally looked good to return to the top flight. But as it turned out, if they were going to make it, it would be without John Toshack.

2 A Red Letter Day

Geoff Twentyman fished for a notepad and pencil from his coat pocket, as Toshack took the congratulations of his Cardiff team-mates on scoring yet another goal. Spying from the Ninian Park stands, as the match kicked off, he wrote, 'Ready for the First Division now'.

Liverpool's chief scout hadn't been alone in his assessment. Just before City's trip to Russia, Fulham manager Bobby Robson had made a £70,000 bid to take Toshack to Craven Cottage. Cardiff accepted the offer, but Toshack turned it down. He felt he wasn't ready, and anyway, he preferred to stay at a club progressing in Europe than move to one at the foot of Division One. If Robson was put out, it didn't last, as he recommended Toshack for the manager's job at Besiktas nearly thirty years later. Bill Shankly was different, though. You didn't say no to Bill Shankly.

Brilliant, enigmatic and intensely charismatic, the Liverpool manager was building a new side. His first great Anfield generation, of Hunt, St John and Yeats, was showing its age and, without a trophy in four years, was starting to break up. The impetus had been a humbling FA Cup defeat at Second Division Watford the previous season. Long discussions in the Boot Room, with his lieutenants Bob Paisley, Joe Fagan and Ronnie Moran, resulted in plans for wholesale changes.

'After Watford I knew I had to do my job and change my team,' Shankly would later write. 'I had a duty to perform for myself, my family, Liverpool FC and the supporters, who had been used to success after our winning the Second Division championship, the First Division championship, the FA Cup, the championship again, and reaching the semi-final of the European Cup and the final of the Cup Winners Cup. It had to be done, and if I didn't do it I was shirking my responsibility. That first team we had at Liverpool was lauded as the greatest and songs were made up about the players. They were worth it. They were the fellows who made Liverpool FC what it is today. But the show had to go on.'

With a ruthlessness that would symbolise the Liverpool way for the next two decades, the sixties greats were thanked for their services with a minimum of fuss and sentimentality, and a new-look Liverpool began to take shape. Ron Yeats, Ian St John, Tommy Lawrence and Roger Hunt were past their best, and after filling their sideboards full of medals, the edge had inevitably been taken off their appetite for success.

Ray Clemence, understudy for several seasons, replaced Tommy Lawrence in goal. Alec Lindsay arrived from Bury and eventually found his niche at left back after a spell in midfield. Larry Lloyd joined from Bristol Rovers and Emlyn Hughes was recruited from Blackpool.

Two university graduates also joined the squad. Midfielder Brian Hall stepped up after a couple of seasons in the reserves, while winger Steve Heighway arrived from non-League Skelmersdale United in March 1970. Reminding Shankly of sixties winger Peter Thompson, Heighway was practically thrown into the deep end of Division One at the start of the 1970/71 season, making an extraordinary impact. Blessed with the ingenuity to beat defenders before using his breakneck pace to get to the line and despatch a delicate cross, Liverpool just needed someone to get on them. And that's where Toshack came in.

At the start of the 1970/71 season, the press speculated that Liverpool were considering a bid for him, and in November, prompted by that hat-trick against QPR, Shankly made a £110,000 bid.

'One Sunday morning Jimmy Scoular, the Cardiff manager, came to the house to see me,' recalled Toshack. 'Jimmy lived at the bottom of our road, and strangely enough, as I watched him walking up the hill, I knew what he was coming to see me about. I began to think about all sorts of things. It would not be an easy decision for me. We were sitting on top of the Second Division, I was quite confident that this time, after two seasons of just missing out on promotion, we could make it, and that I would realise my one great ambition to play in the big League with my hometown club.'

His own loyalties, to his club, and to his family, who were making a new home in Wenvoe, made sure it wasn't an easy decision for John, but he began to feel his club's loyalties to him weren't quite so concrete, in the face of the prospect of a big injection into the Ninian Park coffers. 'I must admit that I got the impression that the people at Cardiff would have been disappointed if I had stayed.'

In reality, however, City would have cause to regret letting Toshack go – or at least not replacing him properly – as the Bluebirds would miss promotion once more, finishing third, three points behind Leicester and Sheffield United, and would never come quite so close to the top flight again.

'It was a lot at the time, £110,000,' says Peter Jackson, 'but it was a joke because he was the top scorer in the Second Division, Cardiff were top of the Second Division, they were in the last eight of the Cup Winners Cup. It was no time to be selling your top scorer. I'm quite sure if Toshack had stayed, Cardiff City would have won promotion that season.'

But, says Jackson, Toshack had always given the impression of being slightly apart from his colleagues, almost as if he was destined for better things, and he didn't exactly endear himself to his team-mates when he likened exchanging Ninian Park for Anfield to going from Sunday school to church.

'Don Murray, the old school centre half, he'd kick 'em up in the air, the fans loved him because he'd go through blood and guts for the club, whereas with Toshack, I suppose there was a bit of the "prophet without honour in his own land". It's a shame he doesn't talk with more affection about his Cardiff days, if he has I've never heard him. I always had the feeling he'd come back here, and

I'm sure it would be at the back of his mind that maybe one day he could manage Cardiff. If Sam Hammam gives them the wherewithal, I certainly wouldn't rule that out.

'But he's become a better player *in absentia* perhaps than he was at the time. People look back and say "wasn't that crazy?", so it's become regarded as one of the great landmarks of the club, the day they sold John Toshack was really the day they told the world they weren't terribly interested in promotion to Division One.'

Perhaps it was that underlying lack of ambition that made Toshack feel it was time to move on, and after all, he didn't owe Cardiff City anything – they'd picked him up for nothing and were about to get a six-figure fee. And when the Liverpool manager spoke to him on the phone, his sheer magnetism lured Toshack north.

'As the train pulled into Lime Street station, I could see a lot of people grouped together at the end of the platform. Bill Shankly was in the middle of them, holding court,' recalled Toshack, accompanied by Sue, who was told by Shankly to get her blue coat dyed red. 'He took us for a steak at the Lord Nelson Hotel, told me what a good player I was, what a great player I would become and I couldn't wait to put pen to paper and get started.'

A consistent goal-scorer was something Liverpool had needed, as they struggled to replace the profitable partnership of Hunt and St John. Tony Hateley arrived for a record fee from Chelsea but never really fitted into the Anfield system. In the spring of 1970, Jack Whitham was signed from Sheffield Wednesday but flattered to deceive. Bobby Graham had been tried at centre forward, to no avail, and Shankly had even attempted to sign Peter Osgood from Chelsea.

Toshack's initial striking partner would be the blond Alun Evans, signed from Wolves for a record fee for a teenager. 'He had outgrown his strength,' Shankly later cryptically wrote about Toshack, 'but he had scored a lot of goals for Cardiff and his tremendous potential was obvious.'

He found himself arriving in a city in decline. The optimism of the 1960s, spearheaded by The Beatles, was fading, as the Fab Four disintegrated amid a flurry of lawsuits earlier that year. The docks were in decline, while across the Mersey in Birkenhead, the Cammell Laird shipyard was in crisis.

Still, at least he was joining a club that seemed to be moving in the right direction again, and Toshack, full of self-assurance, was spared the usual initial spell in the reserves that faced most Liverpool recruits. 'He was very confident, he settled in very, very quickly,' recalls Tommy Smith. 'Shankly was breaking the team up from the sixties, he had one or two players left over from the old side, Cally [Ian Callaghan] was still there, I was the captain. Tosh came and he gave the team something. Clemence came in goal, Lindsay at left back before we even knew he was a left back, Larry Lloyd, Steve Heighway . . . things just started to happen.'

But in November 1970, things weren't happening as quickly as the fans would have liked, after five draws in the first seven matches, but Liverpool were through to the third round of the European Fairs Cup after victories over Ferencvaros and Dinamo Bucharest.

John signed his contract on Armistice Day, and made his Liverpool debut during an uninspiring goalless draw at home to Coventry the following Saturday. 'I don't remember too much about it, which probably means I didn't have a good game!' If that baptism was less than fiery, the following Saturday's encounter more than made up for it. On 21 November 1970, Toshack got a breathless introduction to the Merseyside derby.

'I can remember the intense preparations during that week, and it was noticeable that the local players, people like Tommy Smith and Chris Lawler, were worried that they might be unable to get enough tickets for friends and family. I remember wondering exactly what was going on – I had never known anything quite like this, and it all helped me to realise just what football on Merseyside meant.'

It was possibly the youngest, least experienced side Liverpool have ever fielded in the fixture – over half of the team, including the 21-year-old Toshack, were derby virgins. Shankly, in his inimitable fashion, decided their confidence needed building up, telling the media, 'This will be the youngest side Liverpool have ever put into a derby game, and I would like to express the opinion that this present crop of youngsters have done the greatest job I have known since I came here, including all the names and all the big games.'

It wasn't a bad time to be facing Everton, however. Reigning League champions they may have been, with a world-class midfield axis in Alan Ball, Colin Harvey and Howard Kendall, but they came to Anfield struggling in mid-table and with a poor record on their travels, having won just two away games all season. Shankly, perhaps tongue-in-cheek, suggested their midfield three couldn't perform for more than an hour.

Toshack and his team-mates ran out in front of 53,777 fans at Anfield. If the week-long build-up had given some idea of what to expect, they certainly could never have imagined exactly what lay in store, even 45 minutes later after an uneventful first half.

Eleven minutes after the break, Johnny Morrissey dispossessed the usually impregnable Tommy Smith, setting up Alan Whittle who, with inch-perfect precision, lobbed Clemence. Then, seven minutes later Johnny Morrissey linked up with Alan Ball on the left, the cross finding the unmarked Joe Royle at the far post, who headed home. With 27 minutes left, Everton looked home and dry, while Toshack looked adrift amid the muck and bullets.

But, rather than capitulating as their youth might have suggested, Liverpool began to turn the tide. 'At 2–0 I don't think many people gave us a chance,' recalled Toshack. 'Perhaps we remembered what Shanks had told us – Everton's midfield cannot last ninety minutes, he had said.' Tommy Smith released Steve Heighway, whose mesmeric run beat John Hurst down the left. He then cut inside to fire home a perfectly angled shot which evaded the entire Everton defence and keeper Andy Rankin. It inspired Liverpool, who were given fresh impetus by the introduction of Phil Boersma as substitute. And seven minutes later Heighway embarked on another run down the left, almost stumbling in the process, but managing to dispatch a cross into the area. Toshack made no mistake with his header, beating Brian Labone who inexplicably failed to make an aerial challenge. With his first goal for his new club, Toshack had restored the pride of the Red half of Merseyside.

But Liverpool, playing towards the Kop, weren't settling for the draw. Brian Hall went close, before Keith Newton almost rescued it for the Blues, prising an excellent save out of Clemence. Then, six minutes from time, Toshack flicked on a free-kick from Alec Lindsay for full back Chris Lawler, making an imperceptible blindside run, blasted the winner in off the post with just six minutes left on the clock. Lawler exploded with joy, as did Shankly, leaping from the bench with his arms aloft. It was an incredible comeback, made all the more impressive by the fact it had been achieved by a strike force unknown twelve months earlier.

'We threw it away,' lamented Everton manager Harry Catterick, who kept his men locked in their dressing room after the match. But that doesn't do justice to the extraordinarily brave fightback by Liverpool's youthful side. The Kop found themselves unable to drift off for a post-match pint, instead staying on to salute their heroes. One journalist explained to a colleague that the fans were staying to hear the other results. 'Why?' interrupted a hoarse Shankly, 'Were there any other games?'

'Even when we were 2–0 down, we didn't think we were going to get beat,' Brian Hall insists. 'I don't remember many games when we did. We just had that commitment to go out and play the way we always did. We were a bit like a steamroller that day – slow to get up speed but unstoppable once we had. At that time, in a strange sort of way, we were naive. Not in our play, but naive about the consequences. So many of us had never experienced it before, the lashbacks from the fans and the manager if you lost.'

In December, Toshack returned to the European stage as Liverpool headed for Edinburgh and a third-round clash with Hibernian. Liverpool came away with a 1–0 win, thanks to Heighway's inventiveness and Toshack's winner fifteen minutes from time. A 2–0 win in the second leg just before Christmas, which he missed with damaged knee ligaments, meant the Reds were through to a quarter-final against Bayern Munich.

Bayern boasted the likes of Franz Beckenbauer, Paul Breitner and Gerd Muller, the core of the German team that had knocked England out of Mexico 70, and were emerging as one of the clubs that would dominate Europe throughout the decade. The first leg at Anfield proved a personal triumph for Alun Evans, as he bore down on the Bayern goal, bombarding Sepp Maier's goal and hitting a hat-trick. A 1–1 draw, after a 24-hour delay after a downpour in Munich, meant Liverpool were through to the last four. Where they found Leeds United waiting for them.

Leeds were again challenging on all fronts for silverware, a habit which frequently saw them tire and finish runners-up. But they proved just too good for the new Liverpool, the only goal of the two legs coming from Billy Bremner at Anfield.

Shankly's young team were starting to gel, however. If they were still drawing too many games to stand a chance of challenging Leeds and Arsenal for the title, they were making good progress in the FA Cup. Wins against Aldershot, Swansea and Southampton had set up a sixth-round clash with Tottenham, the side that had rejected Toshack six years earlier. But a 0–0 draw at Anfield meant, with fixtures starting to pile up, an unwelcome replay at White Hart Lane, where Liverpool went through thanks to a typically mesmerising Steve Heighway goal and heroics from their prodigious new keeper, Ray Clemence.

'I stood at the other end of the field and watched him perform miracles against Chivers, Gilzean and co, and he was undoubtedly the main reason we reached Wembley that season,' remembered Toshack. That win carried Liverpool through to a semi-final at Old Trafford against . . . Everton.

But for John, the other half of the draw held personal significance. 'Arsenal were drawn against Stoke City, and to me this meant only one thing. As boys John Mahoney and I had played for hours together imagining all sorts of things. Now we were ninety minutes away from a Liverpool v Stoke Cup Final. Toshack v Mahoney.'

In the event, Stoke lost to double-chasing Arsenal after a replay, while the build-up to the first Merseyside semi-final since 1950 proved even more intense than the one Toshack had experienced five months earlier.

'The build-up to the match was unbelievable. Radio and television interviews with players of both sides were constantly being recorded. The newspapers were full of photographs – the usual things, one Everton player seen with one Liverpool player in mock battle, a game of chess, a boxing match, anything to convey the image of competition.'

Liverpool were still recovering from that delayed tie in Munich just 48 hours earlier, perhaps not the best preparation for a semi-final, never mind a derby. The players hadn't arrived back in Liverpool until late on Thursday night, taking part in a light training session on the Friday morning before heading off for their hotel in Lymm.

The match got off to a characteristically frantic start. Everton took the lead in the first fifteen minutes, Alan Ball capitalising on some good work by Morrissey and Whittle by stealing in at the far post. Within a minute Liverpool had the ball in the back of the net, but it was disallowed because of a handball by Ian Callaghan.

During half-time, Shankly refrained from dishing out a rollicking. Instead, he simply told his team to play football – get the ball on the ground and play your natural game. After a half in which the ball had spent most of its time in the air, Shanks's message was simple – if Liverpool carried on where they'd left off, they'd have to get the fire brigade in, because the midfield needed a ladder to get near the ball.

'It was a typical Shanks way of saying, let's get the ball on the ground and push it round a bit, and in the second half we did,' recalls Brian Hall. 'It was that side that began to develop the pattern that served Liverpool so well for the next fifteen years; the push-and-run type of game started with us.'

But the restart didn't promise a change in Liverpool's fortunes. Howard Kendall fouled Toshack in the box, yet Liverpool's pleas for a penalty were ignored. But then Everton's luck ran out. Defender Brian Labone limped off with an injury. Smith played a long ball to Heighway, who drew three Blues defenders before slipping the ball to the unmarked Alun Evans, who netted the equaliser.

Ten minutes later Liverpool took the lead. Toshack challenged Rankin for a high cross, who fumbled the ball and Brian Hall hooked the loose ball home. 'Quite how it got knocked down I can't say, I know some of the Everton lads thought John Toshack had fouled Andy Rankin, but there was the ball bouncing in front of me, and there was Howard Kendall on the line, and I hit it, and the whole ground exploded,' recalls Hall. After just six months with Liverpool, Toshack was going to Wembley.

Arsenal opened Cup Final week by beating Leeds to the championship, defeating Tottenham 2–1 at White Hart Lane, which meant they could succeed their North London rivals as double winners. The match held equal significance for Liverpool. It was their first cup final in five years and was the biggest test yet of the new-look, and still vastly inexperienced team, in front of the nation.

'We've got to Wembley with a team of boys,' insisted Shankly. 'We've a pool of players that will last for ten years. And we've not come just for the fun. We've come to win the FA Cup.'

On the Thursday before the final, Shankly named his team. The only major decision concerned whether to select Alun Evans, who had recovered from a cartilage injury, or the hugely experienced winger Peter Thompson. In the end, Shankly went with youth, with the maturity of Thompson on the bench.

That afternoon, the team travelled down to London, and Toshack and his team-mates headed for the Palladium in the evening to see a show starring Tommy Cooper and

Anita Harris. On the Friday, after a morning training session, Liverpool spent the evening relaxing, and if Toshack felt any nerves, they didn't stop him getting a perfect night's sleep.

It was immediately obvious the next morning, as John and room-mate Ron Yeats awoke to sunshine streaming through the hotel windows, that it was going to be a hot day. A very hot day. Shankly did the rounds of the players' rooms, exclaiming 'Jesus Christ boys, what a day, it's good to be alive!'

It's one of the little details embroidered into the Liverpool legend that the team suffered from the heat, the temperature rising into the 90s, with Toshack's exertions exacerbated by his heavy no. 10 shirt. 'Our shirts seemed to be extra heavy while Arsenal had short-sleeved cotton jerseys,' he recalled. Liverpool's young side failed to rise to the occasion, while Arsenal seemed to be suffering from the pressure of being so close to the double. It wasn't a classic.

Toshack too was frustrated, failing to test the Arsenal defence and suffering from an early knock. 'As early as the tenth minute I had gone over on my ankle and it was beginning to swell. At half-time Bob Paisley soaked it with cold water but was reluctant to take my boot off. I carried on in the second half but I was not having too good a game.'

After ninety minutes of stalemate, with both defences not relinquishing an inch, Steve Heighway galloped down the wing in the first minute of extra time and fired home the opener past Bob Wilson.

'My orders had been to help out the two central defenders, Peter Simpson and Frank McLintock, against the threat of John Toshack, and to go for everything,' recalls Wilson. 'I was edging forward all the time when Steve Heighway caught me out.'

But Liverpool's lead lasted just ten minutes. Eddie Kelly equalised, although George Graham infamously still claims the goal, and then Charlie George, socks round his ankles, sprinted down the left and struck a fierce right-foot shot to make it 2–1 and seal the double for Arsenal.

Flat on his back, George entered footballing iconography. For Liverpool, there was nothing but runners-up medals, and the satisfaction of a successful season for a young team on the verge of great things.

'It was a disappointing end to the season, but looking back on it now, I don't think Shanks was too confident beforehand,' reckoned Toshack. 'We were still a very young side and we would get better. I don't think people could have imagined how much better, though.'

'Years later, I spoke to Bill Shankly about the 1971 Cup Final, and he admitted that he believed if we'd met ten times, Arsenal would have won eight of those matches,' adds Wilson.

'You can learn much more from defeat than you ever can from winning,' insisted Shankly, recognising that despite finishing fifth in the table and conceding fewer goals than any other side, and remaining unbeaten at home, more work was needed. And never again would Liverpool wear the wrong kind of kit on a hot afternoon.

In just six months, the Liverpool manager had made an impact on Toshack that would never be forgotten. 'Shanks was the greatest character the game has ever known. He was unique in his relationship with the fans and his love affair with the Kop. He was also the best public relations officer a club ever had, a great manager in all its meanings, and created a backroom team that was the foundation for continuing success. I've always remembered one bit of advice he gave me – "Never lose your accent, son," he said.'

But as he headed for his summer holiday, Toshack got the feeling that despite a not unimpressive first season, more was needed, especially after going the last eighteen matches without a goal. Clearly, he was in need of a new striking partner. But help would soon be at hand.

3 Mind Games

'We were never short of a trick or surprise,' Toshack once rhymed, 'we were once mistaken for Morecambe and Wise.' Certainly, in the early 1970s, Keegan and Toshack would come to rival Eric and Ernie as the nation's most celebrated double act, even if the resemblance perhaps wasn't quite as striking as the bard of Anfield suggested.

Still, there was some confusion when the perennial working-class philosopher, Terry Collier, managed to mix up Toshack with a cassock, as Bob arranged the church for his wedding to Thelma in an episode of *Whatever Happened to the Likely Lads?*

It was the ultimate striking partnership of football's bubblegum-card era, as Liverpool conquered all before them at home and abroad. Toshack the stormtrooper with 10 on his back, fearlessly leading the line, forever poised to rise imperiously above the defence and powerfully head another centre from Heighway past the keeper, or nod it down for Keegan, perpetual motion in red, to fire it into the net.

'In the eyes of many fans we were inseparable,' says Keegan, 'and even now the older generation ask me where Tosh is and what he's doing, as if we were still playing and working together.

'Tosh was struggling when I arrived. But Toshack and Keegan quickly became one of the first genuine partnerships, the big guy and the little guy hunting for goals in tandem. Basically we were perfect foils for each other. We both had football brains and that was the key. Usually one has the brain, the other the pace, or one has strength and the other the finishing skill, but we were on the same wavelength, almost to the point where I knew what he was going to do and he knew where I was going.'

So perfect and intuitive was their interaction in front of goal, many thought they must be telepathic. It was the era of Uri Geller bending Sheffield's finest live on television, after all, and if that was feasible, perhaps it wasn't beyond the realms of possibility that Keegan and Toshack's brand of footballing alchemy could have a psychic explanation?

Students from Warwick University attempted to prove it, once and for all, under laboratory conditions for the television cameras. Keegan and Toshack attempted, in turn, to transmit to each other's mind colours and shapes printed on 24 cards, hidden from the other's view.

'We sat there back-to-back, and I started off lifting up the cards, and as I lifted up the cards, Kevin had to say the first thing that came into his head, colour or shape wise,' Toshack recalled. 'And they reckoned that if you got 6 out of 24 right, there was some telepathic understanding.'

Toshack went first. He picked up the first card, which had a green circle printed on it. But Kevin replied white. Toshack lifted up a red square. Green, guessed Kevin. Toshack held up a white circle. Kevin said yellow. In the end, Keegan struggled to get more than one out of 24 guesses correct.

Then it was Keegan's turn. 'I was all keen, having failed with Tosh, and worked hard at putting across the shapes and colours. Circle. I thought of the centre circle. Red. I thought of blood. Tosh immediately responded "red circle".'

The students eagerly started to make notes. 'This was where he started sweating now a little bit,' recalled Toshack. 'I'm getting each one right, up to about the seventh and he picked up an orange triangle, and I said orange triangle – and you could see these students scribbling away with their pens, so I thought I'd better get a few wrong here.'

Toshack's score was an incredible 16 out of 24. 'We finished and these students are saying, "That's fantastic." Kevin can't believe what's happened here. I said, "You can see now who does the work in this partnership, it might look as if he's doing all the running but there's a lot of thought goes into what's going on. But what actually happened, we were doing it for television, so as I looked in the lens I could see exactly what he was picking up behind me, and without saying anything to any of them, I just got all these answers right. It was very amusing for about two hours afterwards, until I actually told Kevin what exactly had gone on.'

That legendary partnership had been thrown together by chance during a pre-season training match at Liverpool's Melwood training ground, when the first team took on the reserves.

'We'd been back about nine or ten days, and we had our first little pre-season game,' recalled Toshack. 'Shankly put Kevin straight in the first team, which was unusual, and we beat the reserves 5–1, which was very unusual, because in those sort of pre-season games the reserves usually are more motivated than the first team, they go round kicking everybody and the first-team players are trying to keep out of trouble. But we won the game, we hit it off straight away, a few useful combinations, and Kevin made his debut the first match of the season and he just never looked back from there.'

Keegan's performance in that practice game had planted a seed in Shankly's mind. 'We were due to play Nottingham Forest at home in the first game of the season,' wrote Shankly, 'and I had a problem position at the front of the team. He was a shy boy, and I said, "Would you like to play in the team?"

' "Oh yes, I would like to play in the team," he replied.

' "Right," I said, "you are playing on Saturday in the First Division." '

That Saturday, Keegan partnered Toshack for the first time against Nottingham Forest. Keegan scored after just twelve minutes thanks to a pass from Toshack, and, reckoned Shankly, caused a bit of havoc in a 3–1 win. It seemed that the arrival of Keegan could be the spark Liverpool needed to challenge for the championship once more. Within three weeks Shankly was telling Keegan that he would play for England.

'Incredible really,' recalled Toshack, 'because he's one of the few players if not the only player who's been signed and gone straight into Liverpool's first team and never came out. That didn't very often happen in those days.'

Following that opening-day defeat of Forest, Liverpool won four of their first five games, but their form slumped and they won just one of the next seven. In Europe, they entered the Cup Winners Cup as runners-up, as double-winners Arsenal entered the European Cup. Beating Servette Geneva in the first round, Liverpool then took on Bayern Munich, who were clearly out for revenge for their Fairs Cup defeat of the previous season, and held Liverpool to a goalless draw at Anfield before routing them 3–1 in Munich.

In December, after a run of disappointing games, Toshack was dropped. Determined to prove his manager wrong, he set about working his way back into the first eleven by scoring six goals in just three reserve games.

It must have had an effect. Alun Evans, who had come in for criticism from Shankly following the Bayern defeat, was sidelined. Shankly came to the conclusion that, despite an inauspicious start to the season, Toshack was the man for the future and a Keegan–Evans partnership would never blossom. Evans had never quite imposed his undoubted talent on the Liverpool first team, and had suffered an attack in a Midlands nightclub when his face was smashed by a glass, undermining his confidence, and he was sold at the end of the season to Aston Villa. Keegan and Toshack were in business.

Kevin had arrived at Anfield from Scunthorpe during the run-up to the FA Cup Final. 'He sat on top of a dustbin beside the temporary offices we had at Anfield while the new stand was being fitted out, and it must have seemed that nobody was taking any notice of him,' Shankly recalled. 'But one fellow was taking notice of him, and that was me. I said, "Listen, son, you'll get your pants all dirty on that bin. Don't sit on dirty bins." '

He had been recommended to Shankly by Andy Beattie, a former colleague at Huddersfield. Beattie had urged several big clubs to sign Keegan, but elicited little response, Everton boss Harry Catterick reportedly dismissing him as 'just another busy midfield player'.

During his time at Scunthorpe, Keegan actually played right midfield. And hated it. Liverpool noticed he instinctively appeared to veer to the left, giving him an all-round ability that justified their faith in his ability to play as a front-runner, rather than as a replacement for Callaghan. It was assumed that after a cartilage operation, he would play less of a role in the first team, but he quickly regained fitness and played another six years.

Keegan's skills, passing and control were clearly ready for top-flight football. But it was his determination and enthusiasm that really marked him out. He boasted blistering speed, and seemingly unlimited energy to chase back while Liverpool were on the defensive. Fearless, he was able at hold the ball up and was brilliant in the air for someone just 5ft 8in tall.

'We bought Kevin for £35,000 – in the end it turned out to be robbery with violence,' recalled Shankly. 'You could argue that Scunthorpe should have got another £100,000 after the way this boy turned out.'

Certainly Keegan made an early impact on his team-mates. Just a week after his transfer from Fourth Division Scunthorpe, he announced to his new team-mates at the Cup Final banquet, many of them already internationals, that he was going to make his mark at the club and become a superstar. It would have been easy to dismiss it as the rash boastings of a youngster on a high after a few drinks with some of football's biggest names.

And they were probably not too impressed a few weeks later, on a post-season trip to Benidorm, when he invited them to a party in his hotel room, which broke up after a few seconds when he started handing round glasses of lemonade.

But Keegan definitely made an early impression on Toshack. Sue that is, not John. The eager-to-please new arrival had carried her suitcase from the coach as the players' wives and those not involved directly in the first team arrived at their Cup Final hotel.

And most importantly of all, Shankly had been struck by Keegan's attitude at Wembley. 'When we lost he looked brokenhearted and I thought, "Christ, here is a real character, and he isn't even playing. He probably thinks that if he had been playing we would have won." ' His attitude in pre-season delighted his manager too. 'He wanted to be bloody first at everything in training – sprinting, jumping over the hurdles, playing five-a-sides, everything. He ran his guts out.'

So with Kevin's speed and stamina and John's height and awareness, it was no surprise that their partnership became so successful, so quickly, telepathic or not, as Bob Paisley later acknowledged. 'As time went on, Kevin built up a formidable striking partnership with John Toshack, and without disrespect to Tosh, I have to say Kevin was the major partner. John had the head for it, and I'm referring to brains, as well as aerial ability, but his mobility was limited. Tosh got into positions, Kevin made up the ground by his speed and stamina.

'In fact, Kevin was so quick to move that in a flash, he could remake a situation, and as the understanding between the two men developed, so the goals flowed. In the process, while continental sides worried about Kevin, they also came to fear John Toshack in the air. People even began to talk about Tosh and Kevin having a telepathic understanding. Whether you believe the telepathy aspect of it, the partnership did thrive.'

One of Paisley's key lieutenants, Ronnie Moran, says it was all down to the duo's sheer quality. 'They were both good players, and good players will always work off one another. Kevin was the speed merchant, quick dribbling. John wasn't slow but he was better in the air, got on the end of a lot of crosses and balls played up, and that's why they had success throughout the years. You play to people's strengths, you didn't try to change them. You worked on it a bit in training, but you can't put too much in players' heads. Because when it comes to match day, if they have to think "I've got to do it this way," all of a sudden the ball's lost. I like to see players play to their strength.'

Tommy Smith characteristically had no time for the telepathy theory, either. 'What it was, you've got two great players in Kevin and Tosh, working together, it's as simple as that. It wasn't like they ate together or slept together, and all that stuff with the telepathy tests, that was all just for publicity. Tosh was so good in the air, but he wasn't that bad on the floor either, he was quite nimble with his feet, he could trap a ball, control a ball. And Keegan was very, very quick, very fit, and the longer they played together the better they got.

'But it wasn't something they really practised on the training field. You can't really practise these things – you can work on your heading or your left foot and things like that, but because of the way the game is, you can't recreate it in training, anybody who tells you that, it's a load of crap.'

Toshack might have used his 6ft 2in frame to full effect, but as Smith points out, over time he became something more than just a powerhouse centre forward. He acquired more all-round skills, developing close control and becoming an astute distributor of the ball, and deployed his talents to frequently devastating effect, subtle flicks creating numerous chances for his new strike partner and creating space through intelligent running off the ball. And his goal-scoring tally wasn't rattled up through a series of nonstop headers, either. Many were intelligently placed beyond the goalkeeper's grasp. Perhaps Shankly put it most succinctly when he described Toshack as 'one of the modern game's essentials – and that includes all aspects of his play'.

'Kevin and I hit it off straight away, really,' recalled Toshack. 'I was a tall frontman, less mobile of course than Kevin, and Kevin never stopped running from the first minute of the game to the ninetieth minute; very often balls that were played out of defence that looked bad balls, he would chase them and make them into good balls, and people started hitting balls to me and I would flick them off, knowing where he was going, and it reached the stage where I used to jump laughing, and he would say "Anywhere Tosh," and I'd flick it on, knowing he'd be there, turn round and get a return pass.'

'It worked for us not because we were telepathic, or even solely because we had football brains,' adds Keegan.

'In truth it was because we did the simple things well. We didn't do anything complicated. We worked on the principle of knocking the ball straight on most times so that all the other had to do was get in line. That makes it very difficult for defenders, especially with runners like Terry McDermott or Ray Kennedy coming in from midfield to offer an alternative.

'And Tosh was one of the best finishers I ever worked with. If he was through on goal you could more or less guarantee the finish would be spot-on. One of his best goals was scored against Queen's Park Rangers, when he took a full-blooded clearance straight in the face from about two yards and the ball flew into the net. He never even saw that one, he went down for a mandatory count of eight. After the game he claimed that his fantastic reactions had been responsible for the goal. Good reactions would have got him the hell out of the way!'

It's important, too, to remember that in the early 1970s, Division One was still the domain of the tough, old-fashioned, take-no-prisoners centre half, and goals didn't come cheaply. Toshack himself rated Gordon McQueen, Jim Holton, Norman Hunter and Mike England as the hardest he encountered.

And the role played by their team-mates in creating attacking situations proved an equally important part of the equation. 'Time and again Tosh and Keegan scored goals by getting on the end of one of my kicks,' said Ray Clemence. 'If a goalkeeper can get distance as well as accuracy with his kick he can often bypass opposing defenders and give his forwards a good chance of scoring. It is in these situations that Tosh's great ability in the air can be seen to best advantage – and his heading ability can be lethal in set pieces such as corners and free-kicks. He is a handful for any defence to handle, so capable in the air and deceptive on the ground.'

Then there was the mercurial Steve Heighway out on the wing. 'On those occasions when we were thwarted, Steve could be found causing all sorts of problems down the flanks,' said Toshack. 'He perhaps never received the credit his play deserved. Many people spoke of the Toshack–Keegan partnership, but both Kevin and I were appreciative of the contribution made by Steve Heighway.'

Midfielder Brian Hall says the duo's relationship off the field was integral to their success on it. 'I'll tell you a story. I can't remember the game. Kevin and Toshack were a great partnership, they complemented each other so well. Tosh was through one on one at the Anfield Road end in the first half. He was one on one with the keeper. Kevin came up alongside him. It was a tap to Kevin and an easy goal but Tosh decided to shoot and the keeper saved it. Kevin went ballistic, on the pitch.

'At half-time Kevin went mad with Tosh in the dressing room. Tosh answers back aggressively and there's a real confrontation. In the second half the roles are reversed, but this time Kevin passes it to Tosh and Tosh puts it in the back of the net and immediately puts his hands up to Kevin to say, "Yes, you were right!"

'Now that makes the wee man a bit special to me when he does something like that. He could so easily have said, "Sod it, he let me down before, I'll have a go myself!" Tosh knew straight away that he should have done that in the first half. That little cameo sums it up for me. Despite so many things which pull that harmony all over the place, it still came together on the pitch, week in week out, year in year out.'

The Keegan–Toshack partnership was a gift to sports editors and television producers. In addition to their telepathic experiment, they were never shy of publicity stunts – dressing up as Batman and Robin on one occasion, with Toshack as the caped crusader, naturally, and Keegan the boy wonder. And then there was the poetry.

Toshack was an ardent amateur bard, eventually going on to publish a compilation of his poetry under the title *Gosh It's Tosh*, celebrating his career and his colleagues in verse, and naturally there was a ballad about Kevin Keegan, the shy, embarrassed coalminer's son, who came to Anfield in 1971:

The scourge of defenders all over the land
He relied upon John to lend him a hand . . .

But having seen off the challenge for his place from Alun Evans, Toshack faced another threat. Shankly bid for Frank Worthington, the flamboyant Huddersfield Town forward. It was an exciting prospect, admittedly, the maverick, skilled Worthington alongside the energetic, nonstop Keegan. But there was a question mark over the £150,000 transfer. He failed his Anfield medical through high blood pressure, although inaccurate rumours persist to this day that it was due to a dose of VD. The deal was off.

Christmas 1971 proved another barren period for Liverpool, going five games without a win. In the New Year, however, they fired themselves up the table, remaining unbeaten for fifteen League games, but found themselves out of the FA Cup, beaten by Leeds in a replay at Elland Road after a goalless draw at Anfield.

By the time the season reached its climax, Toshack, Keegan and Liverpool were well and truly in the groove and in pursuit of the title. Their main rivals were Leeds and Derby, who had been propelled from the bottom of Division Two to the top of the First in just five years by Brian Clough and Peter Taylor, with the likes of the cultured Roy McFarland and Colin Todd in defence, the mercurial Archie Gemmill in midfield and Kevin Hector up front.

By May, Derby completed their programme with a 1–0 win over Liverpool at Anfield, with 58 points. Characteristically, Clough took his side on holiday to Spain, unable to control the destiny of the title, which could still be won by either Leeds or Liverpool.

On the Monday night, Leeds travelled to Wolves, needing just a point for the title. Revie's team, despite the exertions of their FA Cup Final against Arsenal just two days earlier, were overwhelming favourites. Meanwhile, Liverpool made the trip to Highbury, needing to win and hope Leeds lost.

Liverpool, with just one defeat in their last sixteen matches, were fresh, but if they hoped Arsenal, also recovering from the final, would take it easy, they were sadly mistaken, as the likes of Frank McLintock, Alan Ball and Peter Storey threw themselves into the match, seemingly to redeem themselves after their Wembley defeat.

It proved to be a frustrating evening for Liverpool. Emlyn Hughes hit the bar after a quarter of an hour, while Keegan, on brilliant form, steered the rebound wide with an overhead kick.

Meanwhile at Molineux, Wolves were playing out of their skins, keeper Phil Parkes pulling off a string of world-class saves. Leeds had two appeals for a penalty turned down after two blatant handball incidents before Munro put Wolves ahead just before the interval, and Derek Dougan made it two with twenty minutes to go, until Billy Bremner gave Leeds a glimmer of hope.

Back at Highbury, the travelling Kop on the Clock End, their ears pressed to the commentary on Radio Two, began to inform their team that just one goal would give Liverpool the title, chanting 'Leeds are losing!' and 'Wolverhampton Wanderers!' Liverpool began to pour forward in search of the goal.

Two minutes from time, Liverpool had the ball in the net – a goalmouth scramble ensued, and it was Toshack who fired it home. It looked as though he'd scored the crucial goal to steal the championship right at the death. But the joy was short-lived. The referee was signalling for a free-kick and the goal was ruled out for offside. 'That result was particularly hard to take,' sighed Toshack.

'We were robbed of a goal,' insisted Shankly. 'Kevin went through and gave a slanted pass to John Toshack, who rammed the ball into the net. Everybody in the ground thought it was a goal, but it was disallowed for offside.'

'I am still convinced it was a good goal,' recalled Toshack. 'You see, when Kevin struck the ball I started to move in on goal from the far side. Invariably Kevin pulls his shots with his left foot and I always followed the ball in, in case of a half-save by the keeper. When the ball reached me I looked offside for all the world to see, but I was there because I had reacted quicker than anybody else. When the ball was struck by Kevin, I was onside.'

In Majorca – or as Shankly described it, 'some holiday camp abroad' – Clough and his team toasted an improbable title success with sangria, while Toshack, hearing the news from Molineux in the dressing room, reflected on two seasons of what might have been. 'The way I saw it, I had been two seasons at Liverpool, and we had been beaten in a Wembley cup final in extra time and cheated out of a championship.'

But Shankly ended the season lauding his new striking partnership, and praising the impact of Keegan. 'He was thrown into the fire and he ignited the new team. He brought it to life with awareness and skill.' Despite the disappointment of the goal that never was at Highbury, Toshack had the strike partner he needed. The following season they would finally bring silverware back to Anfield.

4 Rain Man

The storm clouds were gathering as Toshack prepared for his first European final on a Wednesday evening in May 1973. Borussia Moenchengladbach, a team described by Shankly as the best in Europe, boasting players like Gunter Netzer, Berti Vogts and Rainer Bonhof, awaited him and his Liverpool team-mates at Anfield in the first leg of the UEFA Cup Final.

But after a long, hard but successful season dogged by injury, Toshack's place in the starting line-up for the final was by no means assured. 'I was beginning to feel sharp again, and with ten days to go to the first leg of the final, I was back in full-time training, although I would not be match fit,' he recalled. 'I hadn't played for six weeks, and with the season over there were no reserve games for me to play in. Each day Shanks would jog beside me giving me words of encouragement and I felt sure he would pick me for the first leg.'

But he didn't. Toshack was named only as one of the five substitutes and he was furious. Despite the flourishing partnership with Keegan, he'd been in and out of the team all season, frequently due to knocks, it was true, but he'd sometimes got the impression Shankly wasn't altogether happy with his contribution. On this occasion, however, he felt it was the diagnosis of Bob Paisley and Joe Fagan, who'd been forced to deal with his constant injuries all season, that had ruled him out of Shankly's plans.

Liverpool started with just Keegan and Heighway in attack. Borussia, who had intimated they were coming to Anfield to attack, did anything but, deploying midfielder Netzer as a sweeper, and he managed to contain Liverpool's attacking intentions quite easily. But the heavy rain above Merseyside became a torrential rainstorm, making it impossible for the players to keep their feet, while the ball kept slipping in the mud. After thirty minutes, the Austrian referee had no option but to take the players off.

'I had been down to see him and he had said, "If it doesn't get any better, we will have to stop it because the ball won't shift. It won't move," ' recalled Shankly. 'I said, "It's not too bad," because I knew these continentals. If I had said, "Oh yes, put it off," he might have thought, "Oh oh, he *wants* it off." So I said, "It's not too bad really. I've seen worse grounds than that." He said, "No, I was on it. I know. I'll go out and try to kick the ball on it." So he went out and when he came back he said, "No, the game is off until tomorrow." Boy, was I glad to hear that.'

Back in the dressing room, Shankly informed his players that the match was to be replayed in 24 hours' time – and Liverpool would start with the same eleven. Toshack, who had been brooding all evening, finally snapped, and confronted Shankly. 'The conversation went something like this. "I'll tell you what, boss, you must be the luckiest man alive. You've gone out at home in a European final playing with two men up because the Germans kidded you into believing they would attack. Who picks the team here – you, or Paisley and Fagan?"

'With that Shanks blew his top. "Get out of here, who the hell do you think you're talking to?"

' "You can stuff your team," I retorted. "You'll be lucky to get a corner tonight." '

The manager slammed the door on Toshack. Driving home to Formby, John wondered whether his confrontation spelled the end of his Liverpool career.

Shankly normally wouldn't have countenanced mutiny, but deep down he knew Toshack was right. In the thirty minutes before the match was abandoned, he'd noticed the German defence were vulnerable in the air. 'We'd seen something during that half an hour's play in the rain – something that was to win us the cup. The German defenders weren't very big and they never came out of the penalty box. None of them was brilliant in the air. I was a little bit annoyed with the men who had vetted the team for us.'

Shankly mulled it over with Bob Paisley and knew what he had to do. After all, Borussia had been coping quite well with Liverpool's tactics in the half hour that was played, and Toshack would be nothing if not fired up by his omission. Shankly phoned Toshack to tell him to get a good night's sleep, as he could be playing tomorrow night. Toshack knew he was in.

However, Toshack's account of what happened that evening differs from his manager's. In his autobiography, Shankly makes no mention of the row, merely that straight after the abandoned fixture, he said to Toshack, 'Get away home to your bed, son, and get a rest for God's sake – you are playing tomorrow night.'

Tommy Smith is unequivocal about what went on after the game. 'Don't believe Toshack,' he laughs. 'Shanks spotted it straight away, and he wouldn't have been influenced by anybody. You can't take anything away from Shanks, he brought Tosh back in and he did tremendously. Tosh didn't pick himself. Maybe he thought he did . . .'

Whatever the truth, the rearranged game kicked off 24 hours later, as Toshack recalled. 'Shanks closed the dressing-room door and said, "Boys, I'm going to make one change from last night's side. John will replace Brian Hall." Poor Brian was shocked.'

Liverpool had started their bid for the UEFA Cup with a clash with Eintracht Frankfurt, easing through 2–0 on aggregate. In the next round, AEK Athens were dispatched 6–1 over two legs.

They then faced tough ties against Eastern European opposition in Dynamo Berlin – Toshack scoring the third in a 3–1 win at Anfield after a goalless draw – and Dynamo Dresden, before being drawn against holders Tottenham in the semi-finals. Liverpool won the first leg at Anfield 1–0, and some felt it wasn't enough. And at White Hart Lane, Martin Peters levelled the tie just after half-time. Seven minutes later, however, Keegan's solo run drew out Pat Jennings and he squared the ball to Heighway to make it 2–1. Spurs now needed two to reach the final, and they got one back, but it wasn't enough.

Now with the final at last under way, and John restored to the no. 10 shirt, the stage was set for a brilliant night and Bill Shankly's tactics were clear. 'From the start we were pumping the ball into the middle and John was flicking it on with his head.'

Toshack enjoyed a brilliant evening. Repeatedly he leaped majestically above the flat-footed Borussia defence, causing havoc as he won cross after cross to create chances for his fellow strikers. Keegan put away two of his flick-ons in little over thirty minutes, while Larry Lloyd also got on the scoresheet, heading in from Keegan's corner. Liverpool won 3–0, Ray Clemence saving a penalty from Heynckes. 'Bringing back Big John was a masterstroke,' Shankly loudly told the assembled media. 'He destroyed them in the air.'

'The reporters hailed it as a piece of Shankly brilliance,' recalled Toshack, 'but I think that but for that blazing row, I would not have played.'

For the return match in Germany a fortnight later, Liverpool had to rely upon all their powers of survival. Borussia had learned from the first leg, bringing in tall defender Ulrich Surau to shackle Toshack, who had kept his place, despite feeling a reaction to his achilles injury after playing for Wales. Borussia scorched out of the blocks, Jupp Heynckes scoring two, and Liverpool didn't know what had hit them. They found themselves 2–0 down by half-time in a match played, like the abandoned first game, under thunder and lightning.

'Moenchengladbach overran us in the first twenty minutes,' recalls Tommy Smith. 'Gunter Netzer was running the show at this stage. I couldn't believe what was happening. We were 2–0 down at half-time and needed to regroup or sink. I remember sitting in the dressing room and being given the simple orders, "keep it tight".'

In the second half it was all hands to the pumps as Liverpool faced an onslaught of attacks, but they clung on to win the club's first, and Shankly's only, European trophy. 'I remember big John Toshack was too shattered to be elated. It wasn't just the game that had tired him out, it was the whole season of games he had played for us and games he had played for Wales.'

Toshack could feel his achilles tendon throbbing as his manager came over to congratulate him. 'I remember him coming over to me and putting his arm around me. "Well done, son, Christ, well done." That was unusual for Shanks. I think he knew the pain I was in.'

Liverpool placed the UEFA Cup on the Anfield sideboard alongside the League championship, a prize which Shankly rated highest of all in his roll of honour. 'Winning the championship for the third time, with a brand new team, possibly gave me more satisfaction than anything. The policy of the new team was the same as that of the old. We played to our strengths. We devised a system which minimised the risk of injuries. The team played in sections of the field, like a relay. We didn't want players running the length of the field, stretching themselves unnecessarily, so our back men played in one area, and then passed on to the midfield men, in their area, and so on to the front men. So while there was always room for individuals within our system, the work was shared out. I would always try to put the players at ease by saying things like, "Don't think any individual is expected to win the game by himself. We're not expecting you, John, to win the game by yourself, or you, Kevin, or anybody. Don't take too much on your plate or put too much in your thoughts and frighten yourself to death." '

The players had all the motivation they needed from the previous season's disappointment at Highbury, reckoned Shankly. 'I saw the emotion in players like Kevin Keegan and Emlyn Hughes when they were in tears after we got pipped for the League.'

The season hadn't exactly begun auspiciously for John. He scored a header in a pre-season friendly against Blackburn, but had been bothered by a thigh injury. He put it to the back of his mind, thinking it was just another pre-season strain.

But at Melwood on the Monday, it was evident to the backroom staff that he was in some pain. Coach Joe Fagan pulled him to one side and examined his thigh. Fagan deemed it serious enough to stop him going on Liverpool's tour of Germany. 'It was to be the start of a permanent condition that would restrict me throughout the rest of my career,' remembered Toshack.

Liverpool started well with four wins from their first five matches, including wins over Manchester City and Manchester United, but lost at Leicester and Derby. Peter Cormack, a stealthy midfielder full of craft who had completed Shankly's team rebuilding when he arrived from Nottingham Forest for £110,000, had gone straight into the reserves in the Anfield tradition, but was quickly promoted to the first team. He helped Liverpool climb to the summit at the end of September after a win against Sheffield United, and Liverpool would prove hard to dislodge, losing only one match until the end of January.

But Toshack wasn't having it easy. After an impressive start to the season, netting six goals in seven matches, the goals dried up, and he lost his place to Phil Boersma. By mid-winter he'd reclaimed it, however, marking his return against Chelsea with two goals.

January saw yet another threat to Toshack's first-team place, however. Shankly had been struck by the potential of Lou Macari, Celtic's attacking midfielder, and made a bid of £200,000, which the Glasgow club accepted. Macari came down to Merseyside as a guest of honour as Liverpool took on Burnley in an FA Cup replay at Anfield.

It was assumed that Shankly planned to use Macari, a prolific scorer, upfront, a real threat to Toshack's place, despite his burgeoning relationship with Keegan. However, Macari had to watch Toshack score twice in a brilliant performance, and began to realise that getting into the Liverpool team might not be so easy after all. He stalled on the deal, alerting Manchester United and Tommy Docherty to the possibilities, and Macari moved to Old Trafford.

By the start of March, the race for the League championship had become a four-way battle. Liverpool headed Arsenal on goal difference but had a game in hand. Lurking behind were Ipswich Town and Leeds United, who had games in hand.

But Liverpool's challenge appeared to falter with a run of six games without a victory. They returned to form with a 2–1 victory over Ipswich, but it would be one of the last League matches Toshack would start that season. Despite scoring some crucial goals, including strikes to seal victories over Newcastle and Birmingham, and two goals each against Chelsea and Coventry, frustratingly he found himself in and out of the team.

During the second half of that season, he managed to keep secret for four whole months an achilles tendon injury, a symptom of the thigh injury he'd suffered at the start of the season. It was only when his nosediving form bottomed out in April that he confessed. 'I must have been a real headache for Joe Fagan and Bob Paisley, I can imagine Shanks giving them both stick about my continued injury problems and they were never too pleased to see me.'

To outsiders, Toshack's deception might seem a selfish action – understandable maybe given the pressure to break into and retain a first-team place, but perhaps not a decision that put the interests of the club first. But there are plenty of former Liverpool players to testify that Shankly had a long record of shunning players who were injured, frequently blanking them in the corridors of Anfield. It's not surprising that some preferred to play on through the pain. Eventually that injury would force Toshack to re-evaluate his entire style of play.

The race for the championship reached a climax, and Arsenal's challenge was hampered when seven of their players were ruled out through injury and illness. Toshack too was forced to sit out the run-in that eventually saw Liverpool lift the championship by three points, clinching the trophy with a win at home to Leeds United on Easter Monday.

Between them, Toshack and Keegan scored 26 goals to help seal a memorable double at the end of a pivotal season for John. 'I went to bed feeling that the Moenchengladbach games had been a turning point for me. I had been at Anfield for three years, and I think Shanks had been waiting for me to show the type of aggression I showed before the first leg. It was as though he accepted me after that. After three years at Anfield I could at last call myself a Liverpool player.'

But despite this new-found confidence, for Toshack, the 1973/74 season that followed would closely resemble the previous campaign, blighted by more injuries and yet more discord between him and the management, but ultimately ending in glory.

It was to be a gloomy season for everyone in many ways, as an overtime ban in coal mines meant stocks rapidly dwindled. Petrol coupons were issued, heating in offices was reduced – and floodlit football was quickly prohibited, meaning matches had to be played on Sundays and midweek afternoons.

For Toshack, the campaign began with a meeting with his manager. 'Shanks asked all the players to come back and tell him how much they thought they were worth to the club and what their pay increase should be. I asked for a pay rise of £70 a week and he gave me £90. I wonder what would have happened if I had asked for £100. I remember wondering how much Kevin Keegan, Emlyn Hughes and company were earning, but it didn't worry me because I had faith in Shanks and I knew that he would pay me what he thought I was worth to his team.'

Despite Shankly's deeply held belief that his Liverpool side was well capable of lifting the European Cup, they exited at the second-round stage. The first round hadn't been the best of omens. A visit to Luxembourg to face Jeunesse Esch shouldn't have caused too many sleepless nights, but Liverpool appeared to take the tie too lightly and came away from Luxembourg with a 1–1 draw, a match Toshack missed. At Anfield two weeks later, Liverpool needed an own goal to take the lead before Toshack scored in the 56th minute to give Liverpool the barest minimum of credibility.

In the second round, Liverpool crashed out to Red Star Belgrade after losing 2–1 in both legs, as Red Star manager Miljan Miljanic encouraged his side to attack at Anfield. 'A tall left-footed elegant player by the name of Bogicevic ran the game and he left a deep impression on all the Liverpool lads,' recalled Toshack. 'He scored the first goal in Belgrade and he had another fine game at Anfield where we lost by the same score.'

That loss, Shankly's last match in Europe, marked a sea change in Liverpool's style of play in Europe. Shankly concluded that Liverpool in future would have to play from the back, signalling the end to the 'stopper' centre back, with Phil Thompson replacing Larry Lloyd.

At least that defeat shook Liverpool out of their early-season torpor. The Reds had made an indifferent start in the League, and Toshack began the season out of the first-team picture. But in early September he would again make his return to the no. 10 shirt with a goal in a 1–1 draw at Leicester.

Following the defeat to Belgrade, Liverpool would only lose four more times that season, and again Toshack would find himself in and out of the team. In December, they managed to beat Everton 1–0 at Goodison without Keegan, Toshack and Heighway. But they would struggle to keep pace with Leeds United, who'd taken 23 points from a possible 26 in their first 13 games. Don Revie's team would remain unbeaten for 29 games from the start of the season, losing just four in the end, and finishing five points ahead of Liverpool, whose League form dried up with just one win in the last eight matches.

Despite the ever-improving alliance between Keegan and Toshack, between them they only scored 17 goals that season, contributing to the manager's feeling that he still wasn't seeing the best from Toshack, who would find himself in the team for long spells, followed by equally lengthy stints on the sidelines. He and Shankly rowed sometimes, but by the time he was playing in top gear week in week out, Shankly would be gone.

Liverpool's FA Cup run began in January with a 2–2 draw at home to Doncaster Rovers, who lay 80 places below them in the League, but led 2–1 before Keegan scored the equaliser, and Liverpool went on to win the replay 2–0. In the fourth round, Liverpool could only manage a goalless draw at home to Shankly's former club Carlisle, again needing the safety net of a replay, Toshack making it 2–0 nine minutes from time.

It could have been so easily the last goal that a rash John scored for Liverpool. 'At the turn of the year, I was missing more and more matches. When February came around we were still involved in the FA Cup. About this time I was taken to see a specialist, Lyall Thomson, about my thigh. The fifth round was some ten days away when I saw Mr Thomson. He examined me and told me to do no training for a fortnight, but just to concentrate on swimming daily, and that this, combined with the rest, should guarantee a big improvement.'

But the next day, Bob Paisley told Toshack that he would be playing for the reserves that Saturday, and that Thomson had been in favour of it, to see if Toshack would be fit for the cup tie against Ipswich. It naturally troubled Toshack, given the specialist's diagnosis the previous day. On the Friday, he returned to the hospital, and Thomson asked him if he'd felt any improvement. John told him he hadn't – and that he wasn't looking forward to playing the next day. 'Mr Thomson's reaction told me something that was to upset me and lead me to asking for a transfer.'

Toshack wasn't happy. He got the impression Shankly had instructed Paisley to play him in the reserves to get him fit for the FA Cup tie, undermining any chance Toshack had of shrugging off his thigh injury for good.

'I was continually being troubled by my thigh and I got the impression that it would never get better, with the way I was being treated. I didn't realise the severity of the injury but I was so disillusioned that I went in to see Shanks on the Sunday and asked for the transfer.'

Fortunately for Liverpool, Shankly ripped up the transfer request, and although he missed the 2–0 victory over Ipswich in the fifth round, Toshack was back for the quarter-final at Bristol City, and it was his lone goal just after the break that took Liverpool through to a semi-final against Leicester at Old Trafford. The first match ended 0–0 in spite of a dominant display by Liverpool, with Peter Shilton inspired in the Leicester goal.

'It was one of the most one-sided games I have ever played in and I remember coming off the field and wondering if we might have missed the boat, because Leicester surely couldn't be as bad in the replay,' Toshack recalled.

But Liverpool won the replay at Villa Park with strikes from Hall, Keegan, who hit a right-foot volley that left Shilton helpless, and four minutes from time, a goal which had Toshack written all over it. 'We were back at Wembley, though I had begun to feel my thigh injury again and the time between the semi-final and final was a worrying one for me.'

For John, it was a traumatic time. Desperate to avoid the disappointment he'd felt on being left out of the original eleven for the UEFA Cup Final twelve months earlier, he was receiving regular treatment for the thigh injury, and uncertain whether he'd be fit to run out under the twin towers.

His fitness was tested in a 2–2 draw at West Ham the week before the final, and he made the scoresheet. 'But all week I was dreading a recurrence of the injury. I had a sleepless night before the match. I remember feeling it in training the day before the final and resting in my room virtually right through until kick-off time.'

The build-up to the final, infamously, was dominated by England striker Malcolm MacDonald's back-pages boasts about what he'd do to Liverpool when he got to Wembley. It wasn't a wise move, especially with masters of psychology like Shankly around. He wound up his team with MacDonald's words and made sure they planned to stick them back down his throat.

And just like the previous season's battle for the championship, Liverpool had all the motivation they needed from the memories of the defeat at Wembley in 1971.

The final was goalless at half-time, as new boy Phil Thompson kept MacDonald quiet after Newcastle made a promising start, although Liverpool had marginally the better of it. In the second half, however, Liverpool put on a breathtaking exhibition of passing football. Alec Lindsay had the ball in the back of the net six minutes after the restart, only to be ruled out offside. Tommy Smith created the first goal in the 57th minute, dispatching a cross for Keegan which Brian Hall ducked under, enabling Keegan to chest the ball down and drive it with aplomb into the net.

Hall, Callaghan and Cormack in midfield starved Newcastle of possession, enabling Liverpool to mount wave upon wave of attacks. In the 74th minute, Toshack backheaded on a long clearance from Clemence to slice open the Magpies defence. Heighway brought the ball under control and, running into space, placed it wide of McFaul.

Two minutes from time Keegan popped up at the far post to slide home the cross from Tommy Smith and clinch the FA Cup, after a move involving seven players, starting with Clemence and ending with Keegan, and a dozen passes by Liverpool. Newcastle, as David Coleman resoundingly exclaimed, were undressed. On the touchline, meanwhile, it seemed Shankly, gesturing towards his players, was somehow conducting his team. 'For me, that game was the culmination of things. The ground was suitable for play and we won 3–0. In one move we strung together twelve passes and on the thirteenth the ball was put into the net by Kevin Keegan.'

For Shankly there was no end of adoration. But for Toshack, there was just more injury misery, as he required a course of cortisone injections to ease the pain in his thigh. 'The worries about my injury were justified and the day after the game I saw a specialist who put me in hospital for two weeks. I received a course of injections and got some well-needed rest. It was pretty boring, but I had my medal to keep me company so I wasn't too despondent.'

With two turbulent but profitable campaigns behind him, John might have been forgiven for hoping that his troubles were over. Instead, he was just three months away from the most difficult season of his life.

5 Changing Rooms

Just six months after that emphatic victory at Wembley, Toshack found himself out in the cold at Liverpool. Bob Paisley had taken over as manager following Shankly's unexpected departure, and John hadn't always seen eye to eye with the new manager. Striker Ray Kennedy had been recruited at great expense from Arsenal and, finding himself either left on the bench or playing in the reserves, Toshack was not happy.

'The facts were there for me to see. Bob Paisley the new manager and Kennedy the new striker. I had never been Bob's favourite player, and the introduction of Kennedy seemed to me to say the writing was on the wall. For over two months I was out of the first team and the inevitable talk of a transfer started to set me thinking really hard about my future,' he recalled. 'I had been at the club for more than three years and decided that this was probably a good to time to leave.'

In November 1974, Leicester City made a £160,000 bid for Toshack, and Paisley agreed to let him go. It looked like his Anfield career was over, but as he signed on the dotted line for his new club, he couldn't have known that in reality it was only just beginning. In the space of five days, Toshack's life was about to be turned on its head.

Paisley had succeeded Shankly during the summer, in almost every sense the polar opposite of the irascible Scot. Paisley was reserved and unassuming where Shankly had been passionate and charismatic, but like his predecessor, he had football flowing through his veins. In the dressing room at Wembley, Shankly had made the decision to retire in the afterglow of the victory over Newcastle. History records it was a step he would later come to regret bitterly, but he was still giving nothing away even as he arrived for pre-season training at Melwood one Friday morning in July.

'Shanks was his usual self,' recalled Toshack. 'He was playing in the five-a-side as though his life depended on the result and I remember thinking to myself what a great man he was. Sixty years of age and still able to retain his natural enthusiasm for the game.'

Toshack showered and started the drive home to Formby. 'I noticed that the time was coming up to one o'clock. I switched the radio on to get the local news. The words that followed from the newscaster were to leave many people on Merseyside stunned and shocked.'

A press conference had been called at Anfield, where, it was predicted, the club were about to unveil a new signing, the likes of Mick Channon or Ray Kennedy. But chairman John Smith stunned the city when he told the assembled media, 'It is with extreme reluctance, that we have to announce that Bill Shankly, manager of Liverpool Football Club, has decided to retire. We have accepted his decision and want to place on record our great appreciation for the magnificent job he has done for us.'

'This decision has been the most difficult thing in the world and when I went to the chairman to tell him, it was like walking to the electric chair,' said Shankly. 'This is a decision that has not been taken lightly. It has been on my mind for twelve months, but my wife and I feel that we need a rest from the game so we can charge up our batteries again.'

It's no secret that Shankly rued his decision. Eased out of Melwood, lest he get too involved with 'his boys', Shankly drifted away from a club that hadn't even thought to offer him a directorship, even though he'd have probably turned it down. The board's thinking must have been influenced by events at Old Trafford, where Matt Busby's move upstairs cast a long shadow over his immediate successors.

'In subsequent talks I had with him, I can see there was some bitterness regarding something or other, but we will never know exactly what made him finish,' remarked

Toshack during his own initial stint at management at Swansea. 'I must admit to having felt frustrated at the way some people react to being successful. They start to claim a greater share of the credit than they are entitled to and the manager is often left to feel he has not been recognised in the proper way.'

The press conference ended with the almost casual announcement that Ray Kennedy was on his way to Merseyside, and by 3 p.m., he'd signed for the Reds and became Shankly's final recruit.

It was a double blow for Toshack, saying goodbye to the man with whom he'd argued, yes, but also the man who'd helped him lift European trophies and become an established international. And now his parting gift was to sign a potential replacement. There was no question that Kennedy was signed as yet another potential suitor for Toshack's no. 10 shirt. 'I saw Ray as a man who could shoot with power and accuracy and I think he could have continued to play at the front,' Shankly later wrote.

The new manager sat down with Toshack in his office and explained that he had inherited Kennedy and had no axe to grind with any member of the squad, least of all Toshack. But, given the size of the fee, the reality was that Kennedy would have to start off in the first team.

Liverpool kicked off the 1974/75 season at Wembley for the Charity Shield against Leeds, a match which saw Kevin Keegan and Billy Bremner sent off for trading punches after the Scotsman had tried to intimidate Keegan once too often, and both players flung their shirts to the ground as they trooped to the touchline.

Toshack missed the match, having picked up a mysterious virus in pre-season, and then been hospitalised due to swollen knee joints and ankle, which meant he'd been unable to walk for three days. Meanwhile, Kennedy had been injured on Liverpool's tour of Germany.

John recovered to sit on the bench for an opening day victory at Luton in which Phil Boersma wore the no. 10 shirt. He returned for a trip to Wolves in midweek as Keegan's suspension kicked in, but was substituted in a home win over Leicester. Seven days after their trip to

Molineux, Liverpool again took on Wolves at Anfield, Toshack scoring one and laying on the other. But with Kennedy fit, that would be the last League match Toshack would play for over three months.

Keegan's marathon nine-game suspension after his punch-up at Wembley provided an opening in the team for Ray Kennedy, but his recurring injury kept Toshack on the sidelines. So it was a Kennedy–Boersma partnership that lined up for Liverpool for most of the opening months of that season. Kennedy came in for the fifth match of the season, at Stamford Bridge, and constantly pressurised the Chelsea back four in a 3–0 victory, before scoring in a 5–2 thrashing of Spurs on his home debut.

Under their new management, Liverpool got off to an excellent start. They went seven games without defeat in the League and rattled up their biggest ever win, beating Norwegians Stromsgodset 11–0 in the Cup Winners Cup, but in the second round they ran up against Ferencvaros. Toshack was left on the bench for both legs, as the Hungarians went through on the away goals rule.

But with Liverpool still well placed in the hunt for the title, Toshack returned from an international in Austria to consider his future, and after Paisley accepted Leicester's bid, he discussed terms with Foxes boss Jimmy Bloomfield. He signed the forms at the Football League's HQ the next day, and everything was ready for Toshack to make his debut at Manchester City two days later.

But after the problems of the previous seasons, it was no surprise Toshack was concerned about the impending medical, as Bloomfield drove him back to his Leicester hotel. 'My thigh had been giving me no real trouble, but I was still concerned, and I knew something wasn't quite right.'

Next morning Toshack arrived at Filbert Street to meet his new team-mates and deal with the usual round of media interviews. After lunch Toshack completed his medical, but as the team headed north, he felt all was not right. 'I felt uneasy about something, and I had the feeling that somebody was keeping something from me.'

He was right. Next morning Toshack got a phone call from Bloomfield, asking him to go and see him in his hotel room. 'When I went in he was sitting in his pyjamas looking as though he had been up all night. He informed me that he would be unable to play me against Manchester City because there was some doubt about the condition of my thigh,' recalled Toshack.

He was not surprised. Bloomfield told him the club were seeking a second opinion on the Monday, and a decision would be made about whether the deal would go through the next day.

Toshack met his parents, who had made the journey from Cardiff to watch their son's debut, at the station. 'As they walked towards me I remember for the first time beginning to feel a little bit of a lump in my throat.' He told them what had happened and they got back on the same train to return to South Wales, while John went home to Formby with Sue.

That night, John could only sit and watch *Match of the Day* as Manchester City beat Leicester 4–1. 'All sorts of thoughts were going through my head, and I spent all day Sunday at home just wondering what was going to happen. I was 25, and I didn't feel too pleased about having to finish playing football. With a wife and three children to support, I needed to have some sort of security.'

The following day, Toshack returned to Anfield, where Lyall Thomson, the specialist who had told him not to play for the reserves the previous season, examined him and told him he had calcification in his left thigh muscle. It couldn't be removed, as any operation could worsen the thigh.

But there was a chink of light. 'There is no reason why you cannot carry on playing,' said Thomson, 'but of course your movement is going to be restricted and you will probably have to ease off a bit in training.' With that diagnosis, there was every chance the transfer to Leicester could go ahead as planned.

Toshack drove to Filbert Street the next morning in a more positive frame of mind. Jimmy Bloomfield took him to a restaurant, making small talk before breaking the bad news. There was no way a club like Leicester could risk

£160,000 on Toshack, given the calcified condition of his thigh.

'Jimmy was obviously very disappointed, and I found myself trying to console him as much as he was me,' recalled Toshack. Leicester's specialist told him he would be able to play on, but his movement would become increasingly restricted, and his career would last a little more than two years. Toshack vowed to prove him wrong, but with the transfer cancelled and on his way back to Liverpool with nearly two years to run on his contract, he wondered if he could.

'I have never doubted my ability to hold down a regular place in any side, but I had to be fit enough to make a contribution.' And then there was training. Liverpool's regime had never been renowned as being the toughest – there was no running up sand dunes, instead there was ballwork and the legendary five-a-sides – but Toshack wondered how his colleagues would react if he was allowed to take it easier.

It was thought that diagnosis spelled the end for his career, but Toshack's determination and a switch in style saw a reborn player. He concentrated on developing his positional play, reading the game more and more, so as to reduce the need for flat-out sprinting, reducing the impact on his leg. 'I seemed to be able to do it for about half a dozen games, and then my thigh would begin to start causing me problems and affect my mobility. I decided that perhaps I could think about the game more and study my team-mates more closely.'

Toshack developed a tiptoeing style of running that proved particularly effective on hard ground. And he worked closely with Paisley in tactical sessions that whetted his appetite for management. 'John was a good thinker of the game,' recalls Ronnie Moran, 'he had his own inside confidence in his own ability. He'd listen and ask questions. He used to come in on a Sunday morning, when the coaching staff would go in to tidy up, and he'd collar Bob Paisley in his room, talking about the match the day before. He was that type of bloke.'

From seemingly being at the end of his Liverpool career, Toshack was merely at the start.

Perhaps the biggest problem facing him as he started again at Liverpool was the psychological aspect of playing under a physical handicap. 'I'm sure Tosh was deeply affected,' reckoned friend and rival Duncan McKenzie. 'I don't think anyone ever forgets anything like that and somehow, it breeds an extra maturity and makes you realise values a bit more sharply.'

'It was hard for the player, the manager and the rest of us,' adds Kevin Keegan, 'but we got on with it and so did he. Because he was bright, he was able to live with it, cope with the problems it brought and still score lots of goals. In the end he hardly trained during the week, just turned out on match days.'

So with the backing of team-mates and fans alike, John knuckled down. Returning to the reserves, he scored twice against Bury and did the same against Manchester United's second team a week later. But thanks to his relationship with Paisley, he knew it wouldn't be easy. 'I remembered my feud with him when Shanks was in charge, and knowing him to be a very stubborn type, I was aware that I would have to be doing something special to get back in.'

Eventually, Lyall Thomson diagnosed the cause of the thigh problem. A strained muscle a couple of seasons earlier had not been given enough time to heal properly. Returning to action too soon, the strain became a pull, causing a serious haematoma. Ironically, once the injury had been diagnosed, he would actually play more games than ever he had before. He became a fixture in the no. 10 shirt for the rest of the season, displacing Ray Kennedy, whose initially promising rapport with Keegan had faded. 'I used to bring the ball down,' said Kennedy, 'whereas Toshack always flicked it on and as a result my game suffered.'

From now on, Toshack scored at a rate of one every two games, starting with a strike in a League match at home to Luton, prior to which he had received a rapturous reception from the Kop.

After their impressive start, Liverpool remained in contention for the title, lying fourth in the table in the middle of March, with just four points separating the top seven sides. But Liverpool's hopes went on the line in their penultimate match at Middlesbrough. The match was scheduled just four days after a Welsh international in Hungary, vital to Wales's European Championship hopes. Paisley told Toshack, who'd scored one and made one the previous weekend against Carlisle, that if he went to Budapest, he wouldn't pick him for the Middlesbrough game.

Toshack scored in Hungary, but true to his word, Paisley replaced him with Boersma at Ayresome Park, where they went down by a single goal, ending their title hopes. Unhappy at being left out, his subsequent experience of management meant Toshack now understands why Paisley omitted him. 'I have worked with players whose fitness over three games a week is suspect. This has given me a better insight into Bob's thinking, and I suppose if I had been in his position I would have done the same, but as a player one doesn't really think that way.'

Liverpool finished second, two points behind Derby County, after Toshack scored twice at home to QPR to secure a UEFA Cup spot. No trophies, but certainly not a disgrace for Paisley's debut season, and a definite portent of better things to come. Despite almost leaving halfway through, Toshack finished that season as Liverpool's top scorer with 11 goals in 24 League games.

The following campaign kicked off in the summer of 1975 with QPR racing out of the blocks, remaining unbeaten in their first ten matches, having beaten Liverpool 2–0 at home on the opening day.

'I struggled in that match, and after a hard pre-season my thigh was giving me some discomfort. I found after the extra running of pre-season training my injury began to play me up a little, and I needed to ease off before I could come back strongly again,' recalled Toshack.

Rangers led the table after ten matches, while Liverpool had won just six of their first twelve matches. Dave Sexton's team had an array of talent – Phil Parkes, Frank McLintock, England captain Gerry Francis, and the maverick talents of Stan Bowles. But many felt their inexperience might tell, as Liverpool moved up a gear in mid-autumn.

The Keegan–Toshack partnership was revitalised, scoring the bulk of their goals, including a hat-trick for John at home to Birmingham in October, while a poor Christmas saw QPR slip to fifth in the table. But Sexton took the Superhoops on a brilliant run, winning 13 of their last 15 matches. The two-horse race which ran all season was set to go to the wire.

Liverpool's inspiration came in part from Ray Kennedy. Finding his way blocked into the first team by Keegan and Toshack, he was dropped into midfield. His touch and class on the left, coupled with his strength and ability to slip his marker gave Liverpool a new dimension as they chased the title.

'When I joined Liverpool I found it hard to motivate myself playing up front,' recalled Kennedy. 'John Toshack is much better in that position than I am. When you play upfront it is a case of waiting for service from the people behind you and then trying to get in the shot.'

Liverpool kicked off their UEFA Cup campaign with a near upset against Hibernian. The Scots went a goal up at home and missed a penalty which could have given them an unassailable lead. But back at Anfield, Toshack scored a hat-trick of headers to take Liverpool through on aggregate, and despite a nervy last twenty minutes, as is often the way on a cup run, Liverpool never looked back.

Next they faced Real Sociedad, flying the flag for San Sebastian, where Toshack would find his adopted home a decade later. Liverpool won 3–1 in the Atocha Stadium, where a cannon on top of one of the stands behind the goals kept ticketless locals in touch with events by firing twice for an away goal and once for a home strike. The cannon fired seven times as Liverpool triumphed.

During Liverpool's stay, General Franco, the Spanish dictator detested by the Basques, was reported to have died in Madrid. The town erupted and was decked in flags as the residents celebrated. But in fact, Franco was very much alive and stayed that way for another month, enabling him to hear that the joy of the fans who'd celebrated his death had been muted by a 6–0 thrashing at Anfield.

Following a comprehensive victory over Slask Wroclaw, Liverpool took on Barcelona in the Nou Camp, in the first leg of the semi-final. Hennes Weisweiler, who'd managed Borussia Moenchengladbach in the 1973 UEFA Cup Final, had built an impressive team around the Dutch internationals Johan Cruyff and Johan Neeskens.

Toshack rated the Nou Camp as the best stage he ever played on. 'I remember going on to the pitch at the start of the game and thinking what a long way I'd come from using coats for goalposts when I played with the children at school. "Here I am at the top of my profession," I thought, and a look at Cruyff and Neeskens in the opposition was ample confirmation.'

But in an impressively mature performance, which demonstrated their growing capability to cope with European tactics and different styles, Liverpool, in all white, slowed the tempo, passed the ball crisply, switched from defence to attack with lightning speed, subdued the crowd and came away with a 1–0 win courtesy of a strike from Toshack, up against the six-foot Spanish international Miqueli, who, John said, created a deep impression on him – just below his knee.

'We played superbly from start to finish,' he recalled. 'We played the Spaniards off the park, in fact had our finishing matched our approach work, we could have won by four or five goals.'

Clemence's long clearance had been chested down by Keegan on the edge of the penalty box, and he turned the ball perfectly into Toshack's path. He cleverly evaded his marker and fired home from twelve yards with a firm right-foot shot to give goalkeeper Mora no chance, and, insisted Toshack, 'Had we shown a little more steadiness in their penalty area we could have won by at least three more goals.'

Emlyn Hughes marshalled the defence so effectively that as Barca left the pitch cushions rained down on their players from the 75,000 fans, although Toshack's Wales team-mate Joey Jones started throwing them back, thinking they were aimed at Liverpool.

'It must have been Liverpool's best ever performance away from home in a European competition,' said Toshack. It was to be a famous goal. Twenty-five years on, as Liverpool under Gerard Houllier travelled to Catalonia in the UEFA Cup, Toshack's goal was dusted down and played and replayed on Spanish television. Not only that, Liverpool remain the only English club to have beaten Barcelona in the Nou Camp in European competition.

Three days later, Weisweiler tendered his resignation. Despite the poor refereeing that had favoured Barcelona who continually committed ugly fouls, Toshack had engineered the result that undermined the security of the *La Liga* coach, something he would be all too painfully aware of two decades later. He had no such thoughts that night, preferring instead to mark the occasion in verse.

A goalden night and what a thrill,
It's Liverpool one Barcelona nil,
One away goal will suit us fine,
And I'm so pleased it was mine.

Two weeks later, Barcelona arrived at Anfield for a second leg that would see Liverpool attempt to make the final in spite of a tremendous defensive performance from the Catalans, some incredible refereeing, breath-taking goalmouth incidents and near hysteria as Barca tried to score the two goals they needed to reach the final.

Liverpool survived the first half, and turned up the pressure on the visitors after the break with constant attacking. Five minutes after the restart, Tommy Smith took a free-kick which Keegan backheaded on to Toshack, who turned the ball towards the far side of the goal. Phil Thompson raced in to ensure it crossed the line.

That goal seemed to awaken Barca, who still needed to score twice, and Cruyff in particular, who raced down the left wing and crossed perfectly to Carles Rexach, whom Toshack would later encounter as a coach in *La Liga*. Rexach blasted it past Clemence, and another goal would see Barca through to the final. They had 39 minutes in which to get it, and predictably the remainder of the match was a frenzied affair. But Toshack and his team-mates flung themselves at everything Barca threw at them to hold on to their place in the final.

Just four days after Barcelona, Liverpool took on Everton in the derby at Anfield at 11 a.m. on Grand National day. Liverpool were down in fourth place, two points behind QPR who were still in first place. It was to prove a memorable occasion for Liverpool, although there's every chance Toshack doesn't remember it to this day.

'John got a bang on the head,' recalled substitute David Fairclough, 'but they treated him and he carried on even though he looked a bit dazed. But then he suddenly ran the wrong way and someone said "Tosh has gone" and they told me to get warmed up quickly and get in the game.'

The dazed Toshack's misfortune proved to be lucky for Liverpool and the 19-year-old Fairclough who replaced him, creating problems for Everton with his confidence, pace and skill. After 88 minutes of stalemate, Fairclough nipped in to steal the ball from an Everton throw-in, embarking on an incredible run to beat five increasingly desperate opponents before he unleashed a brilliant blast which skimmed past Dai Davies. Phil Neal missed a last-minute penalty, but that win put Liverpool back on the title trail.

During the run-in, they beat Stoke 5–3, and demolished Manchester City 3–0 on Easter Monday. But Liverpool were without a game the following Saturday, as Toshack and Jones had been called up by Wales for their European Championship clash with Yugoslavia that day, and Liverpool's trip to Wolves was rearranged.

May 1976 was to prove a personal triumph for Toshack. Liverpool lifted the UEFA Cup again, but he was substituted at half-time for Jimmy Case as Liverpool went 2–0 down after twelve minutes at Anfield to Bruges, thanks to goals from Lambert and Gools.

'I was bitterly disappointed at the substitution, but really Bob was to be applauded for what happened. The Belgians had not allowed us to get near their penalty area so any aerial advantage I possessed had been completely nullified. A change of approach was needed.'

In the second half, Liverpool attacked down the flanks, and recovered to win 3–2, with three goals in five minutes – a long shot from Ray Kennedy, a close-range effort from Jimmy Case and a Keegan penalty. 'The scoreline was a tribute to the tactical knowledge of Bob Paisley as much as anything else,' reckoned Toshack.

He returned to score a week later in the championship decider at Wolves. QPR had finished their programme with a one-point lead 10 days before Liverpool, and watched the decider at Molineux from a TV studio in London. '4 May 1976 is a night I will never forget,' recalled Toshack, who was eager to get his hands on a championship medal, believing that the one he'd won three years earlier was not quite rightfully his, after only playing in around half the games.

The match had an official attendance of 48,000, but many more climbed on the roof, clambered up floodlight pylons or even filed through the dressing rooms after Phil Thompson had covertly opened an outside door during Paisley's team talk.

Wolves took an early lead through Steve Kindon and were still ahead with 13 minutes left. 'The fans must have thought the title was slipping away,' said Toshack. But Liverpool, who had dropped only one point in their last nine, drew on their reserves of experience. Keegan and Heighway, who had troubled the Wolves defence all night, eventually made the difference. In the 77th minute, Keegan powered the ball in from Toshack's nod down. In the last five minutes Toshack and Kennedy scored to make sure. Those three late goals sewed up their ninth championship and condemned Wolves to relegation.

'It could not have been more dramatic if it had come out of a Boys Own Annual,' said Toshack. 'I felt very proud that night and it remains one of the greatest moments of my career.'

Toshack and Keegan scored 28 goals between them that season, as their revitalised partnership blasted Liverpool to success and gave First Division defences sleepless nights.

But there was still European glory to play for, as John and his team-mates travelled to Belgium for the second leg of the UEFA Cup Final to protect that 3–2 lead. And they soon found themselves one down from the penalty spot. Bruges coach Ernst Happel had been confident his side could grind out the 1–0 win which would have given the Belgians the cup on the away goals rule, and it looked like he might have been right when the referee awarded a penalty for a handball by Emlyn Hughes and Raoul Lambert fired it past Clemence.

But within four minutes, Keegan curled in a free-kick to restore Liverpool's advantage. Bruges pounded the Liverpool goal, and the Reds were forced to pull everyone back into defence, blocking every shot Bruges could muster. The cup was theirs for the second time in four seasons.

Toshack and Liverpool embarked on a post-season jaunt to Spain. 'Joe Fagan chatted to me and finished off by saying, "Well son, you've had a fair old season." Indeed I had, and as I sat on the coach, I was able to reflect on my best ever season.'

John had been selected for the PFA First Division XI by his peers, and also chosen for a Europe representative 16 to play in a South American challenge that never materialised. But although the Leicester debacle now seemed half a world away, there were problems on the horizon.

Keegan had been named Footballer of the Year, and began to attract the attention of Real Madrid and Barcelona, among others. He announced he wanted to leave for a new challenge in Europe and, after talks with the club's management, agreed to stay for another season. Liverpool said they would not stand in his way.

'It's not all honey and cake abroad and I don't want to lose Kevin,' said Paisley. 'But freedom of contract is looming and there could come a point if he wanted to go, he'd just go. He says if he went abroad he could become a millionaire in five years. You couldn't deprive a player of his age that sort of opportunity. If you did, he wouldn't be happy. But we'll cross that bridge when we come to it.'

For Toshack it was the beginning of the end of an illustrious partnership. And the effects of his marathon season would linger on.

6 Nothing Can Stop Us

The name of St Etienne will never be forgotten by Liverpool supporters, linked forever with an emotional night that kept alive the club's dream of winning football's greatest prize. But for Toshack, it represented the end of the perfect partnership he had formed with Kevin Keegan.

Liverpool faced the French champions in the quarter-finals of the 1977 European Cup, as Paisley's team chased an unprecedented treble of League, FA Cup and European glory.

St Etienne were becoming a potent force on the continental stage, their green shirt a symbol of the club's indomitable spirit. *Les Verts* had been on the climb since the early 1960s, but had peaked in the early 1970s, when they lost key players whose contracts had run out. Now, under new coach Robert Herbin, they were ready to hit new heights, having lost the 1976 final to Bayern Munich at Hampden Park.

Prior to the tie, the spotlight had been on the impending duel between Toshack and Osvaldo Piazza, St Etienne's 12st 7lb defensive anchor and Argentinian international, nicknamed The Beast by PSV Eindhoven's Ralph Edstroem. 'He's an animal, a beast. I've never played against anyone like him. He's a machine.'

Toshack wasn't fazed, however. 'I have weight advantage, tipping the scales at 12st 12lb. I'm going to make it tell when I meet The Beast, even though they do call me The Gentle Giant.'

Such was the perceived threat to St Etienne from Toshack that Piazza immersed himself in an intensive training routine, concentrating on his aerial abilities, fully aware of Toshack's power in the air. He compiled a dossier on the Welshman, watching videos of Liverpool matches and quizzing French-based Yugoslav defender Josef Katalinksi, who'd faced John in the previous summer's European Championship quarter-final.

'He played against Toshack twice and during our conversation he told me a lot about him,' said Piazza, who also spoke to Dragan Dzajic, the Bastia winger who'd faced Toshack when Liverpool played Red Star Belgrade in 1973, taking the winger out to dinner to quiz him about Toshack.

John wasn't an unfamiliar figure in France, however, as Liverpool matches were shown regularly on French television, and seven years earlier he'd scored a hat-trick against Nantes while with Cardiff.

'Piazza could have phoned me at home in Formby,' said Toshack. 'I would have told him everything he wanted to know in two minutes and saved him a few francs on the telephone bill. I would have told him about my superior class and how I feel sure it will triumph over brute force. Duncan McKenzie did battle with Piazza before he left Anderlecht. He assures me that The Beast is no tougher than Tommy Smith. I always thought Piazza was something they served in Italian restaurants but I'll be sure to recognise him on the field. I have his picture pinned above my bed just to avoid making a mistake and start battling with the wrong player. We've trained and worked hard for thirteen years to become champions of Europe. It's going to take more than Mr Piazza to stop us. He doesn't worry me. I think the battle will go the distance and I anticipate winning on a split decision. I have height and reach advantage, being two inches taller.'

Toshack was even moved to anticipate the duel in verse, Muhammad Ali-style. 'The Anfield fans will have their feast, when the big man tangles with the Beast.'

But despite the hype, the bout wouldn't go all the way. Toshack hobbled off in the first leg with achilles tendon trouble, while Piazza picked up a yellow card to earn a suspension ruling him out of the second leg.

The first half was a classic European chess match. Liverpool, without Keegan who'd failed a late fitness test, were cagey to begin with, as St Etienne started on the offensive. But gradually Liverpool began to assume command. St Etienne came out firing on all cylinders in the second half, however, going close through Patrick Revelli and Dominique Bathenay. But Phil Thompson headed wide for the Reds, while Steve Heighway hit the post with an effort that looked destined for the back of the net.

Ultimately it was St Etienne who made the breakthrough with ten minutes left, from a corner. Jean-Michel Larque found full back Gerard Janvion unmarked at the far post. His mis-hit shot fell to Bathenay, who fired a half volley with the outside of his left boot into Clemence's net. It was the only goal.

In the fortnight between the two legs, Toshack preserved his stamina and did very little training. 'On the day of the second leg at Anfield, I declared myself fit to play. Joe Fagan spent half an hour with me in the morning and we were both aware of the risk involved in me playing. Psychologically though, it would improve our chances, and I knew that by now Bob Paisley preferred to have me in the side against foreign opposition.'

There was an incredible atmosphere as Toshack and his team-mates ran out for the second leg, as a crowd of 55,000 somehow crammed themselves into Anfield. The St Etienne fans meanwhile, wrapped in green and white, hollered their battle cry of *Allez Les Verts*. Liverpool's mission was simple, to win by two clear goals.

And less than two minutes had gone when Keegan wiped out St Etienne's advantage. He fired in from the left, and his shot, intended as a cross for Toshack, curled over the surprised keeper Ivan Curkovic and into the net.

It was a dream start, but despite their relentless pressure, Liverpool couldn't add to it. St Etienne, well organised and ruthless on the counterattack, stormed back, Clemence making some acrobatic saves from Larque and Rocheteau. But he couldn't stop Bathenay's dipping shot from thirty yards six minutes after the break.

St Etienne's goal meant Liverpool now had to score twice in 39 minutes. They abandoned their careful approach of building gradually from the back and threw caution to the wind. On 58 minutes, Ian Callaghan's centre from the right found Toshack, who breasted the ball down to the influential Ray Kennedy, who steered a low shot past Curkovic to make it 2–2 on aggregate, but Liverpool needed one more.

Four minutes later, Piazza's replacement Mercadier collided with Toshack, who was forced to limp off. It was to prove an historic moment for Liverpool in so many ways. David Fairclough ran on as substitute with destiny at his feet, that much everyone remembers. But equally momentously, it also signified the end of the Keegan and Toshack partnership. They would never play together again.

There were just six minutes left on the stopwatch when Fairclough chested down a through ball from Kennedy, catching the French off balance. Forty yards from goal, Fairclough ran and ran towards the St Etienne goal, beating three defenders and evading a challenge from Christian Lopez before hitting the ball low past Curkovic into the net. Liverpool had done it.

But with his leg in plaster, Toshack was unlikely to be involved as the race for the treble approached the last lap. 'It was the most miserable time of my life, the season was drawing to a close and watching the lads going for the treble was sheer hell.'

Liverpool's European Cup run had begun against Irish side Crusaders, Toshack scoring the second at Anfield, as Paisley's team ran out 7–0 aggregate winners. The second round against Turkish outfit Trabzonspor was most memorable for the appalling conditions.

The team's hotel on the Black Sea was disgusting, infested with rats and cockroaches, and there were stomach upsets in the squad, who were awakened in the early hours by chanting from a nearby mosque and a tannoy calling the faithful to pray. The dressing room had moss on the walls, and there were rocks on the pitch. Even the match ball was substandard, likened by Paisley to a pig's bladder. After all that, it was no surprise Liverpool lost 1–0. But they won the return at Anfield 3–0, and following the emotional victory over St Etienne, they dispatched Swiss champions FC Zurich – without Toshack – in the semi-finals to reach their first European Cup Final.

Their opponents in Rome would be Borussia Moenchengladbach, a repeat of 1973. But for John it was touch and go whether he would enjoy a final reprieve like he had four years earlier. He was undergoing regular cortisone injections for his achilles, bathing it in salt water twice daily.

In the Liverpool camp, it was felt that Borussia were susceptible to big target men like Toshack, just as it had proved at Anfield. So Paisley played a tactical masterstroke, convincing Borussia he would play. 'No doubt remembering the problems I had caused them in 1973, Bob Paisley told the press I would be available for the final.'

It wasn't to be. During the final training session Toshack was in so much discomfort that he had to withdraw from the squad, bitterly disappointed.

When Emlyn Hughes and his team walked out at the Stadio Olimpico, they couldn't believe the sight of 30,000 Liverpool fans, every one decked in red and white. Ian Callaghan wore the vacant shirt, with Liverpool's attacking impetus coming instead from Keegan and Heighway.

On 27 minutes, Heighway delicately rolled a superb pass into the path of McDermott, who curled a shot past the diving Kneib to give Liverpool the lead. But Borussia threw men forward, and when Jimmy Case misplaced a back pass six minutes after the restart, Allan Simonsen nipped in to make it 1–1. The Germans besieged the Liverpool goal, and Clemence had to make a brilliant reflex save from Stielike.

Liverpool countered, however, and from Heighway's floated corner, Tommy Smith leaped above the Borussia keeper and headed Liverpool in front again after 65 minutes. And thanks to the irrepressible Keegan, Liverpool started to put on a real show. Eight minutes from time, he was hauled down in the box and Neal calmly stroked home the penalty.

Liverpool had finally earned European football's greatest prize after thirteen seasons of European competition, inspired as they were by Keegan, playing his last match for Liverpool before leaving for Hamburg.

'I rate Kevin's display in the European Cup Final in Rome as his best ever for Liverpool,' reckoned Paisley. 'He refused to be intimidated, and simply got on with the game.'

After the match, Toshack celebrated in Joe Fagan's room with Tommy Smith, Ian Callaghan and Jimmy Case, and Berti Vogts and two or three Borussia players came in to congratulate them.

It was an emotional night for everyone connected with the club, the mood transformed five days on from a dispiriting afternoon at Wembley, when the Reds had taken on Manchester United in the FA Cup Final in the second leg of their treble bid.

Liverpool had reached the twin towers in controversial fashion, after a heated semi-final against Everton at Maine Road which Toshack missed. Terry McDermott had given Liverpool the lead with a beautiful chip over the stranded David Lawson. Everton equalised through Duncan McKenzie following a mistake by Emlyn Hughes. Jimmy Case looped in a 15-yard header to make it 2–1 only for Bruce Rioch to equalise.

Enter referee Clive Thomas. Mick Buckley knocked the ball back to Ronnie Goodlass, who went round Tommy Smith, and clipped it back from the by-line. McKenzie launched himself forward and got a head on the ball. But crucially it clipped the front of Bryan Hamilton's hip. Thomas, forty yards away, disallowed it, despite there being no reaction from the linesman. Everton insisted that it wasn't offside, and there was no way Hamilton had handled it.

'Clive would never say why he gave the decision,' said McKenzie. 'He was even approached by John Toshack, who was out of the Liverpool side, injured. I was standing in my shorts just outside the dressing room when John came down the stairs. "My God," he said, "What did you disallow the goal for?" And Clive said, "An infringement occurred, John, and you should know better than to ask." And that was the end of it. But Tosh turned round and said to me, "Well, I'll be the first to admit – you were robbed." '

Liverpool won the replay 3–0, and Toshack embarked on that ultimately doomed race to be fit for the two big finals, scoring twice for the reserves against Blackburn on the Tuesday before Wembley. 'I decided to give it one final go. To underline my intentions to Bob, I reported for training the next day, although the other reserve players were given the day off. I was in agony but pushed myself through the training session.'

It was to no avail, and the only team Toshack was part of that day was the BBC's, as John joined Don Revie, Jimmy Hill and Lawrie McMenemy on the Grandstand panel.

David Johnson wore the no. 10 shirt as Paisley led out his team against Tommy Docherty's rebuilt United. In the first half, neither team was able to strike an advantage. Liverpool looked the more creative but David Johnson was unable to capitalise. Soon after the break, Stuart Pearson struck a shot under Clemence's body. But within two minutes, Liverpool were level when Jimmy Case fired a thunderous shot past Alex Stepney. It looked like the scales had tipped in Liverpool's favour. Three minutes later, however, a mis-hit shot deflected off Jimmy Greenhoff and into the net. The season-long dream of the treble had evaporated.

That campaign had begun with yet another threat to Toshack's first-team place, as David Johnson arrived for a club record fee of £200,000 from Ipswich. Johnson had started his career at Goodison Park before moving to Suffolk in 1972. Quick, mobile and useful in the air, Shankly had tried to sign him from Everton, and his acquisition made sense with Keegan moving on and the perennial question mark against John's fitness.

'Johnson was an out-and-out striker who many people thought was bought to replace me in the side. It used to bother me a lot when the club made new signings, people like Alan Waddle, Ray Kennedy and Peter Cormack, but I had seen them all off,' said Toshack, who had also managed to outstay Alun Evans, Bobby Graham and Jack Whitham.

'Now, though, I did not mind too much just who the club signed. I was 27, playing at my peak, I had come to terms with my thigh injury and was happy at the club.'

The no. 10 shirt might no longer be guaranteed, but John was certainly not lacking in confidence, especially after scoring the winner in the Charity Shield against Southampton at Wembley. 'Given freedom from injury, I knew that place was mine.'

Bob Paisley seemed to recognise that the signing of Johnson would create competition for places, but with Liverpool battling on four fronts, they needed quality in every department. 'I've got to choose eleven from sixteen but I hope they'll all be patient because, if the season goes as we hope it will, we're going to need all of them.'

Toshack was on target as Liverpool won 3–2 at Derby in September, after early defeats to Birmingham in the league and WBA in the League Cup. And they slipped up at Newcastle before embarking on an unbeaten run that stretched into December.

In October, Toshack crowned a 3–1 derby win against Everton, Martin Dobson's consolation becoming their first goal against Liverpool since November 1971. The month ended with a victory at Leicester, Toshack netting the only goal against the club he'd nearly joined, and at home to Aston Villa 3–0.

Leicester were beaten again a fortnight after their first encounter, Toshack bagging the second in a 5–1 demolition. Liverpool then went to Highbury and drew 1–1, Paisley's anger being roused as Clemence was booked for abusing the four-step rule.

In their next match, a 2–1 win against Bristol City, Keegan, tired of all the speculation regarding his imminent transfer, scored a first-half goal before signalling to the bench that he wanted to come off. In the event, he did complete the match, but things seemed to be going wrong. Liverpool's unbeaten run ended at Ipswich 1–0 in the first week of December, and Bobby Robson's team won their game in hand at Birmingham to go top by a point.

Liverpool returned to the summit after beating QPR 3–1 at home, Toshack breaking the deadlock. But he had to go off with concussion for the second time in two months. 'For some time afterwards I felt anything but a hundred per cent. My reactions were a lot slower and very often at Melwood I would begin to feel unwell and have to stop. I was going to sleep in the evening at about six or seven o'clock.' The club sent him to a specialist, who advised him to rest for a few weeks.

At least he had things to occupy him during his lay-off. In December, his book of poetry, *Gosh It's Tosh* was published, while he and Duncan McKenzie, who'd recently arrived at Everton, were approached by local station Radio City to co-host an hour-long weekly music and sports programme, inevitably entitled *Mac'n'Tosh*, every Sunday at 5 p.m.

'I hadn't met John before I joined Everton and we'd never had a conversation,' recalled McKenzie. 'Tosh was always ready with the quick quip and lighthearted re-mark, but beneath that exterior lies a deep thinker on football, and many other subjects. But working with him was tremendous and often very amusing, particularly when he did a live impression on the air of Johan Cruyff and even his own wife wouldn't believe it was him.'

The poetry anthology originated after John had decided to celebrate the Football Association of Wales centenary game against England in verse, going on to pen poems about his injury and Liverpool's UEFA Cup victory. 'It snowballed from there. Once I get started, I enjoy doing these poems. Most of it is tongue in cheek. The people who know me as a person will know it's me talking, every word in it is my own. Possibly people who don't know me would take some of the things the wrong way, if they wanted to, and think I'm being pig-headed, but that isn't the case – those who know me will laugh, and accept it as being Tosh.'

Back on the pitch, Toshack was still absent for a midweek trip to Aston Villa, and could only watch in disbelief as Liverpool disastrously crashed 5–1, all the goals coming in the first half. It was the club's heaviest League defeat since 1963. 'We got what we deserved,' said Paisley. 'If they were suffering from any complacency, it should have been knocked out of them by now. Looking at our team, you'd have thought they'd never played before and that we had no experience. It was just too bad to be true.

'We've talked about it and some good may come out of it if they realise they get nothing for last season. It's not in my mind to make a string of changes, but they've got to show what they can do, or some of them are going to be in for a shock.'

Toshack returned for the trip to West Ham three days later, replacing David Johnson, but he couldn't improve matters as Liverpool lost 2–0 and surrendered the League leadership. In response, Paisley and his team had a heart-to-heart talk, and the manager named an unchanged team for the Christmas visit of Stoke. Liverpool ran out 4–0 winners and returned to the summit. But bad weather meant Ipswich had three games in hand, and were only two points behind.

'No other country in the world has such varying conditions for football as we have,' remarked Paisley. 'Within six days we've played in rain against Stoke, on ice against Manchester City and in mud against Sunderland. So we've done well to take five points out of six. These kind of things can make or break championships.'

John's bad luck continued as he got flu, but he returned for an FA Cup tie against Carlisle, then scored twice in a 4–1 defeat of Birmingham at Anfield. Liverpool's title bid was momentarily shaken by a 1–0 defeat at Spurs, however, as their title rivals Ipswich and Man City picked up points. That match at White Hart Lane would be Toshack's last League game of the season, thanks to his achilles tendon injury.

Following their victory over Middlesbrough, Liverpool were top with 42 points after 31 matches, Ipswich had 41 from 29 games and Man City had 39 from 30 matches. But while Liverpool were beating St Etienne, Ipswich crashed 4–0 at West Bromwich. In early May, in a dress rehearsal for the FA Cup Final, Keegan got the only goal against Manchester United. The title was wrapped up on 14 May with a goalless draw at home to West Ham. Liverpool had lost only once since 22 January.

'For me, though, it was a very difficult time,' recalled Toshack, who underwent an operation on his achilles at the end of another frustrating season. Liverpool offered him a new two-year contract, but he knew that he would have his work cut out if he was going to hold down a regular place in the side, especially as Kenny Dalglish had arrived that summer from Celtic to join a strike force that also included David Fairclough and David Johnson. Four into two would not go.

Still feeling the effects of his operation two months later, John took pre-season training a little easier, and, three weeks behind the rest of the team in terms of fitness, he began the 1977/78 season in the reserves.

But an impressive performance for Wales against Scotland prompted Paisley to recall him for a European Cup tie against Dynamo Dresden at Anfield. The manager told Toshack 48 hours beforehand, but he managed to keep it a secret from the East Germans, as John was omitted from the 16-man squad handed to the press.

'They were a crack side, and, after being drawn against Liverpool, had set about watching their opponents with their meticulous planning,' Toshack recalled. 'The first the Germans knew about me was thirty minutes before kick-off.'

Liverpool triumphed 5–1. 'It was a personal triumph for me, because although I didn't get on the scoresheet myself, I laid on three goals.'

But John played only six more games in the red shirt, as injury forced him out of the side after a draw at home to Bristol City in November. It was to be his last match for Liverpool.

In January 1978, John Bond, manager of Norwich and later to succeed Toshack at Swansea, offered £80,000 for him, while Newcastle boss Bill McGarry had also been on the phone to Paisley. He was also linked with the player-manager's job at Hereford. Toshack himself fancied a move back to Cardiff, but it seemed unlikely they'd be able to afford the £80,000 fee. 'It was now inevitable I would be leaving Liverpool, and although I had eighteen months of a contract to run I didn't want to hang around just playing the odd game.'

John was contacted by European agent Jean-Paul Co-lonval, who asked him if he would talk to Anderlecht, and Toshack was encouraged to consider a move by Duncan McKenzie, who had played for the Belgian club. Assistant manager Martin Lippens watched Toshack score twice for the reserves against Burnley, and everything looked good for a move to Belgium.

Toshack set off for Brussels, looking forward to the challenge. 'Technically the continentals are not as good at heading as most English First Division players, and the fact that they only played one game a week would also be beneficial to me with my injury problem.'

A training session went well, before John discussed terms, agreed a two-year contract and underwent a medical. He and Sue even looked into the possibility of enrolling their children in an English school in Brussels. But X-rays of his thigh caused concern to Anderlecht's doctor and, after the Leicester experience, Toshack became pessimistic about the deal.

Sure enough, the day after he returned to Liverpool, he was informed the deal was off. 'It was a shame because I was looking forward to the challenge. I had earned a bit of a reputation for myself causing problems to continental defences and was sure that I could do well, but once again the people concerned were reluctant to take a chance on my medical condition.'

Toshack wasn't heading for the Continent just yet. Instead, he was coming home.

7 International Velvet

Toshack's first international experience came at the age of seventeen, when he was selected by Wales at under-23 level. But he had to wait until March 1969 for his full debut, and a friendly in Frankfurt against West Germany, featuring the likes of Beckenbauer, Muller and Maier.

'It was a tough baptism for me, the Germans were at that time probably the strongest side in Europe, but we gave a good account of ourselves and earned a creditable draw.'

Toshack played up alongside Ron Davies of Southampton, another big target man. Back then Wales were something of a ramshackle outfit, managed by former Arsenal player Dave Bowen, who was assisted by Jack Jones, who would run on to treat injured players, despite being in his sixties.

'The whole set-up was a bit of a shambles in those days, and some of the players were not really too concerned about turning up for the less glamorous matches,' recalled Toshack. 'I know for a fact that one particular player was paid the match fee by his club on more than one occasion and stayed away feigning injury.'

John's first goal for his country came in his second appearance, a 2–1 defeat to East Germany in Dresden, Wales's second qualifier for Mexico 70, having lost the first to Italy at Ninian Park.

The return in Rome proved an even more humbling experience, as Wales were thrashed 4–1 as Toshack ran up against Romeo Benetti, the Azzuri's notorious midfield destroyer.

'Benetti's was a great performance,' Toshack recalled. 'He was everywhere winning possession for Rivera to set up all the attacking moves for Riva and company. I know that sounds simple but believe me, that's exactly what happened. Riva scored a hat-trick and each time the pass was supplied by Rivera.'

But John was on the mark again in May 1970 in an extraordinary game at Wrexham, where Scotland ran out 5–3 winners. Big target men were not something Wales were short of at the time, with Ron and Wyn Davies filling the main striking positions, so remarkably Toshack found himself largely confined to the wing. In fact, this match was the only occasion on which he took a corner.

The following week, as the home internationals continued, John ran out at Wembley for the first time, as Wales lost 2–1 to England, before rounding off the home series by going down 1–0 in Northern Ireland.

Next on the agenda were the qualifying matches for the 1972 European Championships, and a tough group containing Romania, Czechoslovakia and Finland. They proved a largely miserable experience for the Welsh, winning just two of their six matches, but at least Toshack was on target twice as Wales managed the consolation of beating the Finns at home and away.

There wasn't much more joy when Wales embarked on the qualification competition for the 1974 World Cup in West Germany, having been drawn against England and Poland. In November 1972, Kevin Keegan and Ray Clemence found themselves making their England debuts against Toshack's Wales at Ninian Park. And Clemence kept a clean sheet as Colin Bell scored the only goal.

'But Tosh and his countrymen got their revenge at Wembley the following January,' remembered Clemence. 'Tosh put one past me in the first half hour and although Norman Hunter hit a long-range equaliser just before half-time, Wales got the draw.'

Toshack got the Wales goal following some good work by Leighton James. 'As hard as the English tried they could not break us down. But for a tremendous 25-yard drive from Norman Hunter, we would have taken both points.'

'People look back and recall that it was Poland's draw at Wembley that prevented England qualifying for the World

Cup in West Germany,' added Clemence, 'But Tosh was equally responsible by scoring that goal against me.'

'Of course it was the Poles who eventually went to West Germany,' Toshack recalled, 'but it could so easily have been Wales.' The decisive result had been Poland's 3–0 win against Wales in Chorzow in front of 100,000 partisan Poles. 'I missed that match through injury, and the frustrations of being out of action were beginning to get the better of me.'

Following their failure to reach the World Cup, and after sixteen years of disappointment after their moment in the sun in 1958, the Welsh FA attempted to put the national team on a more professional footing. Mike Smith was appointed team manager, and he started the process of improving the structure of football in Wales from the grassroots upwards. The old guard of Gary Sprake, Terry Hennessey and Mike England departed the scene, to be replaced by the likes of Brian Flynn, Joey Jones, Dai Davies and new captain Terry Yorath, who had been a schoolboy opponent of John's in his days at Radnor Road.

Despite being an Englishman, Smith decided one of his priorities had to be generating a new team spirit among the Welsh. John and the senior members of the squad were encouraged to make newcomers more welcome than perhaps they had been in the past. And then there was the singing. 'Some of my fondest memories,' recalled Toshack, 'are of travelling in the team bus from Porthcawl to Cardiff or Llangollen to Wrexham with the tape recorder pounding away to the music of the Welsh choirs, and Mike, an Englishman, sitting at the front joining in the singing with the rest of the lads.'

In May 1975, Toshack captained Wales for the first time, and scored past Clemence again at Wembley, as he and Arfon Griffiths helped cancel out a double strike from David Johnson, the man who would eventually replace him at Anfield. 'From a personal point of view, I think this match is the most memorable in my career. Leading Wales on to the field at Wembley was my proudest ever moment. We were only five minutes away from going into the record books. Wales have never won at Wembley, but with the minutes ticking away, our 2–1 lead looked enough. However, David Johnson headed home a Brian Little cross to put an end to our hopes.

'Still, a draw at Wembley is a creditable performance, and the fact that I got one of the goals against Ray Clemence made it a great night all round.'

And the following March, John and his Welsh team-mates faced England once more, for the Football Association of Wales centenary match, but his Liverpool team-mate Ray Kennedy put a dampener on celebrations with the winner in a 2–1 England victory.

By the summer of 1976, Wales were the only British team to reach the last eight of the European Championship. Don Revie's England had been knocked out after a pitiful display in a goalless draw with Portugal at Wembley, after eight matches in which Revie had managed to get through 27 different players.

But Wales had progressed through a tough qualifying group, beating Hungary home and away, the 2–1 win in Budapest becoming the finest result Wales had ever managed abroad, said John. 'I have played in some good team performances in twelve years, but that one takes some beating.'

The match was scheduled in the middle of Liverpool's 1975 title bid, and Bob Paisley had told John that if he played, he would be dropped for the Middlesbrough match the following week. 'I didn't think he was being serious. Wales had a good chance of qualifying for the finals and I certainly wasn't going to miss out on an opportunity to play in that. I decided to play. We were the first team to beat the Hungarians at the Nep Stadium, and the fact that John Mahoney and I had got the goals made it even more satisfying.'

Wales banked another valuable two points as they beat Luxembourg 3–1 away. 'It wasn't a good game and I received a yellow card which put me out of the last game of the group with Austria at Wrexham. I knew as soon as I had been booked that I would miss it, and at the after-match dinner I was feeling far from happy.' Without him, Wales beat Austria 1–0 at Wrexham to top the group and gain revenge for the 2–1 defeat in Vienna on Smith's debut.

Back then, the European Championship was still played on a knockout basis, and Wales were drawn against Yugoslavia in the quarter-finals, with the first leg being played in Zagreb. Smith's team lost 2–0, having never really recovered from going one down in two minutes.

The return leg was scheduled for Ninian Park, ensuring a homecoming for John. 'It was always nice to go back and play at Ninian Park, and in my Liverpool days I always received a warm welcome from the home crowd on international days.' Things didn't start well. In the first half, Yugoslavia extended their aggregate lead from the spot, as the big defender Katalinksi put it to Davies's right. But Ian Evans gave Wales a lifeline as he made it 1–1 just before half-time.

Twenty minutes into the second half, however, the East German official Rudi Glockner disallowed a goal from Toshack. Fans invaded the pitch, hurling bottles and beer cans towards the referee and venting their anger. Play was held up for almost ten minutes. When it resumed, another Toshack goal was disallowed and Terry Yorath had a penalty saved. Four players were booked, and the police had to escort the referee off the field.

'It was a disgraceful spectacle that saw the Welsh FA fined and football at international level banned from Ninian Park for two years,' recalled Toshack. 'The game ended 1–1 and out we went. It was a miserable day all round.'

Yugoslavia lost to West Germany in the semi-finals, who then lost to Czechoslovakia in the final, thanks to Antonin Panenka's cool moment of genius in the shootout, when he flamboyantly chipped the German keeper.

Dejected, Wales picked themselves up and prepared for the qualifiers for Argentina 78, being drawn in the same group as Scotland and Czechoslovakia. They handicapped themselves as they lost to an own goal in their first game at Hampden Park, but hauled themselves back into contention with 3–0 victory over Czechoslovakia at Wrexham, inspired by Leighton James, although Toshack missed the game with his achilles injury.

It became clear that the showdown between Wales and Scotland would decide who'd be jetting off to Buenos Aires the following summer. Because Ninian Park had been banned by UEFA as an international venue after the Yugoslavia debacle, Toshack's home territory of Anfield was selected as the nearest stadium capable of hosting a decisive tie that was likely to attract massive interest.

But with John in the twilight of his Liverpool career, it was far from certain whether he'd be involved. 'I had played about half a dozen reserve games by the time October came round, and this left Mike Smith with a difficult decision. Wales were playing Scotland and I had not played first-class football for over six months.'

John knew things weren't right. It wasn't his achilles tendon giving him trouble, but that old left thigh injury, and to make matters worse, he was starting to develop an arthritic condition in his left knee.

'I badly wanted to play against Scotland, and I knew that I had a couple of things going for me. First of all, Mike Smith knew I'd lived with injury problems for a long time and that if I said I was fit, then that was good enough. Secondly the game was being played at Anfield because of the problem of getting a suitable ground in Wales.'

John eventually proved his fitness, but on the night, a freezing October evening, the tartan army outnumbered the Welsh fans by about five to one at Anfield. Merseyside had been besieged by kilted Scots singing and drinking nonstop in an effort to keep warm. They effectively took over the ground, despite it being nominally a home match for Wales. Some found their way into derelict houses on Walton Breck Road and draped flags and banners out of the windows, and there were stories of Scotland fans scaling the walls at the back of the Kop.

The match itself will be forever remembered for just one incident. During a tangle in the Welsh penalty box, an arm rose from a clutch of players to propel the ball away. It was clearly in the sleeve of Joe Jordan's navy shirt, but the referee inexplicably awarded Scotland a spotkick, which Don Masson scored to make it 1–0. It was a 'terrible error', said Toshack, but the disappointment was compounded when Lou Macari and Martin Buchan combined to send the ball over for the Kop's new idol Kenny Dalglish to rush in and head home.

'It was one of my best performances in the Welsh jersey,' Toshack recalled. 'The result was bitterly disappointing, but I was more than pleased with my own contribution.'

Following a 1–0 defeat in Prague to Czechoslovakia in the last group match, Smith told Toshack that he wouldn't be selected any more, given his lack of first-team football. There was no rancour, Toshack accepted the decision, and would soon have more pressing matters to deal with at the Vetch Field.

But 18 months later, John was recalled to the Wales squad in a 'Swansea front row' consisting of him, Alan Curtis and Robbie James. And he collected a hat-trick in a satisfying 3–0 victory over the Scots. 'It was a dream return, and when I scored the three goals at Cardiff, the home crowd didn't know whether to laugh or cry.'

That afternoon witnessed a forgettable international debut for Alan Hansen. 'A nightmare. Things started badly for me, and got worse. Early in the first half I got caught in possession by Toshack, who put Wales ahead. To add insult to injury, he went on to score his hat-trick.'

But for John it should have been merely a cameo return to the international stage, given the stresses of his managerial workload at Swansea. 'It had been a marvellous return to international football for me, but I was ready there and then to call it a day.'

Instead, Smith persuaded him to play alongside Curtis and James once more against West Germany in Cologne, in the qualifying round of the 1980 European Championships. 'On a cold night we were battered 5–1 and I limped out of international football with yet another injury after an hour. This time I knew it definitely was the last time.'

Wales failed to qualify for Italy, and Smith moved on to Hull City, as Mike England took over the reins of the national team, a post with which Toshack would briefly and disastrously flirt over a decade later. But as he put away his international boots for the last time, there was nothing to regret. 'I have had many great days in my career, but few of them can match the feeling of pride I had when I led Wales out for an international at Wembley in 1976. It was the only time I captained the international side, but I can tell you it was a very special day.'

8 Field of Dreams

His illustrious, if sometimes frustrating career at Liverpool at an end, it was no surprise that Toshack wanted to return home. Cardiff City were in the Division Two drop zone when Jimmy Andrews, the manager at Ninian Park, approached Bob Paisley about the possibility of a loan deal, as the Bluebirds couldn't afford a fee.

Toshack didn't feel he had much to gain from a loan spell, but once Liverpool agreed to give him a free transfer, Toshack met up with the Cardiff chairman Bob Grogan and vice-chairman Tony Clemo.

To John, the duo, who'd received letters from supporters encouraging them to sign Toshack, seemed wary of the club's position, and Andrews' position seemed precarious. Toshack suggested that he could join the club as a player or player-coach, but despite the fans' encouragement, Grogan and Clemo seemed to be cooling on the deal.

And Andrews himself seemed less than keen, challenging Toshack about his lack of coaching qualifications. 'I told Jimmy Andrews he could look in my trophy cabinet at any time and see for himself what qualifications I had. But I didn't like his attitude anyway, and felt a little bit humiliated by my visit to Cardiff.'

He felt frustration at the lack of passion and adventure shown by the Ninian Park regime. 'They lacked any sense of adventure and didn't seem to possess any real passion for the needs of Cardiff City.

'Jimmy Andrews was obviously concerned for his job and I got the impression he considered me a threat. I was at great pains to explain to him that I could sign as a player-coach and would still be able to turn out regularly.

The Cardiff public were crying out for a new face, and surely there would have been an increase in attendances if I had returned.' But it was not to be.

Meanwhile, forty miles west, a local solicitor and successful businessman, Malcolm Struel, was turning on his car radio and starting an improbable six-year chain of events that was the inexorable rise and fall of Swansea City.

It was late on Thursday afternoon in February 1978 when Struel caught the end of a local news bulletin, announcing that John Toshack would be in the city the following day, promoting sportswear firm Gola with Welsh rugby icon Barry John at a trade fair. Struel made a mental note of the time and place – the Dragon Hotel.

Next day, after the fair, Toshack found himself in Struel's home, discussing terms. 'It seemed an impossible proposition. Swansea were in the Fourth Division and I was a Cardiff lad born and bred. Liverpool were the champions of Europe and there was a world of difference between the two clubs.'

That weekend, Toshack played his last match in a Liverpool shirt against Manchester United reserves. On the Sunday, Reds chairman John Smith was approached in London, and by early evening, the board had agreed to release Toshack.

On Monday morning, Swansea's administrative team were on their way to Merseyside to meet Peter Robinson and Toshack and his representatives. By 5 p.m. a deal had been hammered out – Toshack could join the club as player-manager for nothing, becoming the youngest boss in the League, and in return Swansea would give Liverpool first refusal on any player for sale from the Vetch Field. Ironically, the traffic in footballers between Merseyside and South Wales would be exclusively southbound.

After an exhausting day, Struel was happy with the outcome. 'I was determined that there was no way I was going to leave Liverpool before getting things all sewn up.'

'What a difference there seemed to be in the drive and ambition shown by Malcolm Struel, compared with the attitude of the people at Cardiff,' recalled Toshack. 'He was Swansea through and through, and I felt this was a club that had the potential to improve on its Fourth Division status.'

In fact, as Swansea City historian David Farmer notes, Toshack hadn't been the club's first choice, as one of the leading candidates had attended Swansea's fixture with Newport County earlier in the month. 'In the stand for that match was Eddie McCreadie, who had been the manager at Chelsea. McCreadie told the press that he was considering several offers, including one from Swansea.

'Instead he flew to America to manage Memphis Rogues. McCreadie became the third manager to refuse Swansea's offer. Despite the confusion and disappointment, his was a momentous decision as far as Swansea was concerned. It opened the door for chairman Struel to approach his fourth candidate. This time he was to be successful.'

Once the ink had dried on his contract, Toshack didn't have much time to race to Rochdale and link up with his new club, where, as the new manager watched from the director's box, they faced the Football League's 92nd team. And lost 2–1.

'I'd spent the last few days telling him how good we were and then at his first sight of us we played so badly, I didn't have the nerve to ask what he thought about the game,' Struel admitted after the match.

Toshack drove home to Formby wondering if he'd made the right decision. In 24 hours, he'd exchanged the Champions of Europe for a team beaten by the worst team in England. But still, Toshack was fired enough to insist to his passenger and former room-mate Emlyn Hughes that within three years he'd be taking his Swansea City team to Anfield for a League match. 'Little did I realise how prophetic that statement would turn out to be.'

There just appeared to be one problem as Toshack started work on St David's Day. Swansea City already had a manager. Harry Griffiths, however, welcomed his successor with open arms.

'Strange as it may seem, Harry was delighted to see me take over from him,' said Toshack. 'He had been at

Swansea for thirty years and had seen the need for a new young manager at the Vetch.'

Griffiths, who now became John's right-hand man, had been in charge at the Vetch for three years, and had gradually revitalised the club, unearthing local talent and assembling an exciting team which had just missed out on promotion the previous season. But Griffiths openly admitted that he wasn't getting any younger, and it was felt that bringing Toshack to the club would be the final impetus towards Struel's stated aim of reaching Division Two in two years.

'If you believe the authorised version, Toshack took us from re-election to near champions,' insists writer and Swansea fan Huw Richards. 'But this ignores Griffiths, who was resuscitating the Swans when Tosh was still performing his impression of a berserk red-shirted electricity pylon.'

Naturally, one of Toshack's first tasks at the Vetch was to meet the local media, who naturally had just one question. Why Swansea and not Cardiff?

'I ducked that one. It was not so much a case of me not wanting to go back to Cardiff, but more a case of them rejecting me. That hurt a lot, and I was determined in my own way to make them eat their words.'

Toshack chose instead to underline the immense potential he could see at Swansea. 'I believe that I have come to the right place at the right time. When I went to Anfield the place was a shed. Now the club has a cabinet full of trophies.'

But the appointment didn't initially go down well with all of Swansea's fans, reckoned Huw Richards. 'The North Bank weren't that impressed. Griffiths was a popular local hero while Toshack suffered the almost terminal handicap of coming from Cardiff.'

Still, following the press conference, Toshack and Griffiths embarked on their stocktaking. Three players stood out. Robbie James, a gifted, combative midfielder with a cannonball shot, the skilful Alan Curtis, blessed with a brilliant body swerve and an eye for goal, and Jeremy Charles, a promising goal-scorer with the pedigree that came with being John Charles's nephew. All three had been noted by top-flight scouts, and Swansea had recently turned down a £165,000 bid from Sunderland for Curtis.

'I decided that with sixteen games to go, we would throw everything into attack and hope that if we conceded three goals, we would score four,' recalled Toshack. 'With James, Curtis, Charles and myself, it seemed the logical thing to do.'

Fittingly, it was British football's other great upwardly-mobile team of the 1980s, Watford, who presented John Toshack with his first test as a manager. Managed by Graham Taylor under the chairmanship of Elton John, they arrived at the Vetch Field for a Friday night game that attracted more than 15,000 fans, three times the club's usual attendance. It ended 3–3, and Toshack had to wait until his fourth game in charge, at home to Stockport, to win his first match as a manager.

Swansea now lay in eighth position with a dozen matches remaining. And under the inspiration of Toshack, they only lost one of those games, to Northampton on the penultimate Saturday. It meant they needed just a win and a draw from their last two home games to win promotion.

But the optimism soon turned to tragedy. On the morning of the next match against Scunthorpe, Harry Griffiths collapsed as he chatted with Toshack and treated Les Chappell in the medical room.

'He keeled over on the floor and was obviously struggling to stay alive,' recalled Toshack. 'I had never seen anything like it and quite honestly I was scared out of my mind.' Griffiths, who had suffered a massive heart attack, was taken to Singleton Hospital, but died in the ambulance.

Toshack and Struel resolved the game would have to go ahead, deciding that it would have been what Griffiths, who had laid the foundations for the rebuilding of the club, would have wanted.

'We shall leave no stone unturned to do him proud,' declared Toshack, as he broke the news to his players, who naturally took it hard. Young defender Steven Morris broke down in tears, but Toshack decided to play him, as Swansea won 3–1 to put their destiny in their own hands. The following Saturday, Toshack scored with a free-kick that deflected off the head of a defender as Swansea beat Halifax 2–0 to secure promotion.

'Most of the lads had been brought up by Harry, and he was somebody everyone in Swansea knew,' reflected Toshack. Harry's widow Gwen later told John that he'd never been happier than during those fourteen games he'd assisted Toshack, and was planning to sign a new contract to stay and help the new manager.

'He never did, though, and if ever a man died for a football club then that man was Harry Griffiths. Although I had been in charge for sixteen games, the team that went up was Harry's, and he had set the wheels in motion for the success that was to follow.'

Perhaps the biggest tribute that can be paid to Griffiths is the fact that five of the players he nurtured at the Vetch Field went on to play in Division One for Swansea.

In the summer of 1978, season-ticket sales were the best at the club in twenty years, and Struel gave Toshack £50,000 to spend on team building. Some £24,000 went on Leicester striker Alan Waddle, previously a rival for Toshack's no. 10 shirt at Anfield. 'He was some way short of being a First Division player, I felt he could do a job in the Third. I saw him as a player who could fill in for me at centre forward, and as I had played with him in the reserves at Liverpool, I knew there might be times when we could link up once again.'

Toshack, who intended to play himself at centre back, also recruited goalkeeper Geoff Crudgington from Crewe, who had impressed playing against Swansea during the promotion run-in.

Perhaps most crucially, John also managed to secure the signature of Alan Curtis, who was being courted by several top-flight clubs, on a one-year contract. 'There was a buzz of anticipation acknowledging his extraordinary tight control, ability to feint, turn, create space and torment defenders who lacked the contortionist flexibility to keep him in check.'

And he persuaded his former Liverpool team-mates Tommy Smith and Ian Callaghan to head south. Smith had just missed out on the 1978 European Cup Final at Wembley after dropping a hammer on his foot and breaking his toe. Liverpool had made it clear Smith's long and distinguished career at Anfield was over, as was that of Callaghan. Between them, they had played 1,500 matches for Liverpool.

Smith and Callaghan, both still based on Merseyside, were given dispensation to train at Liverpool's Melwood training ground for part of the week, only travelling down in the build-up to games, to avoid having to uproot their families.

Toshack started the season by proclaiming that, 'We are going to put this club back on the map!' and Swansea certainly opened impressively, drawing at Colchester on the opening day. Four days later, Smith led out the Swans at home in front of 20,000 fans. Lincoln were swept aside 3–0 and with a win at Oxford the following Saturday, Swansea topped the Third Division after three games.

'The Swans simply flowed over them,' recalled Huw Richards. 'Robbie James, finishing with thunderous finality, scored in each half as palpable excitement grew among the massive Swansea following.'

In the League Cup, Swansea had been drawn against Tottenham Hotspur, whose manager, Keith Burkinshaw, had signed two of that summer's World Cup heroes from Argentina, Ossie Ardiles and Ricky Villa. Tommy Smith, seemingly affronted by this import, issued his own unique reception with a contemptible tackle on Ardiles after a 50–50 ball.

Smith even earned a condemnation in the leader column of the *Guardian* for his troubles, but he remained unrepentant. 'If these Argentinians want to come over here and play they had better get used to the idea of being tackled. They have won the World Cup and Miss World but that doesn't mean we have all got to stand and admire their skills. Ardiles will do well to remember, that tackle will be the first of many.'

Swansea had been 2–0 up, but Alan Waddle allowed Spurs to get back into the game, conceding a penalty after a handball, and Tottenham earned a draw. Toshack attempted to play down Smith's remarks as his team prepared for the replay at White Hart Lane. Spurs, thrashed 7–0 at Anfield the previous Saturday, were without centre back John Lacy, so Toshack decided to take advantage of Swansea's aerial threat, and it worked, as he and Charles headed Swansea in front. Alan Curtis, who tormented the Spurs defence, added a third and Ardiles and co were out, 3–1. Ignoring Smith's remarks, Ricardo Villa was gracious enough to liken Toshack to his World Cup team-mate, Mario Kempes. Not surprisingly, John picked up his first manager of the month award.

The Liverpool contingent grew as Toshack signed former team-mate Phil Boersma from Luton for £35,000, and he made his debut in an incredible match against Rotherham, as City recovered from 4–1 down to snatch a point. The following weekend, Swansea clawed back from a 3–1 deficit to beat Tranmere 4–3, finding themselves back on top of the table after six games.

But Swansea's promotion bid faltered after two away games in three days. At Chester, Alan Curtis had to be substituted after half an hour with a pelvic injury, before Tommy Smith got a red card and Swansea lost 2–0. Three days later at Carlisle, centre back Nigel Stevenson was unlucky to concede a penalty two minutes from the end when it looked like Swansea had earned a goalless draw. The League Cup run came to an end too, as the Swans went down 2–0 at Queen's Park Rangers, despite a virtuoso display from Robbie James.

'He had an indestructible quality since announcing himself as a sixteen-year-old with his first League goal, a thirty-yard screamer on New Year's Day 1974, and had carried on in the same manner,' recalled Huw Richards. 'He was a streak player who scored goals in bursts. Twenty-one this season included eight in the first four matches, then six in eight on the run-in, most hit with alarming power. Robust and barrel-chested, he looked cumbersome until he had to cover ten yards to the by-line or a loose ball. Then he was quick, adept and competitive.'

Toshack strengthened his squad further when he signed Aston Villa defender Leighton Phillips for a club record

£70,000, as Tommy Smith was finding it tough to complete two matches a week. Phillips slotted into the defence, and like the rest of Toshack's new recruits, quickly gelled with his new team-mates into a formidable unit.

By November, Swansea were lying in third position, one point behind the joint leaders Watford and Shrewsbury. Geoff Crudgington, who'd been one of the side's weaker links until then, saved a penalty against Bury to ensure a Swansea victory.

John decided to escape the pressure and take a mid-season break, leaving Smith in charge, but Toshack found himself unable to switch off. 'He'd gone away for a few days, and Tosh told me he wanted me to look after things,' recalls Smith. 'We'd signed a defender from Everton, Neil Robinson, and he hadn't played. We had a reserve game at Bristol City and he came up and asked me if he could play. So I said yes and I thought nothing more of it. Next morning, there's hammering on the door of the hotel where I was staying. I was told to get down to the club, there's Neil Robinson on the table. His cartilage had popped out against Bristol. The doctor there didn't know what to do. So I told him to get it sorted, have the operation, and I got on the phone to Colin Harvey at Everton and told him we were going to stop the payments.

'But that afternoon, Tosh came back from holiday, asking what I was doing. In the end, he stayed, and he got manager of the month – and he'd been away half the time.'

Robinson's arrival from Goodison didn't prevent the club being dubbed Anfield Reserves by Fleet Street, and any player leaving Liverpool, including Emlyn Hughes, was instantly linked with the club. But as Struel's objective of Division One within 18 months began to look more and more of a possibility, Toshack was more concerned with what he perceived as a lack of ambition within the city. 'They keep asking me to get the Swans back into the Second Division. What's wrong with Division One?'

Following Christmas, and a Boxing Day defeat to Bristol Rovers which included an amazing diving headed own goal from Alan Waddle, it looked like Swansea might be slipping out of the promotion race. The Swans had been dumped out of the FA Cup by Bristol Rovers, and the weather ruled out any football in January, while February saw City, further bolstered by the recruitment of utility man Brian Attley from Cardiff, go without a win for five games.

Two wins in four days against promotion rivals Gillingham and Watford put them right back in it, however, and an Easter defeat of title favourites Swindon in front of 17,000 fans put the Swans in the driving seat. Robbie James blasted the only goal in the first half and Swansea soaked up some immense pressure from Swindon. Fans' favourite Alan Waddle, who scored 19 goals that season and created countless others, was memorably celebrated by a huge banner which declared, 'Alan Waddle lays on more balls than Fiona Richmond.'

But that match signalled the end of Phil Boersma's playing career. 'It was the worst injury I have ever seen,' said Toshack. 'I drove his wife Eva to hospital the following day and had the feeling we had seen the last of him as a Swansea player.'

With just half a dozen matches left, Swansea had their return to Division Two after sixteen years in their own hands. But, says Tommy Smith, the uncompromising style of management that would later become a hallmark of Toshack's coaching career had not fully developed. 'When I first went there he was inexperienced, he had me and Cally, and he relied on us at times to set an example. I remember once after a game we were in the dressing room, and we went round picking up the kit, he couldn't believe it, because the players there then never did that. But that's what we'd done at Liverpool. I think maybe later on when he'd become more established, he took more control.'

Ian Callaghan agrees. 'He wasn't a loud person, what he said you took in, and he spoke to people individually and told them exactly what they wanted. He was a great character, although he was quiet, and players took notice of him, and that's why he was a success, because the players responded. I'd always thought he'd stay in the game in some capacity, you could see the Liverpool upbringing put him on the way to being a good manager. You could see the influence of Shankly and Paisley, the way we trained, the way we played, the influence was always there. And why not, because Liverpool were so successful.'

Of those six matches, Swansea had to come from behind in five. On their first ever appearance on *Match of the Day*, they drew their penultimate match at Plymouth, coming from behind twice as Toshack scrambled home the equaliser from three yards.

John had been alternating between playing and sitting on the subs bench during the promotion run-in. Now for the last match, he was on the bench as his team ran out needing a win over Chesterfield in front of a full house of 25,000 fans on a Friday night.

Chesterfield tore up the script when they took the lead directly from a Phil Walker corner which City failed to clear. Alan Waddle equalised with a header just before half-time, but with twenty minutes to go, Chesterfield remained resolute and Swansea, who came close but were denied by the woodwork, were no closer to the victory that would secure promotion.

'Tommy and I sat on the bench and looked at the big clock on top of the North Stand. "Well, it's now or never," said Tommy, and I knew what he meant,' recalled Toshack. He entered the action in place of Attley, as Swansea, now boasting a strike force of Curtis, Waddle, Toshack, James and Charles, went in search of the goal.

'With five minutes left, Danny Bartley took a free-kick on the left-hand side of the penalty area. I rose to head the ball into the top corner of the net and that was it.' Swansea were promoted for the second time in twelve months.

Toshack felt proud for his team, the board who had backed his vision, and the fans who had to suffer the indignity of seeing their team apply for re-election to the Football League just three years earlier. But even as the champagne corks popped, Toshack was already planning the next campaign, wondering whether Tommy Smith, Ian Callaghan and indeed himself could keep playing, and whether Alan Curtis might finally be tempted by a move into the big time.

He didn't have to wait long for his answer. Less than a week after promotion, City lost Alan Curtis to Leeds United for £350,000. It was money Swansea, despite their new-found status, could hardly turn down, nor could they stand in the way of Curtis's development, even if Toshack had his doubts about his ability to compete at the highest level.

'He was a very gifted player,' recalled Toshack, 'but Alan is very much a home bird and I could imagine him having some difficulty settling away from home.' Toshack joked with Curtis that he would salt half of the fee away in order to buy him back in two seasons. Curtis laughed, recalled Toshack, but didn't argue.

Toshack set about bolstering his depleted midfield. First to arrive was his cousin, John Mahoney, for £100,000 from Middlesbrough, to bring some experience and inspiration to the Swans midfield. He would line up alongside Tommy Craig on the left from Newcastle for £150,000, and Dave Rushbury from Sheffield Wednesday for £65,000.

Toshack believed with this kind of experience, blended with talented youngsters like Chris Marustik and Nigel Stevenson, could see the Swans adapt well to the Second Division. He remained unhappy with the notion that the Second Division was the club's rightful home, but given the club's history, it was not surprising supporters were being cautious.

And after two promotions, Toshack felt the board might be getting carried away. 'They were all seeing success for the first time, and obviously there would be times when they would get carried away with it.'

The playing staff seemed to have their feet on the ground, at least, with the exception of Alan Waddle. Having scored 23 goals in 50 matches, Alan believed he deserved better and refused to sign a new contract.

'Alan is a big likeable lad who occasionally gets carried away and believes he is a better player than really is the case,' Toshack said. 'He had done virtually nothing until he came to the Vetch Field and could quite easily have drifted out of the game.' But Waddle's bargaining power was helped by a hatful of goals in pre-season games and a hat-trick in Swansea's first match, a League Cup tie against Bournemouth, and he eventually signed a two-year deal.

Swansea got off to a flying start, Curtis and James scoring in a win over Shrewsbury, and after the first dozen or so games, the Swans were among the leaders, but their promotion bid was undermined by home defeats to Leicester and QPR. 'The system of play I had adopted was causing problems,' admitted Toshack. 'At home we didn't seem to get men forward quickly enough.'

Toshack adopted the sweeper strategy that was to become a hallmark of his managerial career for the next two decades, initially deploying Leighton Phillips, who was starting to lose his pace, in the role. In order to give the side a bit of flair down the left, meanwhile, he tried to sign Leighton James from Burnley, who had been with City as a teenager. But the Lancashire club demanded a £200,000 fee which Swansea didn't have.

Instead, Toshack turned to David Giles. The Cardiff-born player had left Ninian Park just twelve months earlier for Wrexham, and now here he was signing for his third Welsh club at a cost of £70,000.

'Giles began to give us that bit of dash down the left-hand side,' recalled Toshack, 'but in defence Leighton Phillips was performing so badly we were forced to leave him out.' Christmas loomed with a 3–0 collapse at Chelsea, but on Boxing Day Swansea beat Cardiff City 2–1, Toshack putting one past his old club with a header, but an error by new goalkeeper Glan Letheran let the Blue-birds back in. David Giles got the winner, however, and with a new, more balanced line-up, Swansea managed to halt their slump.

The new decade dawned with an FA Cup clash with the outfit dubbed the Team Of The Eighties. Terry Venables brought his Crystal Palace team to the Vetch Field for a third-round tie that attracted 20,000 supporters and plenty of media interest.

Toshack gave the underdogs a half-time lead, and Swansea's new young defensive partnership of Stevenson and Charles appeared to be working well. But Palace got back into the tie with two goals, and looked to be going through until Toshack got his head on Tommy Craig's corner and earned a replay.

Jeremy Charles failed a fitness test for the rematch, however, and Toshack drafted himself back into the line-up as sweeper. It seemed to confuse Palace, and Swansea raced into a two-goal lead after a quarter of an hour. Palace pulled them back to force extra time, however, and Swansea again took the lead, but Vince Hilaire equalised to make it 3–3 and send the tie into a second replay, at Ninian Park.

Toshack drafted in Ian Callaghan in midfield and played himself upfront alongside Alan Waddle. 'We had played them three times and I had picked three different sides and approached each game with a different style of play. I knew Palace were a better side than us, but I felt that perhaps the element of surprise would be our best way of beating them.'

He was right. Palace took the lead, but Swansea didn't panic and Robbie James and David Giles netted to finally earn them a place in the fourth round, where they beat Reading. In the fifth round, at eventual winners West Ham, Swansea were denied a replay by the linesman's flag.

In the League, Toshack had been concerned by the form of goalkeeper Glan Letheran and resolved to find a replacement. Swansea were too close to the basement for his liking, and he was himself starting to feel the pace of football playing and management. But he continued to select himself and helped Swansea put some wins together and sufficient daylight between them and the drop zone. Toshack took a break, and reflected on the pressures of management. 'I realised where I had been going wrong. Quite simply I had been doing too much. I had been pushing myself to the limit both on and off the field.'

In the end, Swansea lost only one of their last twelve matches. Just before the match at Orient, Toshack was offered £400,000 for David Giles, who had proved a revelation as a forward with the ability to cause trouble for the best of defences. 'I know a large amount of his success was due to the fact that I had been playing up alongside him in attack,' recalled Toshack. 'I was pointing him in the right direction on the field and the more people likened him to Kevin Keegan, the more he continued to impress.'

Toshack turned down what would have been a profit of £330,000, still feeling reluctant to cash in on players with whom he felt a natural bond. 'Of course I have since realised that there is no room for such sentiment in football, but in my earlier days in management, that sort of thing did bother me.'

Meanwhile, Toshack was finally able to prise Leighton James away from Burnley, who seemed doomed to relegation, for £120,000. 'He had not been without his problems or his critics, but I knew Leighton better than most and thought I knew how to get him going again.'

James arrived three days before Swansea's final match with relegated Charlton, and despite his arrival after the transfer deadline, the Football League gave James permission to play in what was effectively a dead rubber. 'Leighton was full of himself,' recalled Toshack, 'and said to me, "Tosh, I don't like that no. 11 jersey," to which I replied, "Oh, that's OK Leighton, you can have the no. 12."'

James thought Toshack was joking until Saturday lunchtime, when he announced James would start on the bench. But Swansea struggled in the first 45 minutes and sent James on at half-time. In no time he'd scored one and made one, to end a difficult season on a high.

9 Tales of the City

Twenty years on, the Division One table of 17 October 1981 is an extraordinary document of a period in football that will probably never be repeated. Leeds United are in the relegation zone, where they would end the season, and Arsenal aren't much safer. Brighton are higher than Liverpool and Notts County can look down on Aston Villa. But to cap it all, top of the League after ten games aren't Tottenham or Nottingham Forest, or Big Ron's new-look Manchester United. In little more than three years since Swansea had said goodbye to Division Four, after a 2–1 victory over Stoke, the number one team in England was from Wales.

Rewind a season or so further to the summer of 1980. Toshack and his players were preparing for their second season in Division Two, and the impressive form they'd shown in the last dozen matches of the previous season meant there was plenty of optimism around the Vetch. Phil Boersma joined the coaching staff after his enforced retirement, replacing Tommy Smith as first-team coach. On the field, Toshack paid West Bromwich Albion £60,000 for goalkeeper Dave Stewart to replace Glan Letheran, who hadn't impressed since arriving from Chesterfield to replace Geoff Crudgington.

During a pre-season tour of Scotland, Toshack was contacted by a Yugoslavian journalist, Borko Krunic, whom he'd first encountered during those stormy matches with Yugoslavia four years earlier. He wanted to know if Swansea would be interested in signing Dzemal Hadziabdic, a defender with 27 caps for Yugoslavia.

Hadziabdic, who hailed from Mostar in Bosnia, was in England looking for a club and was available for £175,000.

Toshack agreed to take a look at him during a friendly with Spurs at the Vetch. Swansea won 1–0, but the result took a back seat compared to Hadziabdic's performance in the no. 3 shirt, outshining Hoddle, Ardiles and Tottenham's new signings, Garth Crooks and Steve Archibald. When he was forced to leave the field in the second half suffering the effects of a heavy cold, he received a standing ovation.

'Hadziabdic stole the show,' recalled Toshack. 'The board held a meeting straight after the game, and twenty-four hours later we had a new player on our books.'

Swansea paid Velez Mostar £150,000, and Hadziabdic was immediately rechristened Jimmy by his new team-mates, who had difficulty pronouncing Dzemal. It was money well spent, as Hadziabdic would be almost ever-present that season, striking up an excellent understanding with Leighton James.

But Hadziabdic's work permit hadn't arrived from the Home Office by the time Swansea kicked off their campaign at Vicarage Road. Toshack played a 5–3–2 system with Leighton Phillips continuing at sweeper, with Jeremy Charles and David Giles in attack. Robbie James put Swansea 1–0 up, but Watford forced their way back into it and took the two points with two goals. Toshack remained philosophical, however, believing that his most successful seasons had kicked off with an opening day defeat.

And after remaining unbeaten for the next six matches, Swansea were well placed to mount a promotion challenge. Alan Waddle forced his way back into the team, scoring twice in a superb team performance as Swansea beat Bolton 4–1. As December approached, Swansea hadn't been out of the top six and were being hailed as genuine promotion contenders, and Toshack also managed to recapture Alan Curtis from Leeds. Their manager Jimmy Adamson had been fired and it seemed that Curtis, recovering from a knee injury sustained in a collision with Peter Shilton, didn't figure in new boss Allan Clarke's plans.

Toshack was quoted a figure of £300,000, which Swansea couldn't afford, but with Leeds under financial pressure, Swansea were able to bargain them down to £175,000 – the figure Toshack had told Curtis 18 months earlier he'd reserve to buy him back.

But November started with City earning just two points from four games, leaving them off the pace and sixth in the table. Curtis's return came in part after Bill Shankly had told Toshack that with a bit more firepower, Swansea could win promotion. Shankly had been surprised as he watched Swansea fold at struggling Oldham before Christmas, and as well as buying Curtis, Toshack resolved to purchase an experienced central defender.

Curtis returned in time for a concerted push up the table. Having waved to the crowd before a 4–0 rout of Newcastle, he scored a penalty at home to Watford three days later that propelled the club into third place. The pessimists were silenced, but Toshack felt moved to quell promotion talk. 'There's a long way to go. Ask me again in the middle of May.'

Two days after Christmas, Toshack took his team to Cardiff City. 'For obvious reasons, I wanted us to go to Ninian Park and put on a display of quality football.' And Swansea did just that. For 80 minutes, at least. They were 3–1 up until the unfortunate Dave Stewart miskicked a goalkick and Peter Kitchen rounded him to make it 3–2. Then in injury time, John Buchanan blasted home a free-kick from 35 yards. Toshack conceded that if the game had continued for another five minutes, Swansea would have lost.

'I had so much wanted to beat Cardiff that day,' he admitted. 'My thoughts had gone back to the day three years earlier when the club had turned down my wishes to return there, and I wanted to show them the mistake they had made, and the best way would be for my team to play them off the park.'

Swansea crashed out of the FA Cup 5–0 at Middlesbrough the following Saturday, but Toshack's priority was promotion, and it left the way clear to concentrate on that aim. Unfortunately, the slump continued. They played host to runaway leaders West Ham, who seized an early initiative and were 2–0 up at half-time. After the break,

Curtis got the Swans back into it, but a blunder by Leighton Phillips let the Hammers seal the points. Swansea lost their next four games and slipped to 11th.

After a 3–1 defeat at Cambridge, the out-of-form Leighton Phillips asked to be left out for the visit of Queen's Park Rangers. Toshack regretted replacing Phillips, as Swansea lost 2–1.

But respite appeared to arrive from the east. Swansea took another Yugoslav international defender, Ante Rajkovic, on trial from Sarajevo. Fittingly, it was his performance for Swansea against the touring Red Star Belgrade team in a friendly that convinced Toshack to spend £100,000 to sign him. 'Phillips reacted angrily and demanded that he be put on the transfer list. This was the first time any player had asked for a transfer. I really was a football manager now, all right, and the problems were mounting up all the time.' But Rajkovic, a strong footballer with the ability to read the game, was to sustain a hamstring injury in his second game for the club.

Swansea crashed to defeat at promotion-chasing Sheffield Wednesday in a dismal performance. A misunderstanding between Leighton Phillips and the erratic Dave Stewart led to the first goal, and Toshack believed that kind of inconsistency had wrecked Swansea's chances of promotion.

He decided instead to bring through youth-team captain Dudley Lewis to give him experience, and thrown in at the deep end, he acquitted himself magnificently as Swansea swept aside Bolton 3–0, thanks to a Leighton James hat-trick. The off-form James had almost been left out by Toshack on the morning of the match, but capped his treble with a 25-yard rocket.

Swansea only lost one of their next eight games to haul themselves back into contention, and with three matches remaining, were vying for promotion with Luton and Blackburn for the third place behind West Ham and Notts County. Just two wins and a draw from their last three games would ensure promotion for Swansea.

Chelsea were beaten 3–0 at the Vetch Field, Hadziabdic scoring to send the crowd into an ecstasy. Dudley Lewis and the recalled veteran Wyndham Evans had by now struck up a useful partnership at the back, and with youngster Nigel Stevenson drafted in too, Toshack pondered whether these three unlikely heroes could help Swansea make it.

'An eighteen-year-old in his first season as a professional, a player in his testimonial season who never dreamed he would be playing in such important matches, and a centre half whom the club had wanted to give away. But they were Swansea City through and through, and the thought of First Division football at their club was enough to make them die for the cause.'

Two days later there were 23,000 fans at the Vetch Field for the clash with promotion rivals Luton, who needed a win to keep their own hopes alive. And after just 20 minutes, Swansea were 2–0 up. Luton pulled one back just before half-time, and took control in the second half as they sought victory. Luton equalised 15 minutes from the end, meaning that Swansea, boosted by a superior goal difference, would have to win their last game at Preston to beat Blackburn to third spot.

But Toshack had a selection problem. Jeremy Charles, returning from injury, had come on as substitute for Tommy Craig against Luton, but now both merited a first-team start, especially Craig who had been inspirational in Swansea's run-in.

It meant a reluctant decision for the manager. 'I decided John Mahoney would have to be the player to stand down. Imagine how I felt. Having to tell any player that is never pleasant, but when it's your own cousin then it becomes even more difficult and I remembered the games we played together as young boys in the streets at Canton. I called him to one side and told him. He was so disappointed that he broke down in tears, and I must admit that I had to wait for a few minutes before I could go into our team meeting.'

Toshack was so confident of victory, he'd arranged a celebration party at the old Holiday Inn in Liverpool for all the players and their wives. He approached the game like Shankly, getting up early and going round the players' hotel rooms, before leading them on a walk in the hotel grounds.

When they arrived at Deepdale, there were 10,000 Swansea fans waiting for them – and Bill Shankly, who went into the Swansea dressing room to wish them luck. Shankly had played for Preston for fifteen years, but now he was eager to see them lose, even if it would seal their relegation to Division Three.

But not everyone was so sure, remembered Toshack. 'Just as everything went quiet in the dressing room at about 2.45, Alan Curtis quipped, "Now, what happens if we win and Blackburn win – are we definitely up?"'

The answer was yes. Leighton James gave Swansea the lead and Tommy Craig made it two following some excellent work on the right wing by Neil Robinson. In the second half, they lost the impetus however, as Preston pushed forward for survival, and with Swansea just twenty minutes from the pinnacle of British football, Preston made it 2–1 when Stewart fumbled a cross and Alex Range tucked it away from close range.

With ten minutes left, Stewart messed up again, coming for a corner but failing to gather, but Preston's Mike Baxter put his header just wide. Toshack finally believed Swansea were home and dry, and with just seconds remaining, Curtis and Robbie James combined to set up Jeremy Charles to fire home the third.

'It was fitting that Charles, Curtis and James should combine to clinch promotion. They had helped take the club from the Fourth Division to the First in record time, a fairytale story.'

But Toshack's first instincts were to race towards Dudley Lewis, who at just 18 and on just £50 a week, had performed magnificently and maturely since replacing Leighton Phillips in defence. He might have admitted to feeling the pressure at times, but had acquited himself brilliantly. The celebrations went on for ten minutes, Toshack indulging in a celebratory war dance as the players saluted the travelling fans.

'Possibly the most remarkable element of Toshack's achievement is that it was as a player-manager,' says Huw

Richards, 'a hugely demanding role, not least because it is generally filled by players at a stage in their career where the simple business of staying fit becomes a burden.'

Toshack returned to the dressing room where he was greeted by Shankly. 'It's a bloody miracle what you've done at Swansea,' he told Toshack. 'The most remarkable thing since the war to go from the Fourth to the First Division in such a short space of time.'

The team returned to their hotel to celebrate, before heading for the Vetch Field, where they were met by thousands of fans at 2 a.m., including Ante Rajkovic who had been waiting for his new team-mates for three hours. It summed up the unique spirit that had been generated among the players and the fans. The season was rounded off with a Welsh Cup Final victory over Hereford United, which meant Swansea would also have European football to look forward to.

The odds of 200–1 for the championship might have been against Swansea City at the start of the 1981/82 season, but as he prepared his squad for five competitions, Toshack was more concerned with some tough decisions. He was faced with the prospect of dismantling the team that had won promotion and building a new one. 'I had built two teams in my three years at the club and the fact that we had progressed again meant I would have to bring in more new players to meet the challenge of the big League. I also knew some of the players who had helped us win promotion would not be good enough to play for Swansea in Division One, and that was the thing that bothered me most of all.'

Only Leighton James and John Mahoney were experienced top-flight players, while Leighton Phillips and Tommy Craig had played in the division before but hadn't performed consistently over the previous season. But having the fit-again Ante Rajkovic would be like signing a new player, and he was poised to bring plenty of character and integrity to the squad.

Toshack had half a million to spend on new players. He thought about buying Ray Clemence from Liverpool – but he wouldn't have been able to sign anyone else. Instead, he moved for the experienced Dai Davies, who had been in excellent form for Wrexham, paying £45,000.

Upfront, he recruited Bob Latchford from Everton for £125,000. A proven goal-scorer, Latchford had been suffering with injury problems, but if it was a gamble, felt Toshack, then the stakes were reasonable and the potential rewards high.

The signing of former Evertonians Davies and Latchford should have put an end to the Anfield Reserves tag. But having initially decided to see how Wyndham Evans, Dudley Lewis and Nigel Stevenson would cope at the back, City conceded five in a friendly against Fourth Division Blackpool. John agreed a deal with Luton for defender Paul Price, but he opted for a move to Spurs, so Toshack went back to Anfield once more to sign centre back Colin Irwin for £350,000. It was the biggest cheque the Vetch Field board had sanctioned yet.

Swansea's preparations were disrupted, however, when Leighton Phillips criticised Toshack's managerial style. 'He said one or two uncomplimentary things about my managerial ability and I was both annoyed and surprised. I had been disappointed that Leighton wasn't able to justify the faith I had placed in him as a player.'

Phillips, who certainly wouldn't be the last to fall foul of Toshack in this way, was sold to Charlton, while Dave Rushbury was off-loaded to Carlisle. But as Swansea flew off for a pre-season tour of Yugoslavia, there was plenty of optimism among the squad, and Toshack felt satisfied that Latchford and Curtis would combine well upfront.

Saturday, 29 August 1981 saw Leeds United arrive at a Vetch Field bathed in sunshine for the first top-flight game staged at the ground in the club's seventy years. City fielded five international forwards, while Leeds named their £1 million recruit Peter Barnes in their line-up. But despite the price tag, he wouldn't be getting among the headlines that day.

Jeremy Charles scored Swansea's first top-flight goal after six minutes, but Derek Parlane equalised, and Dai Davies was forced to make some excellent saves.

In the second half, however, Latchford scored a hat-trick in ten minutes and Alan Curtis rounded off the rout superbly. On a blistering afternoon, City's rout had all of football talking, as they racked up their first three points under the new system introduced that day.

The following Tuesday, Swansea beat Brighton, although when they crashed 4–1 at West Brom the following weekend, many assumed the bubble had burst. But Swansea had played well at the Hawthorns, felt Toshack, and until Jeremy Charles's injury had been the better team.

He put it down to naivety, and hoped the players would learn that indiscipline at the back would always be punished at the highest level. For the next game, he deployed Ante Rajkovic as sweeper, and brought in Max Thompson, recruited from Blackpool, to replace the injured Charles. He also added to the growing Everton contingent at the club, paying £130,000 for the versatile midfielder Gary Stanley.

September saw City travel to Manchester United, where in the corridor outside the changing rooms Toshack heard a voice he recognised. 'Shanks was already talking to some of my players and he greeted me with a warm grin and firm handshake.'

Shankly congratulated Toshack on Swansea's magnificent start. 'I told you before, son, they are only human beings in the First Division, nothing more, nothing less.' But Swansea lost 1–0, despite, as Toshack put it, murdering United. Ante Rajkovic was the star of the show, and Shankly had plenty of praise for John and his team after the match.

It was to be the last time Toshack would see him alive. Two days after defeating Sunderland to consolidate their position in the top six, John was woken by his wife Sue. 'She woke early at about 6.30 and after hearing the 7 a.m. news, she returned to the bedroom to say, "John, Shanks has died." I cried unashamedly.'

In many ways it was not a complete shock, as Shankly had been admitted to Liverpool's Broad Green hospital on the Saturday with a mild heart complaint, suffering a massive heart attack two days later. 'Something had gone out of my life, there was no question about that,' said

Toshack. 'In a strange sort of way, I felt that what I was doing at Swansea was being shared with him. He loved the company of my players, and seemed so relaxed when he was with us. I know that I could not have achieved what I have in the game without him. He took me to Anfield when I was twenty years of age, and although he left the club four years later, he was still a great help to me when I returned to Liverpool after the Leicester business. And when I went into management, he was a constant help to me and his regular phone calls were always so timely. Now there would be no more conversations with him.'

Shankly had a massive influence on Toshack's early managerial success, reckons Tommy Smith. 'He used to rely on Shanks a lot, he'd be on the phone to him every day. Shanks had a formula – to get out of the Fourth Division you needed a big centre forward and a big centre half. Then to get out of the Third Division, you need a centre forward, we had Alan Waddle playing up there, two centre halves, I was playing there, and two wingers. And then once you were in the Second Division you needed better players again.'

Toshack was one of the pallbearers at the request of Shankly's widow Nessie, and the route of the funeral cortege was lined with mourning fans. By coincidence, next day Swansea were playing Liverpool at Anfield. City led 1–0 at half-time and Bob Latchford made it 2–0, but despite giving everything, there was no way Liverpool were going to lose on such an emotional day, and they ended the game level, thanks in part to Swansea's inexperience and naivety.

Naturally, the match was preceded by a minute's silence, as the players and managers lined up in the centre circle. 'We all had our black Swansea tracksuits on,' recalled Toshack, 'and just before the minute's silence began, I took mine off and unveiled a red Liverpool no. 10 jersey. It was meant as a mark of respect for a great man who had given me my chance in the big time, and for someone to whom I owed everything.'

But some Swansea fans were unhappy about Toshack's method of paying tribute, and wrote to the local press insisting that he should have thought more about the fans of his current team, not his old one. 'It may have been a natural emotional reaction to the loss of Shankly, but many crammed into Anfield's excuse for an away end felt he might have remembered whose manager he was,' reckoned Huw Richards. 'After all, we were six places ahead of Liverpool at the time.'

Toshack explained that it had been a spontaneous gesture, admitting that he hadn't stopped to consider the feelings of the Swansea fans. 'With the benefit of hind-sight, I realise that perhaps it was understandable for my own supporters to be upset, but I was still astonished by some of the letters.'

Toshack made amends by wearing a Swansea no. 10 shirt at the Vetch Field the following weekend as he received an award before a 2–0 victory against Arsenal which featured a spectacular volley from Max Thompson. And the following Saturday, Swansea beat Stoke to go top of the League, just four years after being a Division Four club.

But Toshack had problems motivating his players, six of whom had been in the Wales team that had blown their chances of the World Cup four days earlier in a 2–2 draw with Iceland. The first half saw Swansea's worst display of the season, and they trailed 1–0 at the interval. Gary Stanley replaced Leighton James and equalised straight away, before floating in the perfect free-kick for Latchford to earn the three points.

Swansea's touch returned with a thrilling victory at Ipswich Town, which moved Bobby Robson to remark that no team had dominated a game at Portman Road in that manner in five years. But just as quickly they lost it again with a couple of serious defeats, and Dai Davies started to be barracked for his goalkeeping performances after several blunders. One Swansea fan ran on the pitch before one match to erect a huge set of cardboard hands in front of the new stand, and a placard reading You Need Hands. But City managed to regain the top spot before Christmas with a home victory over Aston Villa, to belie their pre-season status as relegation favourites.

In the cups, Swansea had precious little luck that season. Having been knocked out of Europe by Lokomotiv Leipzig, they would need a replay to overcome non-leaguers Colwyn Bay in the Welsh Cup despite topping the League at the time, and they crashed out of the FA Cup at the first hurdle at home to Liverpool.

Not for the first time, rumours were linking Toshack with the Liverpool job, as Bob Paisley prepared for retirement after eight years in the chair. 'I had been very flattered by them. It would be very presumptuous of anyone to think they would become manager of the best club in Europe. But it is also very presumptuous of clubs to think they can just go and get who they want, when they want. I was very happy at Swansea and helped to build the club up from the ashes into a First Division force.'

In the new year, City lost 2–0 at Leeds in icy conditions, Toshack insisting that the game should never have gone ahead. Swansea had now lost three games in a row and the manager searched for new blood. He found it in the shape of Ray Kennedy. His position in Liverpool's midfield had been taken by Ronnie Whelan, and Bob Paisley agreed to release Ray to Swansea in a £160,000 deal on a four-year contract.

Toshack hoped Kennedy would bring motivation and balance to Swansea's title challenge, in addition to the experience represented by 381 games for Liverpool that had brought five championship and three European Cup medals.

'I felt completely stale mentally and needed a change,' said Kennedy. 'Recently my consistency, which has been the secret of my success here, has been slipping a bit and I knew something was not right. Unlike other clubs, Liverpool finds you out straight away if something is wrong.'

Kennedy had opted for Swansea over a return to his native North East with Sunderland, a move described by his biographer Andrew Leeds as a strange choice, as Ray didn't know anyone in South Wales and didn't really trust the Welsh. Kennedy had actually been brought to Liverpool to replace Toshack, and they didn't have much in common.

As Kennedy headed south, Swansea were sixth in the table, four points off the top, and he made his Swansea debut against Manchester United, after two months without a first-team game. City played two upfront and tried to stifle the United midfield of Robson and Wilkins. Swansea scored twice after half-time, and after the match, Kennedy declared, 'How can anyone rule us out? We must still be in with a chance of the championship.'

To recharge their batteries for the final push, Swansea took a mid-season break to the Costa Del Sol, returning to earn their first away win in three months at Notts County thanks to an early penalty from Robbie James, while Dai Davies relished a brilliant performance after his miserable autumn.

But a trip to Middlesbrough proved to be an unsatisfactory experience. Kennedy scored his first goal, courtesy of a Leighton James free-kick; however, despite being bundled over in the area, he was denied a penalty and the match ended in a draw. Ante Rajkovic, earning plaudits from every quarter for his performances at sweeper, had to come off injured at half-time after a kick on the ankle.

The manager was unhappy with the attitude of some of his players, who he felt seemed happy over a draw with a team struggling at the wrong end of the table. He convened a team meeting on the Monday morning, to outline his expectations for the rest of the season, and making it clear that he definitely wouldn't tolerate a lack of ambition. Toshack reacted with typical disdain to the team's pleas of a swirling wind and a terrible pitch. 'Players, of course, will always have excuses at the ready.'

But Tommy Smith reckons that Toshack was sometimes guilty of setting his standards unrealistically high. 'Tosh used to overanalyse. The game can't be planned half the time, because you can't predict what's going to happen. But Tosh tried to plan it all. I remember him playing this system in a Welsh Cup tie, and I think we were 3–0 down at half-time. He told us to carry on, but after we'd gone out on the pitch after half-time I went round everyone saying, "you play there, you play there". But he was a very thoughtful man, possibly he had to go abroad in the end.'

On this occasion, however, his players responded to his rollicking as they faced Liverpool at the Vetch next evening. Paisley's men were on a long march up the table after an uncharacteristically poor start which had seen them lie 13th in the table on Boxing Day. Toshack wanted to show Liverpool what he could do after that FA Cup defeat.

A frantic first half ended goalless. Sammy Lee had been detailed to take on the returning Ante Rajkovic, but the Yugoslav dealt impeccably with Liverpool's raids. Liverpool attempted to run Swansea ragged, as they had at Anfield earlier in the season, but Toshack deployed Leighton James and Chris Marustik to stifle Neal and McDermott, while Ray Kennedy and Robbie James contained Souness and Lee.

Leighton James fired in a free-kick from 25 yards, and Liverpool threw everything forward for an equaliser, until Alan Curtis broke away to make it 2–0. It was one of the most satisfying results of Toshack's career, against a Liverpool side in their pomp, but after the game he was rendered speechless. 'I can't describe how I feel. Our first season in Division One and we beat Liverpool.'

Successes at Sunderland – and at Arsenal, which was graced by a superlative display from Rajkovic at sweeper – maintained the momentum, and it was becoming clear that Ray Kennedy was providing a canvas on which the flair of Leighton James and Alan Curtis could thrive. But Kennedy's influence eventually began to ebb, and the reason for that would not be known for several years.

A further injection of talent came when Toshack exchanged David Giles for forward Ian Walsh from Crystal Palace. It seemed like a good deal, as Walsh was two years younger than Giles, and with Latchford suffering with injury problems, it appeared a sensible move.

City returned to second place in the table behind Keegan's Southampton after a victory over Stoke, but Ante Rajkovic was booked against Coventry and now faced a suspension. It was a real blow to Swansea's hopes as he'd been the chief architect behind their remarkable defensive record, with only one goal conceded in their last eight games. To compound the misery, Jeremy Charles limped off with a cartilage injury, having been plagued with injuries for eighteen months.

But Toshack wasn't altogether pleased with Charles's attitude all round. 'I felt a lot of his trouble had been self-inflicted and I had a chat with him and his wife Pam about the need for him to improve his discipline, determination and application. His uncle John and father Mel had both set high standards, but Jeremy was falling short of them.'

Swansea were back on top of the League after beating struggling Wolves in March as Toshack headed for Buckingham Palace on his 33rd birthday to receive the MBE. 'The Queen seemed to have a word for everyone as she pinned on the decorations, and I can remember her asking me if I was enjoying managing as much as I had enjoyed playing. We were on top of the First Division at the time, so my answer was, I suppose, predictable. "I am at the moment," I replied.'

Toshack's next engagement was with fellow title-challengers Ipswich at home. And City clearly missed Rajkovic as they succumbed to a last-gasp Eric Gates goal after a poor performance. Liverpool and Ipswich climbed above them in the table, and City were now fourth.

But John wasn't giving up hope just yet. He told his players they still could lift the championship, and they responded well with a 3–1 victory over a physical WBA side. However they threw two points away the following weekend. Swansea were leading West Ham through a Robbie James goal, but having been susceptible to set pieces all season, they conceded a Paul Goddard goal from a corner with two minutes left.

The next game was against Southampton at the Vetch Field, with Lawrie McMenemy's men one place below the Swans in fourth. Liverpool had a five-point lead, with Ipswich and Spurs in hot pursuit, but Toshack felt that the title was still a possibility. 'As I saw it, any one of six sides could still win it and I was at great pains to make sure the players realised the need to fulfil the 42 games with 100 per cent effort.'

He brought Leighton James back into the side and Swansea won 1–0 to put four points between them and Southampton, but they were now six points behind Liverpool and one behind Ipswich, having played a game more.

But Swansea surrendered the title with a 2–1 defeat at Birmingham when, with Latchford ruled out, Toshack selected James and Curtis upfront, hoping their pace would unsettle the back four. Swansea's performance on the day was dismissed by the manager as pathetic, and he made certain his players knew how he felt.

Liverpool won 3–2 at Southampton to virtually seal the championship, and with six City players called up for Wales, Toshack resolved to remind players of their loyalties. 'I wanted to make certain that they were all aware of where their bread and butter was.' It had echoes of the time Paisley had left him out after a Welsh international, and John was beginning to see the other side of the coin.

The players responded well in training, but when they faced Everton on the following Saturday, Ray Kennedy limped off after thirty minutes with an injury and Adrian Heath put Everton ahead. Chris Marustik gave away a second-half penalty and Everton went on to make it three. Robbie James pulled one back but as a season in which they had coped superbly with life at the top reached the end, Swansea were punished for making elementary mistakes.

Trouble was brewing off the field too. Toshack had been misquoted by a Sunday paper, which implied that he rated himself better than everyone except Brian Clough and Bob Paisley, when he'd actually stated they were the people he wanted to emulate. Further fuel was thrown on the fire when he was quoted as saying, 'I'm surprised nobody wants to use me in some capacity during the World Cup.' In fact, Toshack had said that if Wales had qualified for Spain, he'd have been there to watch his players in action.

It was a chastening welcome to the top rank of football management. 'I had spent four and a half years earning a reputation for myself and now one article had blow it all up in the air.'

He discussed it with Bob Paisley as he travelled to White Hart Lane to see Liverpool face Spurs. 'I was at great pains to explain to everyone that I had not said half the things that were printed and most of the stuff I had said was taken completely out of context. When I saw people like Bobby Robson, Terry Venables and Terry Neill coming into the room I felt terrible.'

City faced Spurs themselves two days later, and John shuffled the pack, giving Wyndham Evans his First Division debut to become the fifth player to have played in all four divisions with the club. But Evans fell awkwardly in a challenge with Mark Falco and tore his knee ligaments, and Swansea suffered their third League defeat in a row. Toshack was less than pleased about several aspects of Swansea's game, and hammered it out with his shell-shocked troops the following Friday. Top-flight football was finally taking its toll, but Toshack also felt he detected a lack of effort from certain quarters.

The talk had some effect, and the players were desperate not to see their good work wasted and Swansea slip out of the top six. And Robbie James scored twice as City triumphed at Nottingham Forest 2–0. But Swansea's hopes of a place in Europe started to evaporate as they lost at home to Middlesbrough when any kind of luck in front of goal seemed to dissolve.

'I sat at home on the Saturday evening with Sue and the children and I must admit I really did feel down in the dumps,' said Toshack. 'While all the fuss about Welsh Cups, UEFA Cups and championships was going on, I had almost forgotten about the four people who lived with me in Three Crosses. We talked a lot that evening about what the future held in store for us.'

Swansea managed to secure their place in Europe as they beat Cardiff over two legs in the Welsh Cup Final. And the following Saturday, Toshack blooded five teenagers in the final League match at Aston Villa, which ended in a 3–0 defeat.

Despite a disappointing end to a season that hinted at stormier times, there was no reason for anything but a celebration as Swansea ended the season in an amazing sixth place. The club had hit heights previously undreamed of, and their manager had proved himself an inventive and innovative tracksuit manager in a League where his favoured sweeper system was still viewed with suspicion. It was a testimony, as City historian David Farmer points out, not only to the managerial skills of John Toshack, but a tightly-knit group of footballers. 'What was most significant was that none of the many talented players in the squad could think of themselves as the stars. Swansea City's success lay in the fact that they constituted a *team*.'

Above In the Cardiff front row versus Blackpool's Glyn James and Jimmy Armfield, November 1967

Left Portrait of the artist as a young dog at Ninian Park, November 1970

Above left 'Never short of a trick or surprise ...' Beating Leeds United's Jack Charlton, December 1970

Above right Getting the better of Everton's Henry Newton in the air in the Merseyside derby at Goodison Park, April 1972

Left Forcing a save from Peter Shilton at Wembley as Tommy Smith looks on, May 1971

Right Enter the dragon to beat England's Bobby Moore and Peter Storey, May 1972

Above 'Just like a team that's gonna win the FA Cup ...' Wembley 1974; Toshack is second from the right

Left 'Newcastle were undressed ...' Causing Pat Howard problems in the FA Cup final

Right In control at Highbury, February 1975

Above left 'And here's the mighty Toshack to do it once again ...' Clinching the title at Wolves, May 1976

Above right Talking tactics on arrival at Deportivo La Coruna, August 1995

Left Back in the big time with Swansea, August 1981

Right Trouble on the horizon at Besiktas, July 1997

Left Making a point to hi
Real Madrid team, March
1999

Below 'You end up pickin
the same 11 arseholes ...'
Entertaining the Spanish
media, September 1999

10 Everything Must Go

By the summer of 1982, Swansea City fans could have been forgiven for believing their manager was a bona fide miracle worker. And as he recuperated after more than four years of constant progress, even Toshack could be pardoned if he'd started to believe it himself.

'For the first time I could relax and enjoy a long summer break,' he said. 'There would be no new signings to be made this close season. We would be the only club competing in five competitions for the second successive season, and hopefully would be able to make a bit more progress in the domestic cup competitions than we had managed in the previous season. Already I was looking forward to our second season in Division One and I knew that the players would be anxious to improve their game and develop as top performers as well.'

In hindsight, the signs had been there at the end of the previous season. City had won just one of their last six matches of 1981/82. Toshack no longer had the counsel of Bill Shankly, who had been a fount of advice and support throughout the good times. When Toshack really needed him, he wouldn't be there. And his decision not to build on the squad that had performed so heroically the previous season seemed to fly in the face of the old Liverpool maxim of buying when you're strong.

But characteristically, Toshack remained bullish. 'I really feel it signals the end of the beginning at Swansea. Many people have expressed concern about our ability to maintain the standards we have set, and I suppose that is understandable. We will not be surprised by anything that happens at Swansea.'

It's doubtful if anyone, including Toshack, would have been anything but surprised to learn then that within four years, Swansea would find themselves back where they started in Division Four, at the bottom of a spiral of failure, debts and recriminations. Especially after Swansea got 1982/83 off to an excellent start, kicking off with a goalless draw at Notts County, followed by home wins over Coventry and Norwich, leaving them second in the table after three games.

But in addition to the fault lines outlined above, there was one major problem facing Swansea in 1982. In many respects, City were a Division Four club playing in Division One. In contrast to the tightly run ships like Luton Town and Watford who'd emulated Swansea by breaking into the top flight, City had spent big. And they weren't skimping on the wages, either. In 1982, thirteen employees were earning over £20,000 a year.

None of which might have mattered if the club had been able to sustain footballing success and maintained an even keel. But that meant keeping a lot of balls in the air at the same time. Crowds remained relatively small, especially during the recession of the early 1980s which hit South Wales particularly hard. Despite the construction of the new East Stand, the Vetch still held only 26,400, including just 800 seats. 'It means we will always have difficulty in competing on a financial footing with some of the big guns in the Football League,' insisted Toshack in 1982.

With limited income through the turnstiles, it meant that Swansea were in no position to buy new players and would soon have trouble paying the ones they did have. This in turn would affect results on the field, which in turn would hit crowds. And smaller crowds led to even less income through the turnstiles . . .

'In this period the bottom's beginning to drop out of the transfer market,' notes Huw Richards. 'One of the reasons Swansea got into trouble is that they bought towards the top of the market in 1980/81, then when they needed to sell, transfer prices dropped back.'

It seemed like the infrastructure of the club was beginning to crumble. The club hadn't paid off the transfer fees of Colin Irwin, Ray Kennedy and Gary

Stanley, and they were barred from buying any more players until the debts were recovered.

In his autobiography, Kennedy alleges more sinister goings-on at the Vetch.

Swansea was about to blow up when I arrived, but I wasn't to know that. The club was rotten to the core, in debt with underhand payments going on as well as wage top-ups. The Vetch Field is opposite Swansea jail and I used to say we should go across the road to get our pay.

Kennedy, it should be stressed, at no point implicates Toshack, who meanwhile was starting to feel aggrieved by the attitude of the local media.

Some people, including the local media, still have not really come to terms with the sheer professional approach needed to succeed in the First Division and it has bothered me that I have had to upset a few of them over the years.

It all pointed to a siege mentality as Swansea failed to capitalise on their excellent start by losing the next four games, despite the return to fitness of Jeremy Charles. They went down 2–1 at newly promoted Watford, before a 4–1 rout at Stoke where some of Toshack's tactical switches went badly wrong and Ray Kennedy ominously reported feeling tired and sluggish.

Swansea were completely outplayed as they lost 3–0 at home to Liverpool. Dai Davies dropped the ball following a shot from Alan Kennedy, presenting Ian Rush with the simplest of tap-ins. Kenny Dalglish strolled through a bewildered Swansea defence to set up the second for Rush.

Toshack, having started out with 5–3–2, altered his tactics again, deploying four upfront and only three at the back. But it seemed like Swansea's cutting edge was nonexistent. Bob Latchford seemed only interested in heading the ball and Alan Curtis couldn't find his touch as

Craig Johnston made it three towards the end. Seven months earlier, Swansea had been the last team to beat Liverpool, but already it seemed as if they were in a different division.

The following Saturday, Swansea's fortunes stubbornly refused to improve. Colin Irwin broke his leg in a defeat at Aston Villa and wouldn't play again all season, presaging a horrendous year of injuries for City. Four or five players would find themselves out for long periods including Ray Kennedy and John Mahoney, and with no strength in depth, raw youngsters were thrown in at the deep end.

Having conceded eleven in four games, Toshack asked Kennedy to play in central defence against Spurs to counter striker Steve Archibald. And it worked, as Swansea, more organised and resilient, won 2–0 with goals from Max Thompson and Bob Latchford. Toshack's sweeper system coupled with some effective man-to-man marking shackled Tottenham's creative department, while the emerging Chris Marustik raided from his right-back spot. Swansea climbed into mid-table, and a draw at Brighton with Kennedy orchestrating back in midfield seemed to put City back on an even keel.

But despite a couple of encouraging results, team spirit was beginning to fray. Toshack's relationship with Kennedy was becoming more fraught, while the midfielder became unsettled by what he perceived as a split in the camp between the Welsh contingent and the rest. 'Some of the Welsh boys like Alan Curtis, Jeremy Charles and Robbie James were OK, but there was no real knitting together of the team as had occurred at Liverpool, and no forward planning.'

He felt that more often than not, the Welsh players would pass to each other, while there were smirking remarks about sheep on the team coach. Kennedy had actually informed Toshack about the split during the previous summer when by coincidence they both found themselves on holiday in the Algarve. Toshack had been dismayed, sighing 'Oh, don't say that, Ray,' before appointing Kennedy club captain, no doubt hoping he could bring together the two factions.

Certainly there seemed to be some camaraderie remaining as Swansea, inspired by the unsettled Leighton James, fought back to snatch a point after trailing 3–0 at West Bromwich Albion with twenty minutes to go. City had looked utterly dispirited, Albion's keeper Tony Godden even roamed into the centre circle looking for some action. But Leighton James gave Swansea a glimmer of hope when he lobbed Godden, before sending in an immaculate cross for Jeremy Charles to hit home. Three minutes later, an almost identical cross was met by a free header from Robbie James to equalise. It might have suggested there was still some fighting spirit left at the club, but the fact that an average WBA team had been allowed to go 3–0 up in the first place demonstrated the weakness in a Swansea team that had already featured 23 different players that season.

Encouragingly City started December by beating Luton Town, but followed up with a disastrous run of six games without victory, and Christmas 1982 arrived with Swansea in the relegation zone with Birmingham and Sunderland. Toshack became ever more anxious to motivate his team, and even took to visiting the younger players at home in the evenings to fire them up and tell them how he wanted them to play the following weekend.

Meanwhile Ray Kennedy was suffering with a niggling hamstring injury that had kept him out of the team, and when he had played, his form had largely been poor, except for the times he had been played out of position in defence. Toshack accused him of not keeping fit, and after a reserve game in which Kennedy came off injured after seven minutes, the manager, believing Kennedy to be a bad influence on the club's younger players, suspended him for two weeks, without any explanation, and stripped him of the captaincy.

'I have done this in the best interests of the club,' Toshack told the media. 'It is always sad when you have to take this action, whether it be Ray Kennedy or anybody else. You have to do what you think is right. You can be patient and let it go for as long as you can, but there comes a time when something has to be done and enough's enough.'

Toshack handed the captaincy to Robbie James. 'He cares about Swansea City deep in his guts. That's the kind of player we want in the tough months to come.'

Meanwhile, Kennedy was forced to train away from the rest of the squad, cutting a lonely figure as he did laps on his own of the training ground. PFA chief executive Gordon Taylor was eventually brought in to mediate, decreeing that the two weeks be regarded as a 'cooling-off period'. But it was mooted that he would be allowed to join Newcastle for a bargain £30,000, as Swansea, desperate to slash their wage bill, couldn't afford to pay him £800 to sit on the sidelines. Leighton James had already been dispatched to the Northeast on a free transfer to Sunderland, while Kennedy was joined in the sin bin by Bob Latchford, another player Toshack had begun to regard as a bad influence.

It was even reported that at one point, according to Huw Richards, he made 'the extraordinary decision to split his squad between two dressing rooms, rather than allow them [the young players] to be infected by what he saw as the cynicism and time-serving of older professionals'.

Toshack meanwhile attempted to bolster his coaching team, bringing in former manager Harry Gregg as assistant boss prior to a mid-season team break in Spain. But Gregg walked out just two months later, claiming he hadn't been sufficiently involved with the first team, a claim Toshack described as staggering. 'I brought him here, realised it was a mistake and I dismissed him,' insisted Toshack. 'Apart from his obvious talent as a goalkeeping coach, I could not see anything else that would have benefitted us. He was involved right up to the Tottenham game and also went with the seniors to Spain. You can't be more involved than that.'

February dawned with Swansea three positions from the bottom as Ray Kennedy returned to the first team at home to Watford. 'You can count on me to battle all the way and help John Toshack get Swansea out of trouble,' he declared. 'I've had my own problems, but if it's left to me I'll see out the last two years of my contract here.

Since Tosh arrived at Swansea it has been success all the way until this season and how he copes with the first setback of his managerial career will be crucial for both the club and himself.'

Ray showed flashes of his old composure but the Swans lost 3–1, before he performed well in defence as City went down by one goal at Spurs. But Kennedy quickly lost form again. Says Kennedy's biographer Andrew Leeds, 'John Toshack kept on at Ray, saying that his attitude was all wrong, that he was lazy and overweight and accused him of hating the Welsh.'

Neither was to know the real reasons behind Kennedy's loss of form. He was suffering from the onset of Parkinson's Disease. He had exhibited difficulty stretching for balls on his right side, and his leg continually felt taut, his right thigh muscles being constantly stiff and in spasm.

Kennedy played in a long-sleeved shirt, gripping the cuffs, with one arm sometimes fixed to his side, and had problems putting his foot on the ground when he started to run, while he lost concentration during games and his normally immaculate distribution had started to disappear in the run-in of the previous season. In training meanwhile, he felt a hot, dry, choking sensation in his throat. It might be unfair to point the finger twenty years on, but the club's insistence on extra training was possibly the worst remedy they could have prescribed.

Toshack would later raise the possibility that it was caused by a cumulative injury from repetitive heading of the ball, although Ray refuted this, saying Toshack himself had headed the ball much more than him and not contracted it.

The exodus from the Vetch Field continued; Robbie James was sold to Stoke City, as Swansea lost to Tottenham at White Hart Lane leaving them just a point above the relegation zone, their one solitary shot on goal coming on the final whistle.

Swansea, this season, are a mere memory of the lively team which surprised so many First Division clubs when they were fast promoted [wrote Brian Glanville in the *Sunday Times*]. Judged on this leaden performance, their present position in the League and the way I saw them awkwardly survive at Brentford in a League Cup tie earlier this season, they will do quite well to avoid returning to the Second Division. At the moment, there seems little sparkle and little appetite for the game among their ranks.

In early March, as Toshack marked five years at the Vetch Field, during the coach ride to Southampton, he had a long heart-to-heart with Kennedy, that seemed to have sorted out their problems once and for all. But it didn't work out like that. Kennedy was so clumsy and sluggish that he had to be substituted at half-time. He went on the transfer list.

'Ray has had difficulty settling here in Wales and we feel the time is right to release him,' said Toshack. But nobody wanted to sign him.

Since the turn of the year, Swansea had notched up just one victory, over Notts County, in thirteen games, when they thumped fellow strugglers Man City. It proved just a blip. By April they were well and truly in the mire. They drew 1–1 at Birmingham, after leading until the 87th minute, compounding a damaging trait that season of throwing games away in the last ten minutes, symptomatic of a team that just wasn't good enough. As Toshack blooded more and more youngsters, including goalkeeper Chris Sander and midfielder Jimmy Loveridge, they were thrashed 5–1 at home to West Ham and lost 3–1 at Luton.

A brave draw at home to Ipswich and an excellent win over Aston Villa staved off the inevitable, and on the penultimate Saturday of the season, a 2–1 defeat at Old Trafford relegated Swansea back to Division Two. It was their 21st away match of the season, and they hadn't won a single one.

'It has been a Liverpool-style run club here at Swansea for the last six years and for a small club that is incredible. But Swansea are not Liverpool or Arsenal,' said Kennedy. 'You can't expect to compete with the big boys year in, year out unless you have solid foundations.'

It might have seemed unavoidable for so long, but relegation still came as a shock to supporters, players and management alike, after that extraordinary surge from the basement to the penthouse. But instead of bringing the club together, relegation almost tore the club apart.

Swansea City were over a million pounds in debt. The club were still saddled with expensive contracts signed at the height of their success, which rival clubs, also feeling the pinch of the football recession, were loath to take on. PFA representative Bob Latchford called the players together to persuade them to take a pay cut to keep the embattled Toshack in the manager's chair, while the directors were battling for boardroom control.

The bitter atmosphere at the Vetch Field festered as the 1983/84 season kicked off. In the preliminary round of the Cup Winners Cup, at home to East German side FC Magdeburg, Swansea were winning 1–0 when the still inexperienced Chris Marustik hit a suicidal backpass to recently signed veteran goalkeeper Jimmy Rimmer. It allowed striker Streich to nip in and score. Ray Kennedy recalls that, 'after the game, Toshack kept mentioning the error over and over and wouldn't let it go'. Swansea lost the return leg 1–0 and missed out on a profitable tie with Barcelona.

In the League, Swansea's form was equally appalling, picking up just one point from the first 15 after an opening-day defeat at home to Sheffield Wednesday. Their first victory didn't arrive until the last Saturday in September, a 2–1 win at home to Cambridge, a team so dismal that later that season they would go 28 games without a win. At least Swansea never got that bad. But it was close.

Toshack was forced to field a team comprising the handful of top-class players still on the books, a mixture of youth-team hopefuls, veterans like Rimmer and loan signings, and even Emlyn Hughes answered the call and headed south to help out in defence. On 16 October, after a 2–1 defeat at home to Newcastle United, which left Swansea rock bottom of the Second Division, chairman Malcolm Struel and his vice-chairman Tom Phillips resigned.

'I have been privileged to serve the club for fourteen years and have twice saved League football for Swansea and southwest Wales,' said Struel. 'I am vacating the chair because I have become completely disillusioned with the way the game is going. In fairness to the club, I do not consider, feeling as I do, that I can any longer summon the necessary motivation. It is my intention to remain a director of the club for the present.'

The financial situation was causing anxiety, as new chairman Douglas Sharpe, managing director of a Swansea construction firm, took office. One of his first jobs was to meet with the club's bankers. Swansea City were £1.7 million in the red and losing £10,000 a week. 'League football at Swansea is safe – at least for a few weeks,' announced Sharpe.

He met with Toshack to spell out the terms and conditions of the club's commitment to the bank. To stay alive, Swansea had to raise £200,000 by the end of November. Clubs were circulated with an announcement that Alan Curtis, Ian Walsh, Bob Latchford, Ray Kennedy and Neil Robinson were all for sale 'at realistic prices'. Kennedy was less than eighteen months into a four-year contract worth £800 a week.

On the field, Swansea still couldn't win away as they plunged headlong towards the Third Division. They collapsed 5–0 at Fulham, and threw away a 2–0 lead with 15 minutes left at Charlton, Derek Hales taking a penalty twice after Rimmer had moved before Steve Gritt was gifted the equaliser four minutes from time. It would have been Swansea's first win in eighteen months, and Toshack was rendered so speechless he refused to speak to the press after the match.

His relationship with his own players wasn't much better. He'd fined two players for urinating by a bush in training, while Neil Robinson had sworn at Toshack and his coaching staff during one match. Robinson apologised, and assumed the matter would be dropped. But Toshack called him into his office and fined him a week's wages.

Unrest in the changing room and upheavals in the boardroom. There was no money and the real prospect that Swansea could go bankrupt any day. Even by the end of October, it was clear to supporters that City, rooted to the bottom of the Second Division, were doomed to relegation. It's no surprise Toshack felt he'd had enough. On 29 October, he threw in the towel.

'I had battled as hard as I could to make him stay,' insisted Doug Sharpe, revealing that Toshack had resigned, asked for no compensation for the remaining eighteen months on his contract, and donated £1,000 to the club's youth team.

In retrospect, while it's probably fair to say Toshack had made mistakes, he was still inexperienced as a manager – he was still only 34, an age when most of his contemporaries would still expect to be playing and counting down to their testimonial. Toshack *had* worked a miracle at Swansea, but the luck was bound to run out sooner or later. He'd lost his mentor, while the club had become crippled by debt and internal politicking.

Toshack was replaced temporarily by coach Doug Livermore, and the club eased their financial worries when they sold Jeremy Charles to QPR and Alan Curtis to Southampton, accruing £180,000, while Ray Kennedy was released on a free transfer and ended up at Hartlepool. But the bank deadline for reducing the £1.7 million overdraft at the end of November came and went and the directors ended up paying the wages out of their own pockets.

But at the start of December, Livermore quit. Having won just one point in six games in charge, he announced, 'I'm just not up to the job.'

Sharpe remained upbeat as he advertised the post. 'We'll probably go for a player-manager much along the lines of six years ago when we were in the Fourth Division and we persuaded John Toshack to join us.'

The new manager was very much like Toshack. In fact, it *was* Toshack. Less than two months after resigning, he agreed to return to the Vetch Field – on a short-term contract and wages slashed from the £45,000 a year he was reported to be earning before he quit. And what's more, with Swansea's roster utterly threadbare, he was back in the team.

His first game back in charge was, appropriately enough, at Cardiff City on Boxing Day, but despite getting on the scoresheet with a spectacular shot following a creaky run from halfway, Toshack couldn't work the magic as the Swans went down 3–2. It was followed the next day by another loss at home to Shrewsbury. But despite a predictable lack of mobility on his part, he managed to inspire his team to a 2–0 victory over Derby on New Year's Eve and the mini-revival continued with a draw at Cambridge. They fell back to earth, however, with a 6–1 thrashing at Sheffield Wednesday, in which Toshack managed to score an own goal.

With both Livermore and Boersma now gone, Les Chappell became Toshack's assistant manager and the dedicated Wyndham Evans, who had left Swansea in the summer of 1983 to manage non-League Llanelli, returned as player-coach.

But the nightmare run of results continued. There was the odd draw, and a victory over Charlton thanks to the only goal from prodigious young forward Colin Pascoe. It wasn't enough, however, as Swansea slipped further and further behind, and in March, Toshack left the club for the second time, only this time it wasn't his decision. Doug Sharpe said he had been very despondent about the succession of defeats. 'I feel a new face in the club would give the lift which we desperately need.'

While Les Chappell was put in charge of the team, Toshack said he had been asked to resign but had refused. And Malcolm Struel, still on the board, said he was refusing to recognise Toshack's sacking, as it had been made without prior agreement between all the directors, and called for a full board meeting. But Toshack wasn't coming back this time. There was speculation that he might return to managerless Cardiff, but it came to nothing. Inevitably, Swansea were relegated at the end of April after a 2–0 defeat at Shrewsbury.

Swansea had become a victim of football's very own boom and bust. Promotion to the first division had meant the wage bill exploded from £528,000 in 1981 to £826,000 in 1982. Toshack was on £45,000 and a dozen players earned between £20,000 and £35,000 each. The new £800,000 East Stand became a white elephant, and most crucially of all, the club had spent £2.2 million on new players and recouped just £1 million in sales. Record signing Colin Irwin was ruled out for almost two seasons through injury, while Ray Kennedy, through no fault of his own, had proved a very pricey liability. The maths were simple. And the few decent young players graduating from the youth team, like Darren Gale and Colin Pascoe, never quite fulfilled their potential after bearing the scars of that nightmare season, although local star Dean Saunders managed to shake off the stigma of relegation to become one of British football's most reliable goal-scorers.

But, says Huw Richards, despite the switchback ride, Swansea fans wouldn't have had it any other way. 'Very few fans experience that, to go from one end of the League to the other in such a short period of time, but I think a lot of supporters would say it was worth it, and I think he's still regarded as a hero at Swansea. Whenever there is speculation about the future, his name will come up, "Perhaps Toshack will come back and buy the club." When they formed the supporters trust this season, Toshack I know was the one of the first people who sent a message of support. He still has that standing. I think, I know, he was a miracle worker. In those three or four years, he earned a permanent position as one of the great heroes in the club's history.'

11 Home Thoughts from Abroad

One year after his departure from Swansea City, as he relaxed at home in South Wales, Toshack's phone rang. On the other end of the line was Inaki Alkiza, the president of Real Sociedad. Senor Alkiza was looking for a new coach ... and would he be interested? Exit John Toshack, enter John Benjamin.

It was to be the first of three occasions that Toshack would answer the call from the Royal Society Club of San Sebastian, the Basque city that he has called his home for most of the last seventeen years. He remembered the time he'd faced Real with Liverpool in 1976, and how welcome he'd been made on that occasion. Now, touching down at Bilbao Airport, he was impressed by the fact that the club's welcoming committee all spoke English.

Toshack had spent the last year managing Sporting Lisbon in Portugal, guiding them to second place. But Real Sociedad, he decided, represented a bigger challenge. Once more, he would be stepping into the shoes of a local folk hero. Alberto Ormaechea had taken Real to the championship twice in the early 1980s, based on a counterattacking system and a solid, defensive team that provided the bedrock of Spain's team for the 1982 World Cup. But finding themselves slipping down *La Liga*, Real had decided it was time for a new approach, and for Toshack, it helped that British coaches were in vogue in Spanish football, Terry Venables having just steered Barcelona to the title.

'By the 1984/85 season,' says journalist Phil Ball, based in San Sebastian, 'those players who'd won them the title like Jesus Zamora and Jesus Maria Santrustegui were in the twilight of their career, as they say, and Ormaechea hadn't really replaced them. He was a really nice guy, but

I think they felt they couldn't really go any further with him, times were changing. I think what they were looking for was someone a bit high-profile, a bit international, in inverted commas. Someone with a name.'

Toshack's name, it was decided, was certainly big enough for Real, if not quite long enough. 'He is invariably called John Benjamin Toshack by Spanish journalists,' says Huw Richards, 'whose taste for full names is matched only by the rugby commentator Bill McLaren.'

Founded in 1909, Toshack's new club was a canvas for the expression of Basque nationalism, refusing to sign non-Basque players for much of its history. 'It was always a bastion of Basque pride,' explains John Aldridge, who became a rare import in 1989. 'Outsiders were so mistrusted that Real had only employed ten foreign players in all their history. It hardly mattered if you were Spanish. You had to be Basque to be fully accepted.'

When Aldridge arrived, the Sociedad supporters club president was quoted as saying, 'I'd rather see Real in the Third Division than see a foreigner wear the club shirt.' But it helps, reckons Aldridge, that Basques loved English football. 'They appreciate the unique talents of English players. They watched English football matches as often as they could on television.'

John Benjamin quickly cottoned on to the fact that the Basque country, like his homeland, had its own unique culture. 'He'd go to a Basque *derbi*, and put his Basque beret on, and be seen doing Basque things,' says Phil Ball. 'Being Welsh was very useful as well, I think he pushed that a lot, because he realised politically the Basques would be sensitive to that, and that culturally they would accept a Welshman more than an Englishman. He's a clever guy, he realised that would work.'

It did. And the Real supporters responded warmly. 'When I was scouring Europe looking for players for Newcastle I fancied a big centre forward Tosh had at Real Sociedad called Meho Kodro,' recalls Kevin Keegan. 'Tosh collected me at the airport and I was amazed at the esteem he was held in Spain. Everyone wanted to shake his hand and say hello.'

But he wasn't the first non-Basque manager of Real Sociedad. In the 1930s, a Brit called Harry Lowe had taken charge of the team. 'It's not really been a big deal in the Basque country,' adds Phil Ball. 'Athletic Bilbao had lots and lots of English managers, right from the 1920s, so it's not a paradox, they're supposed to be only Basque, but managers don't count . . .'

Toshack also realised the importance of communication, declining the use of an interpreter even in the most difficult situations, and despite a grammatically suspect grasp of Spanish, he usually managed to get his message across.

He had already experienced a mixed start to his managerial career on the continent. Following his second and final departure from the Vetch Field, he had been head-hunted by Sporting Lisbon, who had just finished third behind champions and city rivals Benfica. 'Looking back he was obviously always destined to go abroad,' reckons Phil Ball, 'he's not a parochial bloke.'

And when he guided Sporting to a 3–1 pre-season tournament victory over Benfica, followed by an opening day 3–0 triumph at home to Victoria Guimares, it looked like the continental life suited Toshack perfectly.

'I was excited by the prospect of learning a new language and finding out about a new culture as well as a different style of football,' he said. 'Sporting is one big club. Their derbies against Benfica are as big as anything I had experienced. They had also had eighteen managers in fifteen years, so the job was a big one in itself.'

Toshack's Sporting had undergone a radical makeover. Between the posts was a new goalkeeper, Victor Damas, at 36 a sort of Iberian Dai Davies. He'd begun his career at Sporting back in the late 1960s, spending more than a decade crisscrossing Spain and Portugal, before deciding to return home. In front of him would be defensive midfielder Oceano, recruited from Nacional of Madeira, and upfront, Brazilian striker Eldon from Victoria Guimares.

And from Porto, midfielders Jaime Pacheco and Antonio de Sousa arrived fresh from Portugal's thrilling run to the semi-finals of the European Championships in France.

But when Toshack returned to Porto to bid for defender Joao Pinto, they'd had enough of seeing their team decimated, and were about to take their revenge.

Toshack had clashed with Sporting's prodigious Paulo Futre, at nineteen destined to become the golden boy of Portuguese football. Toshack wanted the forward to go on loan to a lower-division club to 'grow up' as a player, but Futre, a die-hard Sporting fan, believed he was already ready. Porto pounced, stealing Futre away for a ridiculously low sum. 'At Sporting they had told me for so long that they were nursing me,' said Futre. 'I felt I must be in hospital. Now I believe I have joined a club who will give me a regular place in the team so I can show what I can do.' Sporting's fans were outraged, but Toshack remained typically phlegmatic. 'At this rate, maybe we'd better have a new team picture taken.'

Despite the trauma of losing Futre, Sporting maintained their good start in the League, vying for the championship with Porto. And in the UEFA Cup, they saw off Auxerre in the first round, despite managing to throw away a two-goal lead from the first leg during the return in France, only for Oceano and Lito to restore it again in extra time.

But Toshack's innovation of a sweeper system did not go down well with the fans. And Sporting crashed out of Europe to Dynamo Minsk at the second stage, again managing to throw away a home 2–0 first-leg lead in the second match, this time losing 5–3 on penalties.

Back in the League, Sporting headed for Oporto for a top-of-the-table clash that ended in a goalless draw but a moral victory for Porto, who dominated the match. It was a bad-tempered game, too, with the referee flashing seven yellow cards – including one for Toshack himself for his angry reaction when one of his players was badly fouled. Porto now led Sporting by a point.

In the derby game, however, Toshack managed to restore some local pride in front of 75,000 fans, defeating Benfica thanks to Manuel Fernandes's goal after just three minutes, following a characteristic error by the perennially hapless Benfica keeper Manuel Bento.

In January, Toshack boosted Sporting's title bid with the signing of Argentinian Sergio Saucedo, from Deportivo Quito in Ecuador. The 25-year-old made an instant impact, scoring twice on his debut, once from the spot, in a 4–4 home draw with Academica, following up with a strike at Farense before scoring again in 4–1 win over Salgueros.

But Sporting's title bid was badly derailed by a sustained injury crisis, and by the spring, Porto were five points clear at the top of table. And there was another row when club president Joao Rocha suggested that four Benfica stars had asked one of Sporting's players to let the directors know they were interested in defecting. The quartet denied it, though, and as a rocky season ended with Sporting finishing runners-up to Porto, Toshack quit.

It had been an invaluable introduction to European football, however, as Toshack took up residence in San Sebastian. It was clear that Real's present team were a shadow of Ormaechea's title-winning side. 'The side really started to go over the top and decline,' he explained. 'The players dropped a lot in morale. It became mostly defensive, it had a terrible record for playing with everybody back, which really started to take people away from Atocha, so when I arrived I had the job of trying to introduce younger players and trying to get them to play with a little more ambition.'

As at Swansea and Sporting, Toshack imposed his own tactical imprint on Real Sociedad, deploying his sweeper strategy, and what was to become known as the *sistema Toshack*.

'They say now – I've got my own theory about it – but they would say and he would say that he brought in Toshack's famous 3–3–3–1 system,' says Phil Ball. 'A lot of European clubs would play with twin strikers, but Toshack suddenly dispensed with that. Later on he stuck Bakero upfront, he went on to become the midfield crux of Barcelona's Dream Team. Bakero was about 5ft 2in tall and he stuck him upfront. And it worked a treat. If you're going to play a lone striker, you can afford to have that extra man at the back, or play around with defence systems.

'Satrustegui, the top scorer was fading, Zamora was fading. I think in what he inherited, Toshack was lucky where Ormaechea was unlucky. When Toshack took over, with a fresh face, fresh ideas, the youngsters all came through, he got Bakero, Beguiristain, Goicochea, Lopez Rekarte, who all ended up at Barcelona. Without those four the Dream Team wouldn't have happened, really, and they were all just coming through.'

But as the 1985/86 season kicked off, there was a desperate early blow for Toshack when Real's talismanic keeper Luis Arconada damaged his right knee making a brilliant save in a match against Celta Vigo. Arconada's knee blew up like a balloon, and it was thought the injury might not be that serious. But once the swelling had gone down, the X-rays revealed major damage to both ligaments and cartilage, ruling Arconada out for six months.

Restricted by Real's non-Basque policy, Toshack was unable to buy a new goalkeeper, so he was forced to throw the inexperienced Gonzales in at the deep end. 'He was so involved with his own game, it was natural,' said Toshack.

But it soon became clear that Real were missing the natural authority that Arconada had on the central defenders. 'Arconada had always organised everything for them,' said Toshack. 'I realised we had a communication problem. Basque people are generally regarded as a closed type of person, the character is not very open. The players here are a very introverted type of person, as well.'

Instead, he deployed a midfielder, Juan Antonio Larranaga, 'a good talker on the field' as a sweeper behind the two central defenders, encouraging them to play further up the field. But beset by injuries, Real struggled for consistency, and in the first clash of British coaches in *La Liga* for fifteen years, were crushed 5–1 at home by El Tel's Barcelona, with the imperious Bernd Schuster running the show. And when they lost 1–0 at home to Real Madrid before Christmas, Toshack's team were struggling in the lower half of the table.

But in the new year, Real won five out of five, scoring a hatful of goals in the process, culminating in a 6–0 thrashing of Valencia who promptly sacked their coach. Toshack had been criticised when his defence was shipping water in the autumn, but his team was now beginning to make real headway, eventually finishing seventh.

And he demonstrated that he wasn't prepared to settle for anything other than a hundred per cent effort, when one of the Real players dared to laugh during the post-match meal after they'd been defeated 2–1 at Oviedo in a limp fashion in a cup tie. Toshack stood up and ordered the players to be on the coach at 4.30 a.m. to return to San Sebastian. When they arrived at 9 a.m., he ordered them off the coach and straight on to the training ground.

Toshack's authority was further reinforced in 1987, when he decided to sell winger Lopez Ufarte. The idol of the *socios* on the terraces and popular with his teammates, the Little Devil had been a regular goal-scorer and renowned for his amazing runs, if not his work rate. When Toshack, believing him over the hill, agreed to sell him to Atletico Madrid, he was resisted by a display of player power, the Real team signing a petition demanding that Ufarte stayed, and that Toshack be less dictatorial in his running of the club.

'There was almost a civil war about that,' says Phil Ball. 'It was pretty radical stuff. He did suggest the folk hero was not doing the business, and he wasn't, his knee had gone and Toshack was right. Once he gets across to people he never backs down.'

The president and directors backed Toshack, who knew he could replace Ufarte with youngsters keen to prove themselves. 'But that's the mark of Toshack,' adds Ball, 'someone prepared to come into another culture and say no, and he was proved right in a sense, because there's no bad blood between them, Ufarte's now his deputy, his second in command.'

That season, Real reached the final of the *Copa del Rey*, the King's Cup, beating Basque rivals Athletic Bilbao thanks to a gritty second-leg display and a goal from Bakero, following a goalless first leg.

So for the final they travelled to Zaragoza to face Atletico Madrid, who had beaten champions Real Madrid in their semi-final. Ironically, it was the unwanted Ufarte who shot Real Sociedad into the lead after just ten minutes, but fifteen minutes later, Jorge Da Silva levelled for Atletico with a memorable individual effort.

Real regained the lead just before the break, however, through Aitor Beguiristain. Atletico then turned up the pressure after half-time, substitute Julio Salinas playing a perfect pass to set up veteran Rubio who made it 2–2, sending the final into extra time.

Just two minutes from the end of the additional period, Real Sociedad were mightily lucky to avoid handing the cup to Atletico, when the referee ignored a foul in the box on Julio Preito. The final was settled from the spot, and when Atletico's Da Silva blasted wide, the scales tipped in Real's favour, before Arconada saved acrobatically from Quique Ramos. The cup was Real's.

'Toshack has said that was possibly his proudest achievement in football,' says Huw Richards, 'and the subsequent procession through the villages which form the club's hinterland showing off the trophy.'

In the League that season, Real had finished eighth. It hadn't been the best of starts, and the media were quick to forecast a struggle against relegation for Toshack, but they gradually climbed the table, and had been unlucky not to beat Barcelona, Real fans pelting missiles at the Barca players after a late 'winner' was disallowed for a foul on goalkeeper Zubizaretta towards the end of a 1–1 draw.

Having put some silverware in the cabinet, Toshack and Real started the 1987/88 season determined to repeat the feat. But they were dispatched from Europe at the first attempt, exiting the Cup Winners Cup on away goals to Dynamo Minsk. And their by now obligatory poor start to the League was anything but encouraging. But once into their stride, Real looked to be a strong pretender to Real Madrid's throne.

They were led in attack by Jose Maria Bakero, a skinny but powerful striker who became a national team hero when he scored a hat-trick against Albania. Meanwhile Toshack had converted central defender Lorenzo Loren into a centre forward, and he emerged as the leading scorer for the Spanish Under-21 team.

Larranaga had become known as the 'lungs of the team', blessed with a footballing brain and plenty of strength, alternating between sweeper or in midfield, while left back Lopez Rekarte became renowned for his overlapping runs.

And at the heart of the title push were Real's two veterans, keeper Arconada still performing as consistently as ever, and the midfield creative Jesus Maria Zamora seemingly rejuvenated since Toshack's arrival. 'Zamora is in his second youth,' enthused Toshack, 'and both he and Arconada are outstanding examples for the youth team players and reserve team here.'

Both were outstanding as Real routed Barcelona, who had recently sacked Venables, by four goals to one. Arconada made two brilliant saves early on from Gary Lineker, while Zamora netted twice. Real repeated the scoreline in the *derbi* at Athletic Bilbao, and entering the new year, Real lay third in the table, coming from behind to beat Murcia 2–1 before defeating Cadiz to lie four points behind Real Madrid.

In their defence of the *Copa del Rey*, meanwhile, Real faced a rerun of the previous season's final in the last eight, and went down 2–1 at Atletico Madrid in the first leg. In the return at Atocha, however, as Real managed to draw level, Arconada again proved to be a penalty hero, stopping a weak effort from the spot by Brazilian Alemao. Arconada had now faced four penalties that season, and saved the lot. Real ran out 3–1 winners with goals from Loren, Beguiristain and Lopez Rekarte, to set up a semi-final clash with Real Madrid.

In the first leg in San Sebastian, the in-form Bakero scored the only goal after eight minutes to give Toshack's team the slenderest of advantages as they headed for the Bernabeu and the second leg. If they were worried it might not have been enough, their fears were proved unjustified. In a stunning second-half display, Bakero and his team-mates tore Madrid apart, the new idol of Spanish football scoring twice as the Basque side ran out 4–0 winners.

'It was like the end of the world,' groaned Madrid coach Leo Beenhakker. But his side were victorious when

Toshack's side returned for a League match played on a quagmire pitch still recovering from a U2 concert the previous summer. Real Sociedad had looked good for a point, until Emilio Butragueno slammed in a late winner off the post to send Madrid five points clear of Real Sociedad.

And Toshack's side slipped up again in the season's second *derbi*. Athletic Bilbao's Joseba Aguirre scored the only goal after nine minutes, scoring from a rebound after heading against the post. Real pressed forward incessantly for an equaliser, but Howard Kendall's team held out.

With just eleven rounds of the championship remaining, Real Madrid were seven points clear as their nearest challengers, Real Sociedad and Atletico Madrid came face to face. Atletico held the upper hand in the first half, but after the break, Bakero and Beguiristain hit the back of the net to keep Toshack's flickering title hopes alive.

But first was the final of the *Copa del Rey*. Real Sociedad prepared for the final by beating Logrones 4–0, while opponents Barca crashed at home to Betis. Barcelona's ageing team had been written off by just about everybody, but lagging well behind in *La Liga*, Barca desperately needed to win a trophy to maintain their unbroken record of European participation.

The Stadio Bernabeu was only about a third full for the final, 25,000 from San Sebastian and 5,000 from Catalonia. Barca coach Luis Aragones, who had replaced Venables, decided to play Real at their own game and play on the counter. Meanwhile, their central defence pairing of Migueli and Jose Alesanco prevented Sociedad from creating a single chance in a tense, drab game in which Bernd Schuster pulled the strings in midfield. And Barca's Alesanco scored the only goal with thirty minutes left, from the rebound after Gary Lineker had seen his close-range shot parried by Arconada.

It was a disappointment, especially as Real Sociedad's title ambitions had expired by the time the newly-crowned champions Real Madrid travelled to San Sebastian in May. Butragueno scored twice for a Madrid side heading for victory before Luciano Iturrino made it 2–2 a couple of minutes from the end. Madrid endured a nasty reception in San Sebastian, with Michel hit on the leg by a bottle from the stands. Real Madrid finished eleven points clear of Real Sociedad in second.

Toshack had managed to resurrect the club through willpower and ingenuity, with relatively little money to spend, and restricted as to who he could spend it on. Success had come in part due to Toshack's blooding of many talented players from Real's youth ranks, Bakero finishing second only to Hugo Sanchez that season in the race for *El Trofeo Pichichi*, awarded to the League's highest scorer.

It wasn't surprising that Real Sociedad wanted to extend Toshack's contract, which had only one year left. 'The fact is that most of the clubs in Spain would like Toshack as their manager,' wrote journalist Brian Glanville, 'and when his agreement with Real Sociedad does come to an end, he will surely be in a position to pick and choose.'

In April, however, Toshack signed a new three-year contract to keep him at the Estadio Atocha. But the team he'd built was about to be ripped apart. Rumours spread of a triple raid on San Sebastian by Barcelona, who wanted Lopez Rekarte, whose contract was up, as well as Jose Maria Bakero and Aitor Beguiristain, and that summer, all three headed for the Nou Camp.

Toshack had secured striker Juan Antonio Goicoechea on loan in return, by the time Rekarte, Beguiristain and Bakero returned to the Estadio Atocha for a rerun of the cup final in October 1988. But Real suffered the same result, Julio Salinas scoring the only goal in the tenth minute for Johan Cruyff's team, after some good work down the right by Roberto. Real were unable to unlock Barca's three-man defence, until their slender young forward from the French Basque country, Michel Loinaz, only 21, burst through with only Andoni Zubizaretta to beat, but could only shoot straight at the keeper.

In the first round of the UEFA Cup, Real defeated Dukla Prague 2–1 at home, with goals from Loinaz either side of half-time, the second cancelling out Dukla's quick equaliser.

In Czechoslovakia two weeks later, Jiri Nemec equalised for the Czechs in the 17th minute, and they edged ahead ten minutes after the break through Ales Foldyna. And when Dukla added a third from Gunther Bittengel 18 minutes from the end to make it 4–2, it looked like Real were out. But just three minutes later, Lorenzo Loren hauled Real back into it, and with eight minutes remaining, substitute Loinaz, another youngster starting to repay Toshack's faith in him, hit the away goal required to put Real through.

In the second round, Toshack found himself returning to Sporting Lisbon, and it was a victorious return, as Iturrino and Loren scored the goals in Portugal that would see Real through a goalless second leg in San Sebastian.

The third round saw Real at home in the first leg to Cologne, and in the first half, the German team came closest to making the breakthrough, Pierre Littbarski shooting over the bar and Arconada making a memorable save from Thomas Hassler. But Loinaz was on target again, fourteen minutes from the end, after Cologne keeper Bodo Illgner could only parry a shot from Juan Maria Mujica.

In the second leg, however, Falko Gotz equalised for Cologne after just two minutes, converting Littbarski's corner. And Stephen Engels put Cologne in front on the half hour when Arconada failed to deal properly with a shot from Hassler.

Real then dug deep and rediscovered the spirit that had brought them through the previous round. On 35 minutes, Illgner brought down Zuniga and Goicoechea put away the penalty to give Real the lead on away goals. Cologne could have taken the lead again, however, only for Klaus Allofs to miss a penalty. Real eventually put a seal on it a minute from time, through substitute Fuentes.

Returning to League action, after 15 matches Real had slumped to 15th in the table, and were just three points off the relegation zone. Their League form had headed downhill since a decent performance at the Bernabeu in September, when Real Sociedad had earned a draw against the team Toshack regarded as favourites to finish first once more. 'Madrid will win the League again, they're still the best side in the country. They just might have to sweat a bit more this time.'

In November, Real lost 2–1 at home to Ron Atkinson's Atletico Madrid, but that month the papers seemed more interested in speculating that Toshack might be the next coach of Real Madrid when Leo Beenhakker departed as expected at the end of the season.

In the new year, Real Sociedad picked up their challenge for the UEFA Cup, facing German opposition for the second round running, when they travelled to Stuttgart for the first leg of their quarter-final. And the German club's Fritz Walter scored the only goal after 34 minutes, before frittering two clear-cut chances to extend their lead in the second half.

After seventeen minutes of the second leg in San Sebastian, however, Real were level. Stuttgart's attempt to play the offside trap failed as Lasa crossed, before veteran Jesus Zamora turned it in. Real kept pushing forward, earning eleven corners in all, but got more cautious as the whistle approached.

A place in the semi-finals was on the line as the match went into a penalty shoot-out. But Real were denied by the reflexes of German keeper Eike Immel, who saved the third and fifth kicks from Carlos Martinez and Gajate.

It was to be the final bow for John Benjamin. 'I had four very happy years in San Sebastian, it's a lovely city and the Basques are smashing people. I would have happily gone on working there for a long time to come. But the offer came to manage Real Madrid, which must be the most famous club in the world, and when something like that happens in your life, you say to yourself, what are we here for? What's this all about? An opportunity like that comes once in your life. You have to take it. My son can turn round one day and say to his friends, "My dad managed Real Madrid," and that will mean something. For me, that's what it's all about.'

12 The Real World

Ramon Mendoza was not a happy man. He might have been president of a football club that had just won *La Liga* for the third season running, but at Real Madrid, sometimes success just wasn't enough.

It was the European Cup that really mattered at the planet's biggest football club. The supporters harked back to the glory days of the late 1950s, when, inspired by Di Stefano, Puskas and Gento, Real had dominated the pioneering days of European competition. By 1989, however, they hadn't been crowned European champions in 23 years, and under Dutch manager Leo Beenhakker, their latest assault on the competition had ended in ignominious failure.

Real had been torn apart by Milan in the semi-finals, losing 5–0 to a team that had imperiously swept all before them that season, spearheaded by the exhilarating Dutch trio of Ruud Gullit, Marco Van Basten and Frank Rijkaard. It spelled the end for Beenhakker. 'I could have signed a new two-year contract but it was clear to me that there was no point in doing so if they couldn't change the team. I talked about it for many hours with Ramon Mendoza and he agreed it had to be changed, but there were financial problems.'

The club was millions in debt, after lavishing exorbitant transfer fees and spiralling wages on its superstars. And the problems at the Stadio Bernabeu ran deeper. Just two years into his contract, Beenhakker had found that a changing room full of superstars had stopped listening to him, reinforcing his belief that the manager of a blue-chip club like Real Madrid had a life-span of three years at the maximum. 'After that the players have heard it all before, that is the problem.' Beenhakker's hair had been red when he took over in 1987. Now it was white.

He also realised his team was growing old. 'Coaching this club is like no other. The pressures, the expectations here are enormous. This club craves the European Cup once again, it is a part of its history and to be so long without it is a source of great frustration and dismay. But my inclination is that the side is now grown too old. Certain players should probably leave, but maybe they will not do so.'

It was into this bullring that Toshack stepped in the spring of 1989, when he signed a contract worth £250,000 a year. 'I could not have come straight into a job like Real Madrid,' he said. 'I think it was important to have worked up towards it. I had a very good – I won't say apprenticeship because that would be an insult to my other clubs – but a very good grounding or education in the game over here. The four years with Real Sociedad were a very valuable part of preparing for this – although I never envisaged it. I know it's a cliché but in this job it really never pays to look too far ahead. But it meant I knew Spanish football and the set-up. I had seen Barcelona v Real Madrid games from a distance. I knew about the players at Madrid and I knew what to expect.'

Mendoza had been president for four years and knew the players he wanted to see and the style of football he wanted them to play. As Beenhakker put it, Real Madrid doesn't just need a manager – it needs a politician, diplomat and psychiatrist rolled into one. 'What do we expect of him?' Mendoza was asked on Toshack's arrival. 'The usual at Real, to win everything.' Some job description.

'When he arrived at Real Madrid they had a reputation as being a great attacking side,' says journalist Jeff King, 'and wonderful to watch but they were a bit soft, they'd been turned over by Milan. He had this reputation he built up at Real Sociedad, they called him a sergeant major, a disciplinarian. His remit was to toughen them up and do something in the European Cup.'

Toshack had beaten off the likes of George Graham and national team manager Javier Clemente to get the job.

Perhaps Mendoza had been persuaded to recruit him after hearing his analysis of Real's defeat to Milan on Spanish radio, criticising Hugo Sanchez and insisting, 'Real will never win the European Cup with that goalkeeper Buyo, and they need to sort out the centre of defence.' Moreover, Real Sociedad had knocked Real Madrid out of the *Copa del Rey* the previous season.

Despite the accusations that they were growing old, Real's roster was still a formidable one. In addition to the gymnastic Mexican wizard Hugo Sanchez, there was the Bernabeu brat pack, *la Quinta del Buitre*. In Spain, a *quinta* refers to a group of conscripts who have gone through military service together. Real's *quinta*, named after striker Emilio Butragueno, also comprised midfield icon Michel, Martin Vazquez, Manuel Sanchis and Miguel Pardeza, who had all emerged from Real's nursery team Castilla during the 1980s.

Butragueno remained a lethal finisher, if prone to mood swings and indifferent spells, while Michel's flair for organisation had seemingly disappeared and, feeling the discontent of the fans for the first time, he was on the brink of leaving the club. He'd stormed off the pitch during the win over Espanyol that had clinched the championship, blaming his histrionics 'twenty per cent on my ankle, eighty per cent on the fans'. And he was less than impressed by the appointment of Toshack, remembering the new manager's scathing radio analysis. 'If he wants to come here, he must rectify those comments.'

In many ways, Real Madrid had a team that selected itself. It had always been a club where players wielded the power. Their five successive European Cups in the 1950s and 1960s were actually won by four different coaches, with only the name of Miguel Munoz earning more than a footnote in their history, while Di Stefano and his team-mates had infamously held their own parallel team talks. Thirty years on, radio microphones picked up the voice of Real's captain Ricardo Gallego in one match against Athletic Bilbao, pointedly urging Beenhakker to substitute Schuster. The German soon found himself pulling on his tracksuit. Gallego, an influential ringleader in the dressing room, greeted Toshack's appointment by snidely noting that Real Madrid was a very different club to Real Sociedad, and questioning Toshack's tactics.

But the new manager had decided on a policy of keeping his own counsel before taking over from Beenhakker. 'My priority is to say an absolute minimum to the media so that Leo can get on with his job during the crucial final phase of the season. I've asked him to give me the League title as a present so that we can have another crack at the League title next season, but my priorities are just to look the team over and plan a good pre-season.'

Toshack's abrupt departure from Real Sociedad with eight games of the season left had also raised the temperature in San Sebastian. 'I was disappointed some people turned against me because it was something the Sociedad president, Inaki Alkiza, suggested to me. I had recommended the appointment of my assistant, Marco Boronat, as coach for next season and these final matches give him a good chance to ease himself into the hot seat in the dugout, something he is not yet familiar with. At the same time it gave me a chance to look at Real Madrid, find somewhere to live, spend time with my family and have a bit of a break. In the last three years we've played thirty-six cup matches, including two finals and we've had a long UEFA Cup run this year. I need a rest if I'm to do justice to the job at Madrid.'

Suitably refreshed, Toshack took possession of the keys to the Bernabeu and attempted to quell the locker-room storm before imposing his own ideas. One of his first moves was to sell the disruptive Gallego to Udinese. He planned to switch the influential midfielder Bernd Schuster to replace him at sweeper, a move some felt a waste of the German's talents. 'Schuster is a magnificent player who has tremendous vision over the whole pitch as soon as he lifts his head,' said Barcelona's Ronald Koeman. 'He sees things that the rest of us simply don't see. And his passing is out of this world, not only the long ball but also the short pass which destroys the opposing defence. He is a superb midfielder. As backstop some of these qualities are wasted. He is not special in the air, and there are question marks over his tackling.'

Toshack decided to stick to the strategy that had served him well at Real Sociedad, however, with Schuster at sweeper, two new strong central defenders, Fernando Hierro from Valladolid and the Argentinian Oscar Ruggeri from Logrones, with attacking full-backs raiding down the wings. He gave Michel a new, freer role, whereas under Beenhakker he had been largely restricted to the right flank. Hugo Sanchez became Real's most advanced forward, while Butragueno was deployed more deeply, to become more involved and make more use of his blistering pace.

The critics branded Toshack's new approach a defensive one, something outsiders might have felt a good thing after that five-goal defeat in Milan.

But left-back Rafael Gordillo disagreed. 'This is anything but a defensive system. If anything I'd say it's a risky system. But I think it works and it's a system that the players will enjoy putting into practice.'

Emilio Butragueno seemed equally enthusiastic. 'It's early days, but the system seems very valid and I am sure it will bring good results for the team. I know I'm playing in a deeper role, but I enjoy what I'm doing and I think I can speak for the other members of the squad in that respect.'

And the new system also met with the approval of the unsettled Michel. 'Under Toshack, I have much greater freedom to express myself in midfield and I feel a lot happier.'

Real warmed up with a friendly against Liverpool, and Toshack was keen to renew acquaintances with his old mentors, as Ronnie Moran recalls. 'We played a friendly against them when Kenny Dalglish was manager, they beat us 2–0, he was made up that night. The afternoon of the game I'm reading my paper in my room, we'd finished training, had lunch and got the players all to bed, John knocks at my door and spends an hour and a half with me talking about football.'

It was to be an uneasy start for Toshack in *La Liga*. On the opening day of the season, he was jeered by fans during the second half of a 2-0 home win over Gijon. And after a 0-0 draw at Castellon, there were mutterings from the players about his tactical changes. Predictably, despite the appreciative reaction they had met in the summer, they were meeting increasing resistance from the senior players. So Toshack quickly reverted to Beenhakker's tactics, and perhaps wary of the dressing room politics, resisted the temptation to undertake the pruning of the squad's ageing members.

Toshack proved at least that he had the coaching and man-management skills to get the best out of players. One of his most positive achievements at Real was in sparking the emergence of the least prominent member of *la Quinta*, midfielder Martin Vazquez. 'One of the main things he's remembered for that spell at Real Madrid, he discovered Vazquez,' recalls Jeff King. 'Of that whole batch of homegrown players, he had always been a bit of an in-and-out player, until Toshack came along, and for whatever reason, got the best out of him.'

But while Real Madrid led *La Liga* and dispatched their rivals for the title with ease, none of the tactical battles or changing-room politicking seemed to matter. It was an extraordinarily free-scoring team that Toshack had inherited, going on to score 107 goals in 38 games, a record that still stands in 2002.

So it would be on the battlefields of Europe that Toshack would be judged. 'I'm fully conscious of the responsibility of this job,' he announced. 'When we were kids at home in South Wales we heard of Real Madrid – about Di Stefano and Puskas and Gento. I've got to try and improve on what Beenhakker has done here, but it will be very hard.'

In the first round of the European Cup, Luxembourg champions Spora Luxembourg were swatted aside 9-0 on aggregate. Following the easiest of ties, Toshack was presented with the hardest. In the second round, Real Madrid were again drawn against Milan.

'If we were to beat Milan we could forget about the European Cup until next March and concentrate on the League,' he said. 'But if we lose to Milan, then there's a danger that heads will go down and we will suffer a reaction in the League. That's what management is about. There is always something going on which needs your attention.'

Real travelled to the San Siro for the first leg, but the tie was almost over before it had begun. Frank Rijkaard headed Milan into the lead within nine minutes, following a cross from Marco Van Basten, and five minutes later the Dutch predator converted a penalty after he'd been pulled down by Buyo, to double their advantage. Television replays showed the foul had been committed outside the box. But, with Real missing the injured Butragueno, that was how it stayed for the next 76 minutes.

In the second leg, with Real needing to score three to progress, they just couldn't make the breakthrough and at half-time it looked like their European dream was over for another year. But three minutes into the second half, Emilio Butragueno scored to created a glimmer of hope. However, they just could not score again. Real were out.

Three months into his new job, Toshack had practically already been dealt a fatal blow. Cruising to the championship was one thing – they'd done it four years running. It was European glory they coveted. And now they were out, to Milan for the second season running.

In November, John Benjamin returned to San Sebastian for the first time since quitting Real Sociedad, resting – or dropping, depending on who you believed – several first-team regulars in the wake of the Milan defeat. If the Basque fans were happy to see him back, they didn't like the company he was keeping these days, as John Aldridge recalls. 'Real Madrid was known as the central government team and all Basques loved to beat them. "We must win this game, Aldo," one of the players told me. "We don't like Madrid." '

But as it rained non-stop for two days before the match, it looked like Toshack's homecoming might be put on ice. Until Real Sociedad realised that postponing the match would mean forfeiting the £200,000 fee from live television coverage. The game went ahead. 'It turned out to be a bit of a farce,' says Aldridge. 'There were puddles of water all over the pitch and it ruined the match as a spectacle. Not that it mattered much to the Sociedad supporters. I scored in our 2–1 win and they went home happy enough.'

It was to be one of only two defeats Real, largely inspired by veteran midfielder Rafael Gordillo, would suffer that season in *La Liga*, the other one being an early 3–1 defeat at Barcelona. Real won 17 of their 19 home games, hitting seven past the hapless likes of Real Zaragoza and Castellon and six past runners-up Valencia.

Of the century of goals they scored that season, 38 of them were scored by the supposedly past-it Sanchez. 'Hugo always gave the wrong impression to people who didn't know him,' recalls Aldridge. 'Some thought he was lazy but I found him to be among the most hard-working footballers I've come across. When he was man-marked, as was usually the case, he would run to the touchline, taking the defender with him. With the defender out of position, Hugo would run back into the penalty area and would revel in the space his intelligence had created. It took an amazing amount of fitness to do that successfully. His finishing was good too. He knew it. People would say he was bigheaded and arrogant but when you're that talented you can get away with it.'

Inauspiciously, however, Real lost the final of that season's *Copa del Rey* to Barcelona. Still, at any other club on the planet, Toshack's first season would have been deemed an overwhelming success, lifting the championship with ease and only going out of the European Cup by a single goal after an unlucky draw against the best team in the world. But not at Real. He now only had one chance to get it right, or else. And the omens weren't good.

Due to the proprietorial nature of Spanish football clubs, Toshack's influence in the transfer market was negligible. It was Mendoza who held both the shopping list and the credit card. Toshack wanted to sign Des Walker, the Nottingham Forest defender who had proved with England at Italia 90 that he was among the most cultured and composed performers on the international stage. But with Real still millions in the red, Mendoza decided to ignore Toshack's recommendations and shop at the cheaper end of the market, bringing in Yugoslavian Predrag Spasic from Partizan Belgrade.

But failing to bring in the best new talent is one thing. Mendoza managed to compound his folly by losing two members of Real's engine room. Martin Vazquez, who had become the team's backbone under Toshack, was allowed to leave after a long-running pay dispute, and ended up at Torino. Then the influential Schuster was released, in order to fit in with the Spanish federation restrictions on foreign imports, and he eventually crossed the city to join Atletico Madrid.

Mendoza intended Luis Milla, signed from Barcelona, and Gheorghe Hagi, who'd starred for Romania at the World Cup, to take their place in midfield, while Oscar Ruggeri returned to Argentina with Velez Sarsfield.

The 1990/91 campaign kicked off with the visit of Castellon, and Real recorded their 1000th win in *La Liga*, but whereas the previous season they had put seven past the minnows, this time they were restricted to a single goal from Manuel Sanchis. 'I wasn't too pleased with the way my team were playing,' said Toshack after the match, 'they weren't aggressive enough.'

It soon became clear that although Mendoza's meddling could be tolerated when the team were on a roll, once things started to slip it only managed to make matters worse.

The departure of Vazquez and Schuster left Real lacking creativity in midfield, while Hagi largely failed to adapt to the pace and style of Spanish football. Then Milla sustained a ligament injury, leaving a huge hole in midfield. Gordillo then got injured during the third game of the season. Toshack tried moving Michel back inside from the right, and Manuel Sanchis out from the defence, but both failed to deliver in their new roles. Only Emilio Butragueno managed to show anything like top form.

In Europe, at least, things were on course, as Real beat Danish side Odense 10–1 on aggregate in the first round of the European Cup, before an extraordinary second-round tie at the Bernabeu, in which Tirol Innsbruck were routed 9–1, Butragueno notching a hat-trick and Sanchez scoring four times. 'For me, goals are like food,' announced the Mexican, 'when the team wins and I don't score I'm not fully satisfied, as if I haven't had my dessert.'

But in the League, it was all starting to fall apart. Despite beating Real Zaragoza, who had had a defender sent off, 3–1, Toshack was scathing in his post-match analysis. 'There were times when we looked like the team with ten men.' Worse was to come as Real found themselves unable to beat lowly Logrones, drawing 0–0 at the Bernabeu. In an attempt to improve the team's flagging productivity, Toshack pulled Butragueno back again to act as playmaker, but he clashed in midfield with Hagi, and Sanchez remained starved of service. It was clear that Real seemed to have no real definitive formation. The embattled Logrones nearly won it, only for Real keeper Buyo to keep out a point-blank header while Real could hit only the woodwork at the other end.

During the second half, Spasic and Hagi were substituted by Toshack, Hagi running off to a torrent of boos, meaning Real had £6 million worth of talent on the bench. The alarm bells were sounding as Barcelona pulled ahead at the top of the table, but Toshack remained unrepentant during the post-match press conference. 'We lost a point we should have won. We posed no threat in the first half and although we dominated towards the end, the goal just didn't come.'

Real's crisis was about to deepen, however. In their next game, they travelled to minnows Burgos, Toshack naming a conservative line-up featuring five defensive players – Chendo, Tendillo, Sanchis, Hierro and Spasic. In the first half, Burgos wasted plenty of chances but would still have been happy to go in goalless at half-time. Toshack again substituted the listless Hagi, bringing on Villarroya, which appeared to breathe new life into Real, and when Michel directed a great cross into the centre, Hugo Sanchez pounced to make it 1–0. But twelve minutes later Juric seized on a rebound from Buyo after a shot from outside the box to level the match. The embattled Toshack decided that what Real had, they held, and replaced

Butragueno with Aldana to reinforce the midfield. But Burgos continued to pressurise, and with two minutes left on the clock, Juric picked up the ball in midfield and lobbed Buyo from fifty yards. Burgos won 2–1.

Juric had been one of the players Real had considered recruiting before the signing of Spasic, who had been detailed to mark the matchwinner, but nobody really appreciated the irony. Real, four games without a win in the League, were now fourth, four points behind Barca and trailing Seville and Logrones.

Mendoza was quick to give his manager a vote of confidence. 'Toshack is still Madrid coach and he'll be on the bench next Sunday. Real Madrid is not on its way to the intensive care unit and never will be.' And Hugo Sanchez also offered his backing, admitting that Real's dismal form had been due to the players' poor form, and that to sack Toshack would be unfair. 'What we need now is a tranquilliser rather than antibiotics.'

But Toshack's licence for the last-chance saloon was about to expire. Real travelled for the next game to 18th-placed Valencia, and played appallingly. Sanchez got sent off for violent conduct in a 2–1 defeat. Real slipped to sixth place in the table, five points off the lead.

Next day, Real Madrid sacked Toshack. 'There comes a time when you have to say yes or no,' he said. 'In the last months each Saturday has been a game of life or death, and a club like Real Madrid could just not go on like that. This is not meant as a criticism, it is probably my fault. If you ask me what hurts most about this, it's that I won't have the chance to win the European Cup with Real Madrid, which is the thing I think I was signed up for.'

He must have reflected ruefully on the fact that the previous season had been deemed a failure due to the team's early exit from Europe, despite winning the championship. This time round, he'd been dumped due to Real's poor League form, despite being through to the last eight of the European Cup. In his 63 games in charge of Real, they lost only eight.

Toshack might have made mistakes, especially with his tactics against Burgos, but he had been let down by his players and by his president. Hagi had been one of the most promising stars at the World Cup but he failed to fill the void left by Vazquez and Schuster, now shining at Atletico, who had been allowed to drift away.

In addition, the rumours resurfaced of the dressing-room power clique, headed by Michel, which had under-mined Beenhakker, with vetoes on signings, tactics and team selection. Many felt that Toshack had little or no influence on the team. 'Toshack referred acidly to the power that the *Quinta* had by then established in the dressing room of the Bernabeu, in the presidential corri-dors and in the national side,' reckons Phil Ball. 'The gossip still has it that the *Quinta* did away with Toshack in the end.'

But many commentators felt his cause had not been helped by his aggressive manner and his public criticism of his team. Just three months into the job, he'd upset the players for saying he'd sweated more during a victory over Vallecano than they had. And he had refused to be bullied by Madrid's infamously poisonous football press, and in return they were happy to hasten his downfall.

Toshack had also failed to fix Real Madrid's poor return from their biggest matches. Sure, they had won *La Liga* five years running, but it masked an unacceptable record from the crunch games. In the previous five seasons they had only beaten arch-rivals Barcelona three times, and had stumbled at the semi-finals of the European Cup three years running.

Some felt Michel and his fellow members of the *Quinta* suffered from a lack of self-belief, a theory supported by Beenhakker. 'It's a big dream for players like Michel and Butragueno to enter into the great history of this club. As we got closer to the final there was always more and more pressure from the hundreds and thousands of people all over Spain, from the people inside the club – we have to win, we have to win. I always had the idea they couldn't manage it.'

Like Toshack, Beenhakker had been a victim of Real's player power, and Mendoza's insistence on doing the wheeling and dealing. 'I'm sure Toshack also had these wishes to rebuild the team. As I understand it, Toshack's team had problems within and this was reflected in performances on the field. The strength of Real Madrid was always that it was a family, a team, everybody was defending a white shirt with his life. It is not enough to have good players, you have to have a team.'

13 Patriot Games

Over the last two decades, many clubs have attempted to lure John Toshack back to Britain. Not surprising, given a reputation based on a no-nonsense approach in the locker room and a cosmopolitan brand of tactical nous. In the Premiership of Houllier, Wenger and Ranieri, the *Sistema* has an obvious allure to chairmen head-hunting their next boss. But only once has he returned to British football management, answering his nation's call on a disastrous winter's night at Ninian Park in 1994.

Twice during the 1990s, he could have returned to Liverpool as manager. In 1999, he revealed that during his spell at Besiktas, he had turned down the joint manager's job that Gerard Houllier eventually accepted. Following talks with Liverpool's vice-chairman Peter Robinson and manager Roy Evans, he wasn't convinced about the merits of job sharing, and was proved right when the Evans-Houllier partnership lasted just three months.

Seven years earlier, not long after Toshack had agreed to return to Real Sociedad, Kenny Dalglish had resigned as Liverpool manager. Bowed by the emotional baggage of steering the club through the Hillsborough disaster and the pressure of attempting to rebuild an ageing side – like the Shankly of twenty years earlier who had recruited Toshack – Dalglish quit.

Toshack was quickly named favourite for the job by the bookmakers, and more importantly, topped the club's shortlist. Toshack himself remained tight-lipped. 'I've heard what is being said but I have nothing to say myself.' But the deal appeared to founder on Real Sociedad's £1.5 million claim for compensation, and Graeme Souness eventually got the job. 'As a Liverpool fan, I wish them all the very best,' said Toshack, 'and hope to see them on top soon.'

Meanwhile, Everton, Aston Villa, Newcastle, Celtic, Southampton and Manchester City have tried and failed at one time or another to persuade him to return.

'He has succeeded in burying his roots to such an extent that the only place which now seems closed to him is England,' says Phil Ball. 'Once upon a time his name would occasionally be linked with the job at Liverpool, even Newcastle after Kevin Keegan, and although he could undoubtedly contribute his experience to the Premiership, you get the feeling when you listen to him speak that it just wouldn't be his scene any more.'

On one occasion, while acting as studio guest for a live Liverpool match on Sky Sports, he protested, 'I don't really know anything about English football,' as presenter Richard Keys spent an hour attempting to get him to comment on their chances.

Like The Beatles' *Magical Mystery Tour*, Toshack's 47-day spell in charge of Wales is seen as the indelible black mark on his CV, the one great career mistake. But there was certainly no shortage of confidence on his part as he took the job, telling the *Western Mail*, 'My aim is to win the 1996 European Championship in England.'

In the seventeen years since that defeat to the Scots at Anfield, the fortunes of the Welsh national team hadn't exactly improved. Mike England had taken them to the brink of the 1982 World Cup in Spain, only to stumble at the final hurdle with a humiliating draw against Iceland at the Vetch with a team containing six members of Toshack's all-conquering Swansea team. Two years later, they were denied a place at the European Championships thanks to an injury-time Yugoslavian winner over Bulgaria in the final qualifying match.

In 1985, Wales again met Scotland with a ticket to the World Cup as the prize, and with ten minutes remaining, a controversial equaliser from the spot for the Scots cancelled out Mark Hughes's strike and knocked Wales out, although the match will be forever remembered for the fatal heart attack suffered by Scotland manager Jock Stein as the final whistle blew.

England's successor Terry Yorath found the going tough initially, but by the early 1990s he had fashioned a formidable team, augmenting world-class veterans such as Hughes, Rush and Southall with newcomers like Ryan Giggs and Gary Speed. Despite beating Germany in qualifying, Wales narrowly missed out on Euro 92, and a friendly victory over Brazil gave Yorath plenty of optimism as his team prepared for the qualifiers for USA 94. The campaign began disastrously, with a 5–1 defeat in Romania that featured two goals from Gheorghe Hagi, now recovered from his unexceptional stint under Toshack at Real Madrid. But gradually Wales battled their way to the brink of qualification, which hinged on a final confrontation with the Romanians at the Arms Park. Wales needed to win, but after half an hour they were behind to a Hagi goal. Dean Saunders equalised in the second half, before the opportunity emerged. Dan Petrescu fouled Gary Speed in the box. Left back Paul Bodin stepped up. He hit the bar. Raducioiu hammered in the final nail with a goal seven minutes from time.

It was no disgrace to lose to a brilliant team like Romania who, inspired by the devilishly inventive Hagi, reached the last eight of the World Cup. But once again, Wales had fluffed their lines on the big stage, and the inevitable recriminations began. Naturally, the spotlight fell on Terry Yorath's position. However, rather than backing or sacking him, the Football Association of Wales took the curious decision of asking him to reapply for his own job. On New Year's Eve 1993, his contract expired, and he wasn't offered another one.

'I was sent a letter and asked to apply for the job again,' recalls Yorath. 'I was told I had a good chance of getting it but I was very naive. The job was very important to me and I really wanted it. But at the same time, John Toshack was top of their list. In the end, everything was just a shambles.'

It wasn't untypical of a bumbling off the field administration that hadn't improved much since Dave Bowen's reign. Star players were too easily excused international friendlies through dubious injuries, while the FAW had managed to split Welsh club football down the middle with the bungled formation of a National League. If Welsh football was disunited off the pitch, how could it ever succeed on it?

So it was imperative that the FAW proved to the world that Wales could compete with the best, and that meant recruiting a high-profile manager of unimpeachable international calibre. Unsuccessful approaches were made to both Bobby Robson and Terry Venables, who ended up taking the England job instead. There was only one Welsh candidate with the requisite experience of continental football.

On 3 February 1994, John Toshack was unveiled as the new manager of Wales. In fact, Toshack was his country's new technical director, and a part-time one at that. Still very much at the helm of Real Sociedad for the second time, Toshack had agreed to help his nation in a crisis, on a no-contract basis. But he said he couldn't see any problems combining the two roles, pointing out that *La Liga* would close down during international weeks anyway. 'If it didn't work out like that and there was a cup match for Real, for example, which clashed with a Wales match, there would be no argument. Real would have priority.'

Mike Smith, under whom Toshack had played for Wales, was appointed as full-time assistant to act as his eyes and ears in Britain. 'He is a man who I trust and have complete confidence in,' said Toshack. The FAW agreed meanwhile to pay Real Sociedad a 'facility fee' of £4,000 for every Wales match Toshack took charge of.

'He has the desire to win,' enthused FAW chief executive Alun Evans. 'He reminds me very much of Jack Charlton in that he will not be diverted from the path to success.' The reference to Charlton was a telling one. The former Leeds and England centre half had transformed Ireland from a journeyman team of also-rans into regular qualifiers for the big championships, despite only having a handful of quality players to select from. If Big Jack could do it, why not Big John?

But the doubts about Toshack's ability to manage a national team on a part-time basis from Spain were raised

from day one. At the Cardiff press conference to announce his appointment – which had to be hastily
rearranged in a hotel lobby when the 70 journalists who
turned up had trouble fitting into the 25-seater room
booked by the FAW – he underlined his belief that it didn't
represent a problem. 'I can understand people questioning my appointment and whether it can be done, but that
will only motivate me more. I cannot guarantee success
and have no magic formula, but I believe in my ability and
will not need to be told if things are not working out.'

Questions were asked too about Yorath's acrimonious
departure. Evans fidgeted as he was accused of disloyalty
and deceit by the press, but Toshack typically took it all
in his stride. 'I value my friendship with Terry and one of
the conditions under which I took the job was that I spoke
to him and found out exactly what had happened. I have
been aware of the ill feeling about the way it was done,
but it is not something I wish to dwell on. He will sort out
any problems he has with the FAW. I have got a job to get
on with.'

Toshack was quick to dispel any hopes he might have
raised of an instant turnround. 'We are not a big country
and do not have a huge pool of players to call on, so we
will need everyone to be pulling in the same direction. I
have no preconceived ideas but it is important to retain
the experienced players as long as you can. We must get
the balance right, however. Any new manager has to win
over both players and supporters. It is an exciting challenge and something I am really looking forward to.'

He touched on one of his earliest headaches, an ageing
core of talent who had reacted badly to the way Yorath had
been treated, like Ian Rush who had hinted that he was so
incensed that he wouldn't play for Wales again. But Toshack
assured the media that it was heat of the moment stuff.

'John Toshack is a good friend of mine and when he got
approached to become Wales manager he had to tell me
about it – because no-one else told me,' says Yorath. 'I
knew though that if he encountered any problems he'd
just walk away – and he did. I loved being manager of
Wales but my departure was all about political factors.'

There was just over a month until the challenge began with a friendly at Ninian Park against a Norway team that had edged England out of the World Cup with a style best described as efficient, featuring six players from the English leagues in their starting eleven. Toshack, meanwhile, made it clear that he would not be following Yorath's lead and expecting players to play out of position in order to accommodate the attacking quartet of Rush, Saunders, Giggs and Hughes. 'I do not want to play people in areas of the field where they are not comfortable. I would rather have thirty minutes of somebody doing a job he does well than ninety where he is unable to perform.'

Toshack opted instead for a formation less British than the visitors. He opted for the 3–3–3–1 *Sistema Toshack*, with Sunderland's Andy Melville as a sweeper, Jason Perry and David Phillips as wing backs and Mark Hughes on his own upfront, supported by Nathan Blake, Speed and – despite his assurances about not playing people out of position – Rush in deep-lying support. Toshack might have promised evolution rather than revolution at the press conference, but this was more Chairman Mao than Charles Darwin. Still, he stressed it *was* only a friendly, ahead of the more serious business of qualifying for Euro 96. 'I will use the games up to September to have a look at various things. But by then we must have a very good idea of where we are going. Then, the only important thing will be the result, and we will have only one chance to get it right.'

It started badly. Just seven minutes had gone when Chris Coleman headed the ball to Speed who, just 35 yards from his own goal, gifted the ball into the path of Jostein Flo, who drilled the ball into the bottom right-hand corner of Neville Southall's net.

Wales managed to create a couple of chances in the first twenty minutes, a free-kick from Hughes, before he combined with Speed to set up Rush, but he was denied by a combination of Stig-Inge Bjornebye and goalkeeper Frode Grodas. But Toshack's team largely struggled to instigate further attacks. Norway's defensive stance, with five men strung across the middle and only Jan-Aage Fjortoft in attack, meant Wales at least had room to display their creativity, but their passing was so dismal that when they got possession, they immediately gave it straight back to Norway. Rush looked utterly lost in his withdrawn role, and replaced Hughes upfront at the break.

Two goals at the start of the second half killed Wales off. Mykland's intelligent pass found Jakobsen twenty yards from goal and no Wales defender picked up Mykland as he cleverly ran on to the return and executed the perfect finish. Two minutes later, Melville let Flo's low cross from the right run under his foot, allowing the unmarked Jakobsen to take advantage of another gift and score at the far post.

It seemed to many as though Toshack's tactical demands were simply beyond the grasp of the Welsh players, and they eventually reverted to 4–4–2, but it made no odds. Norway could have had six, wasting several chances in a final fifteen minutes in which Wales became a shambles. The last-minute consolation, converted by Chris Coleman from Mark Pembridge's cross, fooled nobody. It had been a humiliating night.

The fans chanted 'There's only one Terry Yorath' and 'We want Terry back', and Toshack partly acknowledged his home town's anger. 'I could understand the crowd's frustrations but I had said that we would have problems early on and what I learned early on and what I learned tonight will stand us in good stead in the long run.'

The long run, as Toshack put it, didn't last more than a week. On 16 March, just seven days after the Norway debacle, rumours reached Wales from Spanish radio that Toshack had been stung by the reaction of the fans and the reaction of the Spanish media to his dual role, and was quitting the job after just 47 days.

Mike Smith told the media that he had tried to persuade Toshack to change his mind. 'He spoke to Alun Evans and myself though our conversation was brief. He is not happy with the situation. He intimated to me that he does not want to continue. We have been trying to get him to change his mind. I think a decision will be given tomorrow. I will be terribly disappointed if he goes through with it.

'It was not just about football or about playing systems. There are other factors involved. Although it was not a good performance against Norway, we were really looking at players, and he was able to work with them. But to do what he wants to be able to do takes time, and we don't have that commodity. It is disappointing, because his ideas have been tried and tested on the big stages. I was excited about working with him. But sometimes you go two paces forward and one pace back. The most important people are the players. They have got to keep going and understand that they have to play for their country. Maybe in the short term I can guide that side of it.'

It seemed that Toshack's words at that press conference had come back to haunt him. 'If at any time the FAW or the Welsh public feel it won't work they can say so. I don't want Real Sociedad to suffer. I don't want Wales to suffer and I don't want John Toshack to suffer. I don't need it.' The Welsh public clearly felt it wasn't going to work, and had said so.

Toshack duly confirmed his resignation that day, with undertones critical of the FAW. 'When I was offered the job I was enthusiastic and full of hope, since I announced I had accepted the job. It is simply that now I have realised some things I didn't know before and I have no interest in continuing. I took the decision to leave the team by myself. It has nothing to do with the position of *libero*, or forwards or goalkeepers. Money does not come into it.'

Whether it was a realisation of just how badly Yorath had been treated, or the discovery that the players were still privately seething at his predecessor's sacking, or he simply just didn't need the hassle, Toshack never elaborated. Questioned about the affair in 1996, he refused to be drawn, responding, 'I've nothing at all to say about that.' In 1999, however, he did hint at one of the problems he faced, after Keegan emulated his old strike partner by taking over as England boss while still managing Fulham. 'For a start, I was in San Sebastian,' said Toshack, 'so I was a long way away from my players. With Kevin, we're only talking about three months and four games, that's all.'

On learning of Toshack's resignation, Wales captain Barry Horne said, 'It's a shock, but I'm not too surprised. Managing a club in Spain and being part-time manager of a national side in Wales was never going to work.' And Ian Rush added, 'There's obviously much more to it than our defeat by Norway. He did get some stick from fans but I can't believe he's jacked it in because of that.'

Meanwhile, the FAW struggled to deal with the fallout from Toshack's departure. 'Perhaps our PR is naive and could be improved, but I don't think it goes beyond that,' said a hopeful Alun Evans. 'I have no qualms about my position. It is only the media who would say my position is untenable. Toshack is not saying Welsh football is in a shambles. The media are saying that.'

But the ire of Welsh football turned on Evans rather than Toshack. Newspaper reports emerged suggesting Evans had been reassuring Yorath he was still in contention as he made abortive attempts to hire Robson and Venables. Then there were allegations that he had kept his fellow FAW members in the dark as he claimed to be in bed with a migraine while he was in San Sebastian negotiating with Toshack.

'Our credibility has been shot to pieces. Welsh football has been turned into a laughing stock,' said one FAW committee member. Evans's optimistic assertion that it was all down to bad PR was laughable. It became a farce, perhaps fortunately so for Toshack, who returned to San Sebastian and escaped the aftermath with his credibility largely intact.

However, Hugh McIlvanney was one journalist less than convinced by Toshack's role in the whole affair.

In spite of Toshack's insistence that his abrupt departure had nothing to do with a raucously condemned defeat in his first match at Ninian Park [he wrote in the *Sunday Times*], that it was inevitable once his eyes were opened to the festering politics of the FAW, does anybody find it easy to believe he would be going if Wales had battered Norway 4–0? Another question concerns the suggestion that, until he reached Cardiff, he somehow failed to appreciate the full depth and bitterness of the controversy precipitated by Terry Yorath's removal. We are told that he and Yorath are good friends. Given that Yorath feels strongly enough about the episode to seek damages for wrongful dismissal, was enlightenment for Toshack not just a phone call away?

Mike Smith took over as Wales manager for a second time, but failed in his bid to guide the team to Euro 96. Perhaps that should have drawn a line under the whole affair, but the embers were still burning three years after Toshack's departure.

Bobby Gould had taken over as Wales manager ahead of the preliminaries for France 98. In August 1997, Wales went down to an extraordinary 6–4 defeat in Turkey, a match on which Toshack acted as co-commentator for BBC Wales. And Gould was less than enamoured by Toshack's caustic analysis. 'I have lodged a complaint with Arthur Emyr, the head of BBC Wales,' said Gould. 'There have been several complaints from my staff's families and committee members back home over the comments. I have asked for a special meeting and I will listen to a transcript.'

The row blew over, but Toshack raised his head above the parapet again three years later, by which time Mark Hughes had become his latest successor as Wales manager. In October 2000, Wales drew 1–1 with, of all teams, Norway in a qualifying match for the 2002 World Cup at the Millennium Stadium. Nathan Blake had given his team the lead, only for Wales to allow Norway to equalise with just ten minutes remaining. And again Toshack was brutal in his post-match analysis for the BBC.

'We've got to pressurise this Welsh side to do better. With the sort of players that Wales have in John Hartson, Gary Speed and Nathan Blake, they should be competing more consistently. And is it too much to ask Giggs to get down the wing on more than five or six times in a game, the way he does for Manchester United? I believe the fans have a right to expect a little better from their national team. Yet at times I wondered if the players really realised just what huge stakes they were playing for. Why do we seem to think we are incapable of qualifying? Wales possess players who have proved themselves in the Premiership. Yet these days it seems we are satisfied if Ryan Giggs just turns up for Wales.'

Hughes responded with his own broadside, insisting that it had been the best performance in his short reign as Wales manager. 'If people want to criticise easy targets because they think they can criticise the senior players in the squad, they have to live with that and be honest with themselves and honest with what they have seen. It's always been the case that criticism works to bind players together, I'm aware of that and maybe some people are not as positive towards Wales games and performances as other people are. But everyone is entitled to their own opinion but it doesn't mean I have to respect it.'

He insisted that his team's performance against a difficult Norway team had been a pleasing one, underlining the fact that Wales hadn't allowed the visitors to play, and citing the excellent performance of Coleman at left back, who repeatedly countered Norway in the air and at the far post.

'My team are together as a group and although they read and hear things, sometimes they feel it's unjust and sometimes they think what's said is correct. You use that to motivate yourself, I don't have to do it specifically for them. It's harder for me to take criticism of my team now I'm a manager than it was as a player. That's because I know how hard they try and the effort they put into everything that we ask them to do. When Ryan Giggs gets the ball there's a thrill going through the crowd, and rightly so. I felt we were the only team trying to play the ball through midfield and have some kind of pattern of play. I'm upset by the comments and I don't see a need for it. The team played really well, certainly in the second half.'

Toshack had certainly aroused antipathy in the Wales camp with his comments, but he had certainly not been unjustified in making them. Wales had thrown away a deserved lead, a trait that would come to dog the side throughout the qualification campaign for Japan and Korea. And the draw with Norway came on the back of four consecutive defeats under Hughes, including an opening qualifying defeat in Belarus. It was not a record to make any team immune from criticism, but to Hughes and his players, it seemed as though Toshack's solitary disastrous game in charge of his country somehow invalidated his authority to comment on his national team's performance ever again, neatly airbrushing out the fact that he had twice managed the planet's biggest club, and few if any British managers could speak with more authority on European football.

'We are not interested in people who criticise us on TV,' said captain Gary Speed. 'We are in the business of getting results for this country. It's important to believe in us.'

'It's easy to point the finger,' added forward Nathan Blake. 'I'm upset by the comments and I don't see a need for it. The team played really well, certainly in the second half. People can sit and pick holes in anybody, but I doubt they played every game brilliantly at international level. They can sit up there and hammer the team because that's what they get paid for but I would say of these ex-players, I don't remember them qualifying for any World Cups or anything like that.'

14 A Sort of Homecoming

He might have just been handed the Spanish equivalent of the P45 by Real Madrid, but characteristically Toshack still had faith in his abilities and remained sure of his own future. 'I consider myself pretty young as a trainer,' he announced, 'and I think I still have a good future.'

Meanwhile, in their first season post-Toshack, Real Sociedad had finished a respectable fifth in *La Liga* under new coach Marco Boronat, formerly his right-hand man, and inspired by the goals of John Aldridge, who had been recommended to the club by Toshack himself during his reign at the Bernabeu. 'I watched Liverpool home and away, and he had been a big hero of mine,' recalls Aldridge.

In September 1989 Aldridge had become the first foreign player to sign for the club in thirty years in a £1.15 million transfer from Liverpool. In the wake of the departure of Beguiristain, Bakero and Lopez Rekarte to Barcelona, and the more recent defections of Iturrino and Loren to Athletic Bilbao, not to mention the retirement of Arconada and Zamora, Real had reluctantly decided to permit non-Basque footballers to strengthen their weakened team.

'Real Sociedad cannot remain impassive before the fact that players we have brought through our youth scheme are being enticed away from the club as soon as they begin to produce their best harvest,' said president Luis Uranga. 'After long discussions we have decided to let our coaches search beyond our frontiers for players who can maintain Real at European level.'

Fortunately, Toshack was able to guide Aldridge through the minefield. 'We spent an hour or so talking through the pitfalls that were likely to confront me in Spain. His advice was welcome. He told me how to handle the press, how to handle living in the town from a political perspective, and how to get the best out of my move.'

At the press conference to announce his recruitment, Aldridge told the assembled media that he was a footballer, not a politician, and had signed to score goals and pay back the money Real Sociedad have spent on him. 'If anyone holds anything political against me, there is nothing I can do about it. Goals are the same in any language.'

And despite being met at the training ground by graffiti announcing 'No outsiders welcome here', Aldridge had scored sixteen goals as Real Sociedad qualified for the UEFA Cup. He even broke a club record when he scored in six successive matches, earning twenty bottles of vintage wine from a local trader.

In the summer of 1990, Aldridge was joined by a couple more exports, midfielder Kevin Richardson from Arsenal, and striker Dalian Atkinson from Sheffield Wednesday. 'Because John Aldridge went there and did so well, they thought this could work,' recalls Richardson, 'and they added myself and Dalian. At times it worked well, other times results didn't go our way, but we won at Barcelona, we won at Madrid, so we couldn't have been doing too much wrong.'

The Basque supporters quickly took the trio to their hearts, adds Richardson. 'The English element of working hard, getting stuck in, shaking your fist, going "come on", they took to that. If they could see you were up for it, that you were giving your all, they responded to us quite well.'

But despite some decent results, the players failed to match the high expectations following the success of the previous season. They were knocked out in the second round of the UEFA Cup by Partizan Belgrade on penalties and as Aldridge suffered an uncharacteristic goal drought, Real flirted uncomfortably with relegation. Luis Arconada, now the club's chief executive, acted after a 2–1 defeat at Atletico Madrid, firing Boronat and calling for Toshack once more.

In the aftermath of his departure from the Bernabeu in the autumn of 1990, Toshack had been linked with a move to Athletic Bilbao, before being approached to take the Liverpool job Bob Paisley had earmarked him for a decade earlier. Instead, he returned to San Sebastian.

'Marco was struggling by the second year and unfortunately got the elbow,' recalls Aldridge, 'and another manager can't take over until the end of the season, so they installed Javier Esposito. John then went upstairs, but he was pulling all the strings, obviously. Javier did whatever John wanted.'

Spanish federation rules preclude clubs bringing in a new manager midway through the season, so veteran youth coach Esposito took up the reins officially, but, having signed a five-year contract, for the rest of that season Toshack was really guiding the club away from the relegation zone.

He was only allowed to watch from the stands, instructing Esposito from the stands via walkie-talkie, as he returned to the Bernabeu three months after his sacking, a ground on which Real Sociedad hadn't won in 46 visits. And it was Aldridge who took the headlines, scoring a stunning solo effort as Real Sociedad bucked their Bernabeu jinx and ran out 3–2 winners.

Toshack had had a remarkable effect on the team, changing their training patterns, having been concerned by their poor movement off the ball, says Aldridge. 'In his first session we played rugby. It was a strange session, but it was to get us passing and moving, because we weren't doing that, and he put it right straight away.

'I remember in one of his first games, we ground out a 1–0 win, it was so, so important, it was one of those games where you don't play well but you work your bollocks off, and we won 1–0. A massive result because we would have gone into the drop zone if we hadn't won. That was the turning point.'

Despite not being officially in charge of the team, says Richardson, Toshack took Real back to basics and back on the winning trail. 'When he took over he did make a difference. He couldn't take training officially, but he did take a couple of sessions that maybe he shouldn't have took. When a new manager comes along, there's always a reaction, and it would have been difficult for him because he'd been there before, but he knows the Spanish League, he knows the Spanish players and he did rescue the club.'

And the memory of Toshack's first reign at Real also played its part, adds Richardson. 'I think he also put a fear into the players, because some of the lads are like "Toshack's coming back . . ." They'd experienced the way he was beforehand, so some of them were a little concerned.'

Real remained unbeaten in their final six matches of the season, finishing in mid-table. But they did at least have a say in the destination of *La Liga*, when they took on challengers Atletico Madrid at home, knowing that a victory would make Barcelona champions. With the match level at 1–1, Aldridge's header clinched the title for Johan Cruyff's men. The following week, Toshack took his side to Catalonia as the trophy was being presented to Barca. But Real gatecrashed the party and won 3–1, with two goals from Aldridge and one from Atkinson.

It had been an encouraging end to the season. Since Toshack's return, Real Sociedad had beaten the top three teams and risen to 13th in the table. But behind the scenes, trouble was brewing.

Dalian Atkinson, a powerful and spirited forward, had arrived from Sheffield Wednesday in September 1990 on a five-year deal, with a probationary year inserted in his contract. And despite several nagging injuries, he started to score regularly, including one stunning strike at the Nou Camp that had left the whole of *La Liga* exhilarated.

But while his strike partner Aldridge had the admittedly difficult problem of being a foreigner in a close-knit and insular institution, Atkinson had the added obstacle of being black in an overwhelmingly white community. 'It didn't go down well in some quarters but Dalian had the advantage of being an exciting footballer,' recalls Aldridge. There were few black footballers in Spain, and Atkinson suffered racial abuse, being told to 'go back to picking cotton' by one fan at Valencia, and to 'go back to the jungle' at Sevilla.

His home supporters at Real Sociedad were at least more supportive. 'Dalian was called the Black Squid, he excited the fans, like all the clubs he played for,' recalls Kevin Richardson. Atkinson was less than enthusiastic about the nickname, although he did tell one local newspaper that it was preferable to being called 'fucking nigger' back in England.

Whether undermined by the abuse or just lacking discipline while playing for a club drifting down the table, his taste for nightlife and fast cars, and his aversion to training, were having a predictable effect on his form. 'People talk too much,' he protested, 'I just like to go out to the discos like anyone of my age. It's all right for John and Kev – they're married.'

Atkinson, then, could hardly have been wild at the appointment of uber-disciplinarian Toshack. 'He never really liked John Toshack and the feeling was mutual,' recalls Aldridge. 'It was a shame because when John came to Sociedad, he took Kevin, Dalian and me out for a meal and had the best of intentions.'

'Tosh never saw eye to eye with Dalian over his off the field antics,' adds Richardson. 'But he was a terrific character, I got on with him but John never saw eye to eye with him.'

It didn't help when Atkinson bought a £50,000 Porsche convertible and managed to prang it on his first outing, accompanied by two female passengers, before proceeding to drive round San Sebastian in a hurry. The police arrived at the training-ground gates the next morning.

Meanwhile, Atkinson's liking for messing around in training – when he turned up – was like a red rag to Toshack. 'I once had to stop Dalian and John having a go at each other,' recalls Aldridge. Matters finally came to a head with a heated confrontation in the shower room, one Toshack was always going to win.

'Dalian saw John and said something disrespectful, and Dalian got very upset,' says Richardson, 'so we had to calm Dalian down otherwise he would have knocked him out. And I mean knock him out.'

Atkinson had failed his probation. Within months he was back in England at Aston Villa. He was soon followed by both Aldridge and Richardson. Despite being the second-highest scorer in Spain in 1991, Aldridge decided to return home. His family were unsettled and his daughter had been bullied at school. He returned to Merseyside and signed for Tranmere Rovers.

Toshack wasn't happy at the impending departure of the club's leading scorer. 'John tried to persuade me to stay, and live on my own there,' says Aldridge, 'but it wouldn't have been right for the family, and I think he was a little bit aggrieved that I never stayed, but hopefully he doesn't hold that against me.'

Luis Arconada was also unhappy about the deal, and refused to release Aldridge's registration. 'He and I had a big argument when I told him I wanted to leave Sociedad,' recalls Aldridge. 'Only the fact that we were responsible adults stopped us coming to blows.' Eventually, over a meal, Arconada assented to Aldridge's departure. But there were soon problems over the deal, as Real tried to make things difficult for Tranmere.

'When a Tranmere official went to San Sebastian to push the deal through, he came back to say he had been treated badly. That surprised me because the Sociedad officials were efficient and fair in their previous dealings with me. To his credit, John Toshack said he appreciated my dilemma. I heard later that he even tried to resign in response to Sociedad's refusal to sell me.'

Real had wanted Aldridge to pay them £25,000 as compensation for not seeing out his contract. Toshack managed to sort it out by threatening to resign.

'The whole affair soured my relations with Sociedad but increased my respect for John Toshack. I didn't want to fall out with anyone in San Sebastian, but I felt I'd been badly treated. The club seemed to be playing games with my career and John was reluctantly caught in the middle of it,' adds Aldridge.

Richardson too had returned to England, with Aston Villa, having gained the impression he was surplus to Toshack's requirements. 'I'd started to play in a lot more positions,' he recalls. 'He'd probably made his mind up that he was going to get rid of me and Dalian. We got knocked out of Europe, and the television money was quite important to the club, I think it was a way of getting some of that back by selling me and Dalian, so he played me out of position and brought in another lad, so obviously he was going to keep him in there, looking to the next season. But I just got on with it, as long as I was playing I didn't mind.

'Later on, he pulled me aside and told me if I could get fixed up he'd let me go, at least he told me straight away the position, rather than letting me rot or messing about. We didn't have any heated discussions, we just got on with it. I don't hold any grudges against anyone, when I was getting played in different positions, I was just thinking of the local lads who weren't getting in the team, it means a hell of a lot to them, they were really good lads. They helped me to settle in, looked after me, the least I could do was try and give them something in return and help them out.'

The midfield vacancy left by Richardson was filled by Portuguese midfielder Oceano, who had played under Toshack at Sporting Lisbon. He became the club's second black player, and enjoyed an easier time than Atkinson. The 1991/92 season kicked off with defeat, however, in a breathless match at Barcelona. Real's Carlos Gonzalez went close before Goicoechea's cross was volleyed home by Barca's Hristo Stoichkov on just seven minutes. Real dominated the first half, though, but they just could not convert pressure into goals. In the second half, Real conceded a penalty when Michael Laudrup was tripped in the box and Ronald Koeman converted.

It didn't bode well for the start of the season, and nor did Real's inability to hit the net. They didn't score in the next match, or the one after that, or the next two. By the fifth week of the season, after a defeat at Osasuna, Real's 'goals for' column read zero.

Almost inevitably, they won their sixth game 3–1 against Valencia, a team with the second-best defensive record in *La Liga*. But Real were staring relegation in the face. They did at least manage to salvage some pride with a 2–0 win over Bilbao in the Basque *derbi*. But most weeks,

Toshack was having trouble getting Real to score or even come close to threatening.

However, in the early weeks of 1992, things were beginning to stir. Real got revenge for their opening-day defeat, beating Barcelona 2-1 at the Estadio Atocha, before massacring Zaragoza away. The prolific Bosnian Meho Kodro was on target at home to Oviedo to haul Real up to ninth in the table.

But the roof seemed to have caved in with a 5-1 thrashing at Atletico Madrid, with both Paulo Futre and Bernd Schuster in their ranks. If they had decided to make a point to Toshack, they certainly managed to do so. Real were 2-1 down and threatening an equaliser before Futre whipped out his wand and created three goals for his team-mates. Toshack fumed, and threatened big changes.

It turned out to be the motivating force for Real to continue their resurgence. They won three on the bounce, Kodro netting the decisive goals in each, and found themselves sixth in the table and now heading for Europe. Defeat at Bilbao threatened to derail Real, but a strike from Bittor Alkiza was enough to earn victory at Gijon and Real were now level on points with fourth-placed Valencia.

Title-chasing Real Madrid were held at the Estadio Atocha, and with Kodro well and truly in the scoring groove, Real Sociedad inched into fifth place and the UEFA Cup with a 4-0 defeat of Burgos. Toshack had managed to turn around a beaten, impotent team into European contenders, racking up one of the best second halves to a season seen in *La Liga* history.

But in 1992/93, Toshack was unable to improve upon his indifferent record in European competition as Real Sociedad crashed out in the first round of the UEFA Cup. Travelling to Portuguese side Vitoria Guimaraes, Real went down 3-0. Jose Mari Lumbreras gave Real some hope after just six minutes of the second leg, and Miguel Fuentes quickly added a second, but Real just couldn't haul them back.

Real started badly in the League, suffering a 4-0 defeat at Burgos on the opening day, and won just two of their first nine matches, including a mauling at Espanyol. A 3–0 win at home to Cadiz brought some hope, as Kodro picked up his goal-scoring form of the previous season, but leading 2–1 at Oviedo, Real threw away two points when Kodro missed a penalty and they ended up drawing 2–2. It left them just one place above the drop zone. Patience with Toshack was starting to run out, and there was talk of the sack.

The nadir came with a 5–1 humiliation at home to Real Madrid in January. Things were so bad that despite a draw at home to Barcelona, Toshack was already talking about the relegation play-offs. Real couldn't even beat Burgos, the team with the League's worst defensive record, after twice taking the lead.

But victories over Sporting Gijon and Albacete meant that Real had won two games in a row for the first time that season. Their improved form couldn't prevent a 5–1 crash at Deportivo La Coruna, however, when Real keeper Javier Yubero, who had been at the heart of so many of their mistakes that season, flapped a Deportivo cross into his own net. Then, poised to pull the match back to 3–2, Real's Luis Perez managed to kick the turf instead of the ball. So hard, in fact, he had to be stretchered off.

Two wins got Real back on track, however, before the emotional final *derbi* at the Atocha, which fittingly Real won 1–0, before moving to the brand-new Estadio Anoeta next season. After weeks in which it seemed he had been hovering over the trapdoor, Toshack finally had managed to get his players playing again, demolishing Espanyol 4–1. There was even a glimmer of glory in the *Copa del Rey* after a 4–0 quarter-final first leg defeat to Real Madrid. Real Sociedad went all out to overturn the lead in the second leg, and almost pulled it off, winning 4–1.

Back in *La Liga*, a 1–0 win over Oviedo appeared to have erased all thoughts of relegation, but a couple of defeats to Osasuna and Sevilla, inspired by Diego Maradona, left Real in tenth, but just three points off the danger zone. And there was little margin for error with a nail-biting schedule for June that included stops at Atletico Madrid, Real Madrid and Barcelona. Real lost them all, but were rescued by a 3–1 win over Tenerife. They finished 13th in the table, but it had been a little too close for comfort.

The following season, 1993/94, didn't bring much further joy. It kicked off at the Nou Camp with Toshack opting for a more attack-minded approach, but Real capitulated 3–0 to a Barca inspired by Romario. The following week saw the inauguration of the new Anoeta Stadium, and the honour of scoring Real's first goal at their new home fell to Bittor Alkiza, who gave Real the lead in the first minute after a pass from Fuentes. But as Real tired late on, they clung on for a 2–2 draw. There was another celebration two weeks later as Real took on Valladolid in their 1,500th match in *La Liga*, and Toshack celebrated by abandoning his new offensive approach for a counterattacking strategy, resulting in a cagey affair not settled until six minutes from time when Oceano pounced on a mistake in the Valladolid defence to net his first goal of the season after returning from a shoulder injury.

Toshack's latest blueprint had its severest examination at title pacesetters Deportivo La Coruna. Real weathered the early storm, before threatening with break after break, and on the hour it paid off, as Oceano's header from a corner hit the post and Alkiza was on hand to tuck it home. Depor threw everything they had at the Real defence, but it stood firm.

The afterglow did not last long, though. Real lost at home to newly promoted Lerida, thanks to some inept defending, and the jeers rained down on Toshack's bench. And in their next home match, Real continued their nasty habit of throwing away games, drawing with lowly Logrones after Kodro had scored twice in the first half. They did manage a 2–1 victory over Celta Vigo, but Toshack managed to upset the crowd at half-time when he substituted Alkiza, who was being watched by Spanish national coach Javier Clemente. The habit continued with a draw with Albacete, which kicked off in a torrential rainstorm, Kodro firing Real in front before the visitors equalised. Then the generator powering the floodlights blew up and the second half was played in a hailstorm.

Toshack wasn't happy about his team's form and fired up his players for the visit of Barcelona. Kodro scored early on but when Laudrup levelled matters, it looked like Real's propensity for blowing leads wasn't going to end. But thanks to a battling performance against a technically superior team, Real didn't give up and, inspired by the tireless Oceano who dominated the midfield, ran out 2–1 winners.

In February, however, there was another row prior to a defeat at home to Deportivo La Coruna and a poor performance by Real in which they did not have a single chance to score. Portuguese star Carlos Xavier was suspended indefinitely by Toshack following a row in training. The two had been feuding for months, after Xavier had been left on the margins of the first team by the coach.

Real Sociedad hovered in mid-table for the rest of the season, the highlight of the run-in being a 2–0 victory over Real Madrid at the Bernabeu, despite not being awarded a stonewall penalty after a first-half foul on Kodro. In the second half, however, he scored after a brilliant pass from Alkiza left him alone in front of the Real Madrid net as the defenders squabbled among themselves about who should have been marking him. Real Sociedad managed to squander plenty of chances, before Imanol made it 2–0 and the cushions rained down on the Madrid bench.

But as Real Sociedad ended another season in mid-table, the talismanic Oceano announced he was about to join the disgraced Carlos Xavier at Toshack's old club Sporting Lisbon the following season. Things were about to get tough. And no longer could Toshack rely on the excuse that Real were poor relations to the big boys of *La Liga*. In the table they had continually lagged behind the likes of Tenerife, Osasuna and the upwardly mobile Deportivo La Coruna. Clearly, as season 1994/95 opened, something had to be done.

It certainly got off to a promising start, with Kodro scoring twice as Real won 2–0 at Compostella on the opening day. But it was followed by four straight defeats, leaving them bottom of the table after a heavy loss at

Tenerife, and despite a brief rally including a draw at home to Barcelona, the pressure was starting to mount as Real languished at the foot of the table.

But Toshack had more important things on his mind. His son, Cameron, now 24, was seriously ill back home in Wales. Cameron had actually followed his father into the Cardiff City first-team front line, albeit for just five appearances, but now he was suffering from an acute diabetic illness. Despite Real's dismal form, his father had made repeated trips home to see Cameron and his family, who had remained at home in Wales throughout his managerial career in Europe.

'The state of mind of our coach has gradually deteriorated because of the delicate family situation, which will force him to dedicate more time from now on to his family,' announced club president Luis Uranga, four days after a home defeat to Celta Vigo.

'Maybe I've been caring too much about things here,' said Toshack, 'and neglecting things at home, where it really matters.'

In some ways it could be suggested that the trips home gave Real Sociedad an excuse to part company with a struggling manager who had won just seven points in eleven games, but that would be to ignore the immense standing and affection that Toshack had earned in San Sebastian, having already become the club's longest-serving coach. It was, it seemed, a reluctant dismissal.

15 House of Cards

Four months after leaving San Sebastian, Toshack was back in football. He'd been linked with managerial vacancies at Leicester and Swindon, but by now, Toshack was well and truly at home on the continent.

'I'd never say never, but I don't see myself managing again in Britain. I know much more about the European scene than I do about Britain now,' he insisted. 'Britain is still cocooned happily in its own world, tactically well behind. Thirteen years after I introduced my sweeper system at Swansea, no British team has played it as well as they did. If you want an indictment, that's it.'

He cited the failure of Howard Kendall at Athletic Bilbao. 'Howard didn't learn the language, watched the English game on television on Saturday afternoon and wanted to talk about what was going on at home. I don't think it helped him adjust.'

Toshack was heading instead for Galicia and joining a club on the rise. Traditionally, Deportivo La Coruna's only ambition every September was simply to stay in the top flight of Spanish football. But president Augusto Lendoiro had embarked on an ambitious and expensive team-building programme, and in 1994 they had been denied the championship in the final minute of the season thanks to a missed penalty that handed the title to Barcelona. After five years in charge their idiosyncratic manager Arsenio Iglesias had been summoned to the Bernabeu to try and do what Toshack himself had failed to do. And Deportivo replaced him with Toshack.

He took over at the Estadio Riazor in the summer of 1995, and began assembling his own team. First to arrive was Martin Vazquez, the former member of *la Quinta del*

Buitre whom Toshack had championed at Real Madrid before he was allowed to leave for Italy. Then there was the skilful and pacy Russian forward Dmitri Radchenko, signed from Racing Santander for £1 million from under the noses of Celtic. Added to the talents of baby-rocking Brazilian World Cup hero Bebeto, it was by no means a weak roster.

In fact, many felt Deportivo had the potential to break the Barca-Real stranglehold at the top of *La Liga*, but Toshack was quick to dampen expectations. 'It's a castle in the air – a squad with an average age of 29 and nobody under 25. I can't think of another team like it in Europe. I know how difficult it is for a provincial club to break through. Since I've been here only Real and Barca have been champions.'

And it wasn't just in the League where fans' hopes were high, as another crack at Europe awaited Toshack. In June 1995, Deportivo had faced Valencia in the final of the *Copa del Rey* at the Bernabeu. The match was level at 1–1 with 79 minutes on the clock, when a thunderstorm meant the final had to be abandoned. Spanish federation rules meant that rather than the whole game being replayed, the time left on the clock only had to be restaged. So three days later, 65,000 fans turned up to see just 11 minutes of football, and after just 58 seconds, Deportivo midfielder Alfredo Santaelena scored to give the club their first major trophy in 91 years.

Any hopes Toshack might have had of playing down Depor's chances disappeared after a 7–0 thrashing of Bayern Munich in their first pre-season warm-up. Bebeto bagged a hat-trick, while captain Fran got two with one each coming from Adolfo Aldana and Aitor Beguiristain, who'd played under Toshack in San Sebastian.

Then came the prestigious Teresa Herrera summer tournament, considered the most important summer tournament in Spain and played at the Estadio Riazor, Depor's home stadium. In the semi-finals, Depor beat Brazil's Flamengo 3–0 to set up a final against Real Madrid. And Real too were dispatched 3–0, despite dominating proceedings. Real keeper Buyo was sent off and

Depor took control with goals from Fran Gonzales, Donato and Bebeto.

In the first round of the Cup Winners Cup, Deportivo travelled to Cyprus to take on Apoel Nicosia, and Toshack was fired up by the challenge. 'I won the British competitions and the other European cups with Liverpool. I've won the three Spanish trophies with three different clubs. The Cup Winners Cup is the one I haven't got.' But in the first leg, Deportivo were surprisingly held 0-0, but more than made up for it back in Galicia, thumping the Cypriots 8-0, with a hat-trick from Radchenko, two from Bebeto, and one each from Beguiristain, Donato and Aldana.

In *La Liga*, however, Deportivo made an indifferent start, prompting mutterings from fans and press alike. The opening day saw them crash 3-0 at home to Valencia, before a 4-0 thumping at Compostela. A win at home to Salamanca took the pressure off, but a string of indifferent results kept Depor firmly in mid-table, and after a defeat at Athletic Bilbao there was even talk that Toshack's head might roll after just three months in the job, with many fans regretting the decision to let Iglesias take his managerial talents to Real Madrid. But a 3-1 victory at home to Valladolid, inspired by the midfield genius of Fran, eased the noose a touch, and Depor followed a thrashing of Rayo Vallecano with a 3-0 home win over Real Madrid.

Back in the Cup Winners Cup, a 4-0 aggregate victory over Turkish side Trabzonspor, again inspired by Bebeto, propelled Depor into the last eight, where they faced an all-Spanish quarter-final against Real Zaragoza. Home for the first leg, Depor established a slim advantage twenty minutes from time by teenage midfielder David, who had impressed after being blooded by Toshack earlier in the season, in a stuttering home display against Valladolid.

But in the second leg, Zaragoza levelled the tie on aggregate through Morientes after 37 minutes. But Bebeto again did it for Depor, sealing their semi-final place with a goal on 64 minutes. 'We're going to win the cup,' insisted the Brazilian, who had been forced to patch up his differences with Toshack after being dropped earlier in the season.

In the semi-finals, Depor found themselves drawn at home to French side Paris St Germain in the first leg, and without injured midfielder Mauro Silva and defender Nando Martinez. It was a crushing blow to Depor's hopes when, with just one minute left on the clock, Youri Djorkaeff scored an away goal.

And there wasn't much more luck two weeks later as Deportivo travelled to the Parc des Princes for the second leg without Yugoslavian defender Miroslav Djukic and midfielder Fran Gonzalez, both suffering from leg injuries. 'All absences are important but Djukic has been a centre-piece in Deportivo's play over the past few years and so has Fran,' said John Toshack.

The second leg was a forgettably tense affair. Deportivo found themselves unable to create chances as Bebeto was marked out of the game. Their best opportunity came after just nine minutes, when Javier Manjarin's header clipped the woodwork following a cross from Radchenko.

Then, 14 minutes after half-time, Djorkaeff controlled the ball, beat Aldana and found striker Patrice Loko, who looked up and fired home from 25 yards past the desperate dive of keeper Francesco Liano.

After the match, Toshack was not happy at the ref-ereeing. 'I think Bernard Lama, the Paris keeper, deserved a red card for handling the ball outside the area. However, apart from the refereeing, Paris are a good side, and I wish them luck in the final.'

In the League, Depor hadn't quite managed to shake off their stuttering form in the second half of the season, climbing as high as sixth in the table as it drew to a close, but falling away to ninth after failing to beat Real Madrid and Barcelona in the final month of the season. It was a disappointing end to the season, but it had not been a bad first campaign for Toshack, as he laid the foundations for a more concerted challenge the following term.

He signed Czech goalkeeper Petr Kouba and Moroccan striker Nourredine Naybet, and powerful French striker Mickael Madar on a free transfer from Monaco, in part as a replacement for Bebeto who had moved to Japan. But undoubtedly Depor's biggest coup was landing Rivaldo.

The mercurial Brazilian, destined to become the world's greatest player at the turn of the century, had originally been bought from Palmeiras by *Serie A* side Parma, however, after a financial dispute he ended up in La Coruna.

Depor had a dispute of their own to deal with, however. Brazilian midfielder Mauro Silva had failed to join his national side's summer tour of Europe, incurring a FIFA ban. President Lendoiro said he would ignore the punishment. For his part, Silva claimed he couldn't join the tour because he'd lost his passport.

Toshack, wisely, decided not to select Silva as Depor kicked off the 1996/97 season at Real Madrid. It took a late equaliser from Real's new Brazilian defender Roberto Carlos to deny Toshack's team the three points. Depor started the stronger, taking the lead halfway through the first half, when Spanish international midfielder Donato flicked on a corner for midfielder Corentine Martins to head home. Then Real had Luis Milla sent off for collecting two yellow cards in as many minutes. Depor couldn't capitalise on their extra man, and themselves were reduced to ten men when Armando Alvarez headed for the showers.

Four minutes later, Roberto Carlos managed to squeeze through the Depor defence and fire past keeper Jacques Songo'o. A dramatic finale saw Depor down to nine men when Donato also got his marching orders. Unsurprisingly, Toshack saw fit to accuse the referee of favouring Real Madrid.

Depor followed up by beating champions Atletico Madrid, with second-half goals from Rivaldo and Martins, and by the onset of autumn, Toshack's team lay second in *La Liga* and looked genuine title contenders, despite losing striker Mickael Madar for four months after breaking his leg.

Just before Christmas, the Spanish transfer window opened up and as the championship contenders set about bolstering their numbers, Depor restocked their squad with two Brazilians, Renaldo from Atletico Mineiro, to replace Madar, and midfielder Flavio Conceicao, who'd attracted the interest of Real Madrid.

Depor found themselves second in the table by December following a 1–0 victory over Valencia, two points behind leaders Real Madrid and two ahead of Bobby Robson's Barcelona. But despite having gone 17 games unbeaten, and breaking a club record, and never being out of the top three, somehow it was never quite good enough for the fans, nor for the directors, with whom Toshack had often managed to fall out with over the team's defensive style of play, in spite of all the pesetas they had spent on attacking talent. Prior to his injury, Madar, a completely different player to his predecessor Bebeto, leading the line and allowing Rivaldo and Martins to feed off him, hadn't managed to excite the fans in quite the same way as the Brazilian hero of USA 94.

In January, Barcelona took over at the top when they ended Deportivo's unbeaten run with an 89th minute goal from substitute Juan Pizza, following a disappointing performance from Depor. 'Not even our most avid fans can argue that Barcelona were not the better side and deserved the points,' sighed Toshack after the match.

He might have pushed the side to third in the table, but it wasn't good enough for some of the club's fans. Prior to that weekend's clash, he and Robson had been dubbed 'farm hands from the museum of British football' in the Spanish media – a massive insult, especially to Toshack who had assimilated himself into Spanish football culture for over a decade. It had been a poor game, admittedly, as the media gleefully pointed out, with *El Pais* writing 'Ronaldo, Renaldo and Rivaldo and Figo, Guardiola, Sergi, Amunike . . . didn't produce a single gram of football.' Robson also came under fire for reportedly encouraging Ronaldo to take a dive.

Typically, Toshack decided he didn't want to stay where he wasn't wanted, and announced that he didn't intend to renew his two-year contract at the end of the season. 'After two years here I fancy a change. Even if we win the League I'll be leaving on June 30.' When he arrived for training that week, he found obscene graffiti painted on the walls of the training ground, with 'Toshack Go Home' being one of the more diplomatic messages greeting him.

There were even reports that he had been threatened with a knife outside his hotel. His defensive tactics had riled the fans who yearned for the return of Arsenio Iglesias's more positive approach, which had taken Depor from the *Segunda Division* to the brink of the championship.

It was a dramatic time in the life of both Toshack and his old Liverpool strike partner Kevin Keegan, who had quit Newcastle United that same week. Unsurprisingly, Toshack was installed as one of the favourites to succeed his old team-mate at St James's Park, but declined to discuss the future. 'I never expected it,' he said. 'After all it's quite a normal thing for a coach to finish his contract and move on. As I said I am stunned by the news from Newcastle and that's all I want to say.'

Favourite for the job on Tyneside was Toshack's fellow farm hand Robson – but he resolved to stay at the Nou Camp, eventually ending up at St James's Park two years later. So Newcastle were reported to have targeted Toshack and Ajax coach Louis Van Gaal – who would actually replace Robson at Barcelona five months later. Newcastle's negotiating team of director Douglas Hall, son of chairman Sir John Hall, chief executive Freddie Fletcher and vice-chairman Freddie Shepherd, were reported as heading to Seville to try to lure Toshack to St James's Park.

Toshack and his team were staying in Seville, after a 2–0 *Copa del Rey* defeat, but he was keen to rule himself out of contention for the Newcastle job. 'I have a contract until June 30, which in normal circumstances I would expect to fulfil,' he said. 'I don't know where I'll be working after that.'

In the event, Toshack didn't take the Newcastle job, which went to the man who had helped hasten his departure from Anfield, Kenny Dalglish. Meanwhile, Deportivo La Coruna unsuccessfully offered Toshack's job to Ottmar Hitzfeld of Borussia Dortmund.

But while the managerial merry-go-round kept spinning, Toshack's position was fatally undermined after a 2–2 draw at home to Athletic Bilbao. In the 29th minute,

Toshack had substituted the £6.5 million summer signing Rivaldo, creating uproar among the fans, and the Brazilian fanned the flames by tearing off his shirt in disgust as he ran to the changing room.

Then, just before the break, Deportivo took a 2–1 lead, and Toshack reportedly turned to the fans in the main stand and shouted, '*Si, auplaudid cabrones!*' (Yeah, you're applauding now, you bastards.)

After the match, Deportivo announced they were planning to discipline Toshack for his insults. President Lendoiro announced after a board meeting that the coach's outburst could not be excused, but wouldn't reveal the sanction he would impose. 'I agree there was a lot of tension in the stadium but the attitude of the coach cannot be excused and he has to be reprimanded.'

But Toshack showed little inclination to make peace with the supporters. In a radio interview he was asked about his tempestuous relationship with the fans, replying, 'It's not possible to talk about a divorce from the fans – we were never married in the first place.'

'He really had problems with the Deportivo fans,' says Jeff King. 'The fans used to hate him, there's some very famous images of him turning round and giving them the wanker sign.'

There was little respite for Toshack – by now linked again with a return to England, this time to West Bromwich Albion – in the next match, as a 1–0 defeat at lowly Extramadura handed more ammunition to the club's restless supporters. Depor were now fourth, ten points behind leaders Real Madrid, whom Depor faced in their next League match.

Depor twice managed to take the lead in the Bernabeu, through Conceicao and Martins, only for Real to level both times, before Davor Suker stole all three points midway through the second half. Depor had played well, however, but the following weekend, Toshack had to endure chants of 'out, out, out' throughout a 2–2 draw with Celta Vigo, and was jeered by the crowd at the end of the game. It was enough. In the early hours he told Lendoiro he was quitting there and then, and Brazilian Carlos Alberto Silva took over for the remainder of the season.

In truth, Toshack never settled in at Deportivo. He'd managed to fall out with players, managers, administrators and journalists alike, true, but it wasn't as if he hadn't delivered success, propelling the team to third place in *La Liga*. But he never quite managed to live up to the high expectations of the fans. 'Every weekend is a drama,' he said, 'you are expected to win all the time.' And his fragile popularity had evaporated when he rubbished his team's chance of winning the title, describing the club as a 'house of cards', and he was never going to follow Iglesias successfully in the hearts of the fans.

'He turned gold into lead,' said one journalist, pointing out that Depor had an array of attacking talent that Toshack illogically underused, preferring to concentrate on the defensive approach that left them fifteen points off the top. Many fans suspected him of spending too much time at home in Zarautz near San Sebastian playing golf, instead of behind his desk or on the training field in La Coruna.

He'd even managed to fall foul of the locals by unfavourably comparing the local confectionary *turron*, a sort of nougat, to the type on sale in San Sebastian. Perhaps that outburst during the Bilbao game had summed up a frustration he'd felt since taking over, as Phil Ball suggested.

'It was a sort of personal challenge to a whole community whose culture, he was implying, was not up to it as far as he was concerned.'

16 Fight Club

Leaving Galicia, Toshack was left to ponder his next move. 'Who knows and who cares? I've travelled round the world getting paid for a job I'd do for nothing. I could retire tomorrow and not have a single worry. Nothing worries me, that's just the way I am. People can take it or leave it.'

In the summer of 1997, he was linked with a return to Merseyside – but this time to Everton. Chairman Peter Johnson needed a big-name replacement for Joe Royle, and like most English chairmen of the time, seemed to have a shortlist of two, Bobby Robson and John Toshack. Johnson came close to offering Toshack the job, it was reported, but was talked out of it by his directors, who felt it would outrage the fans to hire a manager so closely associated with Anfield. Toshack certainly wasn't short of job offers that summer. He was linked with Blackburn, and also met Southampton chairman Rupert Lowe in the Caribbean to discuss the vacancy at The Dell.

'In the last few months,' he said, 'another three Premiership clubs came in for me. This time I did think more about returning than I had done before but there was nothing pushing me. During the time I've been away I've had various opportunities to go home. I've known coaches who have come abroad and after a couple of years have wanted to get back. Maybe in a year or two things might be different and I might return but there is a good chance I may never go back.

'I still feel that when it comes to the European competitions we lack certain things. It's very much a British game even though the imports have come in and when we go abroad, tactically, we are short on certain things. I heard one critic say, "He's been away a long time, maybe he doesn't know the British game." But two London clubs have foreign managers who had never been involved before and they have been very successful so I don't think that's an argument. When people say "He's been away too long", maybe some of them have been at home too long, maybe some of them should see other things and be better for it. At the age of 28 I started something at Swansea that's never been done before and will never be done again, taking a team through all four divisions in record time, so I've nothing to prove.'

Toshack decided that his future remained in Europe. Only this time, he was leaving Iberia behind and heading east.

'Besiktas were originally trying to tempt an old friend of mine, Gordon Milne,' recalls Bobby Robson, 'but he became involved in a wrangle between them and his old club and finished with neither. His club sacked him, Besiktas didn't want him and he was out of a job. Then they came to me, via an agent, and offered me the job. I didn't even consider that one, it was an immediate no. I mentioned to them that John Toshack was available and a very good coach, so they appointed him.' Besiktas had also considered Kevin Keegan, but having left Newcastle seven months earlier, he wasn't eager to return to coaching.

So on 25 June 1997, Toshack was appointed manager of Besiktas on a £1 million one-year contract. And he wasn't sure whether the fans chanting his name when he took control were being entirely complimentary, after he was told his surname meant testicles in Turkish. But he was ready to do his best for the Black Eagles. 'I am pleased by the welcome from the club and the professionalism I have seen so far. I promise not to disappoint the fans.'

Toshack had several problems to face, however. The sale of Besiktas's star player, a host of injuries and above all, a tragedy all impeded his preparations for the new season. 'Sergen Yalcin was sold for £5.5 million to Istanbulspor before I came,' he explained, 'and then one of our best players, Oktay Derelioglu, suffered a tragedy when his wife, Yesim, who was only 21, committed suicide. We were travelling on the team coach when he got the call that she had shot herself, he had a fit and it was terrible. He was left with a five-month-old daughter and he has terrible mood swings.'

It looked as if the club had attracted a more than adequate replacement for midfielder Yalcin in the creative Bulgarian Yordan Letchkov. But Nigerian striker Daniel Amokachi, formerly of Everton, had a back injury making it difficult for him to walk, let alone train. Besiktas's other leading scorer, attacking midfielder Ertugrul Saglam, was also on the casualty list. And captain Recep Cetin was reported to be angry with Toshack for leaving him on the bench for some pre-season friendlies and for playing him on the right, out of his natural position, when he did start.

Toshack got an early taste of the frenzied nature of the Turkish media, when prior to a friendly against Bayer Leverkusen, newspapers claimed that Bayer boss Christoph Daum, himself a former Besiktas coach, had warned Toshack that some Besiktas players would try to undermine him, as they had done to the German. Toshack refuted the story, but it would prove to be a salutary lesson about the Turkish media.

In the opening weeks of the 1997/98 season, his main challenge was to steer Besiktas into the UEFA Champions League, with a qualifying round against Slovenia's Maribor standing between him and another shot at European football's biggest prize.

'To go into the Champions League would be a big thing. They have never done it before and it would give me the chance to pit my wits against the bigger clubs.' But Besiktas looked uninspired as they stuttered to a goalless draw in the first leg at home. Oktay, in his first appearance since the death of his wife, came closest when he hit the woodwork with a header. Toshack remained confident, though. 'It is clear that Maribor are not stronger than us,' he insisted. 'They'll play more open soccer in the second leg, and it will be Besiktas which reaches the Champions League.' And in the second leg they swept

Maribor aside 3–1 with goals from Mehmet Ozdilek, Amokachi and Tayfur Havutcu, to send them into the group stages where they were paired with Bayern Munich, Paris St Germain and IFK Gothenburg.

In the League, however, Besiktas almost got off to the worst possible start at home to newly promoted Seker-spor. The new boys took the lead ten minutes into the game after a Besiktas defensive error and it took them an hour to get on terms. It looked as though Toshack would have to settle for a point until Amokachi stole the three points. 'We must learn a lesson from this match,' said Toshack. 'Everybody should be patient. This team will definitely get better.' But Besiktas had lacked invention in midfield thanks to the spate of injuries, and the defence looked uncertain.

The following week, Besiktas surrendered a two-goal lead, handing Genclerbirligi a 2–2 draw. 'In the second half my players were unrecognisable,' fumed Toshack. 'We made so many mistakes and were just lucky to escape defeat.' But the team's preparations hadn't been helped when striker Ertugrul got injured a day before the match and the recuperating Oktay had to be flown in at the eleventh hour as a replacement. It was just the start that the fans did not want, and they vented their displeasure at what they saw as negative tactics from Toshack. They were especially unhappy at Toshack's continued omission of Recep, who it was felt could bring some creativity to Besiktas's flagging midfield.

Instead, however, Toshack deployed him as a sweeper to bolster his defence for the League visit to Kayserispor. It was a gamble that failed as Besiktas sank to another defeat. Letchkov was struggling for fitness, having not played for six months after falling out with his manager at his previous club Marseilles, and was hauled off by Toshack not long after the break. After just a couple of months, it was already being reported that Toshack might be on his way out, being linked with the job as manager of Nigeria.

But he was firmly in charge as the Champions League kicked off with a tough start at Bayern Munich. Toshack had to field reserve keeper Tuncay Fevzi as the Croatian Marijan Mrmic was injured, while Amokachi was still suffering with his knee injury, and Turkish internationals Erkan and Oktay were also in the treatment room.

There was an unpleasant welcome for Toshack and his team. On cue, hundreds of Bayern fans held up carrier bags from Aldi, the cut-price supermarket chain, as a sick joke about the poor economic fortunes of Turks in Germany. Besiktas got a torrid induction to the Champions League on the pitch too, Thomas Helmer giving Bayern the lead after just three minutes, and twenty minutes from the end Mario Basler doubled the lead.

But two weeks later, Besiktas were rampant as they played host to Paris St Germain. Oktay opened the scoring on five minutes, and headed his second three minutes before the break. At 66 minutes, the Besiktas defence allowed Italian striker Marco Simone to put PSG back in it but with time running out, substitute Ertugrul grabbed the third, after some excellent work from the rampaging Amokachi. 'This was the real Besiktas,' beamed Toshack.

The renaissance continued with another home victory, this time over IFK Gothenburg, through a single goal from the prolific Oktay. It left Besiktas second in the group and well placed to progress to the knockout stages. Besiktas could have rattled up more, if not for an inspired display from Swedish keeper Thomas Ravelli.

But an extraordinary row almost spelled an early end to Toshack's career in Turkey when he managed to outrage the military. The incident flared after Oktay got injured during a spell of national service. The striker had been training with his military unit during the week before returning to Istanbul to link up with his team-mates for weekend matches, but reported for club training one Friday with a damaged right knee ligament.

Toshack was incensed. He respected the fact that Turkish players were obliged to undertake national service, but felt that it was ridiculous for a Turkish international to be forced to endure heavy drill practice. 'The like of this has not been seen anywhere in the world before. Even the communist regimes of thirty years ago looked after their sportsmen better,' Toshack was quoted in Turkish daily *Hurriyet*. The touchpaper had been lit.

The army generals contacted Besiktas chairman Suleyman Seba, ordering the club to warn Toshack of the severity of his remarks, and if necessary, sack him. In Turkey, insulting the armed forces was still a criminal offence. These were not men to be messed around.

Predictably, Besiktas had to back down. 'The board of directors and the technical committee and all our sportsmen apologise for the misunderstanding and extend our thanks to the Turkish armed forces for all the support they have given us to date,' announced a club statement. 'The concern of our trainer Toshack, who was upset by the situation, was unnecessarily exacerbated.'

And Toshack made the inevitable apology. 'I have no business with the military,' he said. 'I showed no disrespect to anybody. I merely felt sorry for the injury to Oktay, who is a member of the national team, and I expressed that. I apologise.'

Predictably, the military were quick to distance themselves from reports they wanted to see Toshack fired, blaming the media. 'When this subject was covered by several newspapers I spoke to Suleyman Seba. I told him to deal with this matter as this could cause misunderstandings,' said deputy chief of general staff, Cevik Bir. 'Seba took the message and said that they are upset to see this news published in several newspapers and that they will explain everything to the public, which they did. But it is wrong to suggest that we want Toshack to be removed from his position. This incorrect interpretation is a result of misreporting, and this has really made us upset.'

Toshack was free to concentrate on the Champions League and the crucial return with Gothenburg. 'Even a draw will not be a good result for us,' he said as his team headed for Sweden. But with Amokachi injured and winger Erkan suspended, Besiktas were lacking in firepower. They fell behind to a penalty on eighteen minutes after Ertugrul was adjudged to have handled in the area. And five minutes later, Alpay bungled a challenge on Niclas Alexandersson and the ball fell loose to Robert

Andersson, who made it 2–0. Just before the break, Besiktas halved the deficit when Oktay rounded off a move initiated by Letchkov and Mehmet. In the second half, there was even more drama, when Marijan Mrmic was red-carded for bringing down Andersson. Toshack brought on substitute keeper Fevzi Tuncay, who became an instant hero by saving the resultant penalty from Pettersson. Despite enjoying the better of the second half, however, Besiktas couldn't hit back. But PSG's 3–1 defeat of Bayern meant there was still all to play for.

In reality, that result meant the Germans would be fired up when they jetted to Istanbul at the end of the month. And Besiktas would be without the suspended Mrmic and sweeper Rahim Zafer. But they warmed up for the tie with a seven-goal rout of Vanspor, including a hat-trick from Oktay, while Letchkov looked to have found his form after an erratic start.

Besiktas started brightly against Bayern, forcing a couple of corners. But just four minutes had elapsed when Bayern were awarded a free-kick deep on the left. It was met by a magnificent leap by Carsten Jancker who steered the ball just inside the helpless Fevzi's left-hand post. Besiktas never really recovered. On the half hour came a carbon copy, this time Thomas Helmer getting the final touch. Besiktas were clearly missing Rahim's presence at the back and the creativity of Mehmet, ruled out at the last minute by a virus. In his absence the creative burden fell on Letchkov, but it was too much. In the second half Toshack brought on Amokachi, still not fully fit, and he made little impact on Bayern's resolute back line. Besiktas were out, and lost the final group game at PSG. It was an unhappy return to the competition for Toshack.

By the autumn, Besiktas were second in the League, a point behind Fenerbahce. They lost 3–2 at Galatasaray, but by November had hauled themselves to the top of the table and looked to be vying with Fenerbahce for the title.

But off the field, Toshack had become notorious for his unsympathetic attitude towards young goalkeeper Fevzi, and his reputation wasn't enhanced when the papers reported that the player had taken an overdose after being relegated to the bench, although there is no evidence to suggest the alleged suicide attempt was related to Toshack. Indeed, Fevzi later appeared on television, explaining that he'd suffered stomach pains after eating a chicken sandwich, taken some pills which hadn't worked and been rushed to hospital with food poisoning.

Now with a clash with leaders Fenerbahce looming, Toshack attempted to motivate his players by accusing them of becoming big-headed after their Champions League excursions. He dropped Oktay and drafted in Amokachi, although the Nigerian limped off after just 25 minutes. Despite leading at the break, however, Besiktas could only draw 2–2. But the real action came at half-time, when, incensed by referee Muhittin Bosat's decision to disallow three Besiktas goals, Toshack advanced menacingly towards the official. He had to be restrained by security guards and was banished to the stands for the second half.

The referee gave his side of the incident after the final whistle. 'I sent Toshack to the stands when he swore in English at the linesman. In addition, I have described this matter in full detail in my report. The federation will decide on this matter and do what is necessary.'

Fenerbahce chairman Ali Sen fanned the flames, insisting he would have sacked Toshack for his behaviour. 'Somebody should explain to Toshack the difference between his country Wales and Turkey, in other words that Turkey is far superior to Wales. Toshack has come and stuck his tongue out at Ataturk [founder of Turkey], attacked the Turkish army and sneered at his players. Such things are impossible. If Toshack had been working at Fenerbahce, I would have put his suitcase in his hand right away.'

Toshack hit back. 'For me, Ali Sen is a clown. He's a very funny man. We all laugh at Ali Sen. I think he should join the circus. We'll go to Paris [St Germain]. There they can ask, "Who's Toshack? Who's Ali Sen?" Then they'll get an answer. I invite him to my home in Wales. I'll show him the cups and medals I've won. He can invite me to his home and show me what he's won himself in so many years of life. Sen is a cowardly man and this is the way cowards talk. Last season he was moaning about the referees. Elephants never forget anything but this elephant has forgotten everything.'

The draw didn't help Besiktas's League position, slipping to fourth place by the turn of the year, nine points behind Fenerbahce. The real killer had been a 3–3 draw at home to Antalya, after Toshack had substituted his best performers, Amokachi and Mehmet, when Besiktas had been 3–1 up. But in December, he had his contract extended until the year 2000. 'I am happy to be working with Toshack for another two years,' announced the taciturn Suleyman Seba.

Toshack explained why he was happy to sign the new deal. 'First, the understanding shown to me by the administration. Second, the hospitality of the Turkish people and the love of and interest in soccer they display. Third, the Besiktas fans. We have not deserved them up to now, but we will pull ourselves together in the second half. I will bring to Besiktas the success I have promised.'

He would certainly have to work to earn his money. The Besiktas defence looked disorganised at times, the midfield less than solid and the forwards unsettled. Oktay was still struggling to come to terms with the death of his wife while Amokachi was fighting for fitness, and, predictably, had fallen out with Toshack after returning late from the New Year break, resulting in a huge fine.

Toshack managed to alienate many of his players, switching some from role to role during matches, with Ertugrul moved from attack to defence and back again, when it was felt his natural position was just behind the main strikers. It looked to many observers as though Besiktas were a team racked by fear, while the fans were divided over Toshack's adoption of a more British style of play than they were used to. His critics had another field day as the second half of the season kicked off with a defeat to lowly Sekerspor.

In the next game against Genclerbirligi, a portion of the crowd called for Suleyman Seba's resignation and barracked Alpay and midfielder Serdar Topraktepe, whose display was visibly affected by the jeers. For once, Besiktas managed not to squander their early lead, winning 3–1.

Still, if Besiktas were struggling for form in the League, they proved more of a success in the Turkish Cup. In the last eight, they beat Istanbulspor on aggregate. 'This victory is our present to the fans whom we have been unable to make happy in the League,' announced Toshack. But they continued to make their fans unhappy, losing 3–1 to Trabzonspor, admittedly with a patchwork side decimated by injuries and suspensions. 'We gave away two bad goals at the start of the second half,' said Toshack, 'and the last half hour was very difficult.'

The rut continued. Against Altay, Besiktas enjoyed plenty of possession but little penetration, as Oktay, Amokachi and young Nihat Kavehci wasted chance after chance. Their 1–0 defeat left Besiktas 14 points behind pacesetters Trabzonspor. Toshack criticised his players for their lack of effort, and was reported as toying with a move back to Spain with Atletico Madrid.

But things were about to get even worse for Toshack. Letchkov, with whom he'd always had a frosty relationship, simply walked out of the club, vowing never to play for them again. The Bulgarian, now beginning to display his true form, initially refused to reveal why he quit, but later explained in various interviews that he'd not been able to get on with Toshack, that Besiktas owed him money, and his wife could not settle in Turkey. Besiktas appealed to FIFA, who slapped a worldwide ban on Letchkov and ordered him to pay £60,000 compensation, but he never stumped up the cash, and there was nothing Toshack or anyone could do.

It was a good job Besiktas still had the Turkish Cup to concentrate on, and a semi-final against Kocaelispor. But Toshack was forced to play with a seriously diminished pack, unable to select Mehmet or Recep, while keeper Marijan Mrmic had lost form and Amokachi looked as though his mind was on the forthcoming World Cup. In the first leg, Besiktas took a one-goal advantage through young prospect Yusuf Tokuc. Besiktas had plenty of chances to extend their lead but squandered them all.

Nobody expected Kocaelispor to overhaul Besiktas's lead in the second leg, though. But it lasted just nine minutes. Ertugrul, playing with a pain-killing injection, failed to clear a cross from the right and Kocaelispor were level on aggregate. They hung on for grim death and Besiktas were unable to breach their defence as the match ticked into extra time. Incredibly, Besiktas scored four times in the additional thirty minutes, and Amokachi had a hand in all of them.

Things turned from sweet to sour for the Nigerian, though, when he was sent off for swearing at an Istanbul-spor defender. 'I only told him in English to go away,' explained Amokachi. 'Is that swearing in Turkey?' It is when it's pronounced fuck off, replied the Turkish press, and Amokachi's suspension meant that with he and Bulgarian midfielder Zlatko Yankov suspended, Letchkov holed up in Bulgaria and Mrmic in Toshack's bad books, Besiktas took on Karabukspor without a single foreign player on the pitch and, looking more interested in the forthcoming cup final against Galatasaray, they were happy to come away with a scrappy 1–0 win.

In the first leg of the final, Buruk Okan earned Gala the lead, and there were just five minutes left when Ertugrul made it 1–1. But the real drama was to come in the return. Mehmet put Besiktas in front at the end of a first half in which Galatasaray had seen more of the ball. In the second half Oktay could have put the cup beyond Gala's reach on 71 minutes but instead shot tamely at the keeper. The ball went straight to the other end, where Arif Erdem levelled for Gala.

Extra time didn't produce a winner, so the final would be settled on penalties. First up was the ubiquitous Gheorghe Hagi. The Romanian saw his kick stopped by Fevzi, who had already kept Besiktas in the game with a number of excellent saves in open play. Erturgul gave Besiktas the edge with his kick. Gheorghe Popescu and Arif Erdem kept Gala in it, while Mehmet, Amokachi and Tayfur converted for Besiktas. Then Gala's Osman

Coskun blasted his kick wide. Besiktas had won 4–2, and as Toshack celebrated with his players, a massive weight had been removed from his shoulders. Despite the rows, the arguments and the controversy, Toshack had shown he was a winner.

Besiktas's League form remained patchy, though, slipping up against teams they'd be expected to beat, finishing a disappointing sixth. Still, there was more silverware when as cup winners, Besiktas beat champions Galatasaray 2–1 in Ankara to win the President's Cup.

But prior to the match, Oktay returned from training with the national team to find himself on the transfer list. Toshack was reportedly angry at disparaging remarks made by the striker after months of friction between the two. Oktay announced that he'd never play for Toshack again and was contemplating a move to Galatasaray. And as negotiations with Amokachi over a new contract broke down, it seemed like Toshack might be forced to pull on his boots again.

It was Amokachi who started the match, however, and he opened the scoring, but Gala levelled in the second half to take the match into extra time and a repeat of the cup final. But there was no need for penalties as Nihat picked up a miscued clearance nine minutes from time to seal Besiktas's second trophy of a turbulent season.

Toshack was linked that summer with a move to Celtic, but remained in Turkey as Besiktas prepared for another season in Europe. But to many observers, the poor finish in the League was due to the players openly challenging his authority by putting in mediocre performances, and practically half of them were up for sale. Recep was now on his way out, but Oktay and Toshack, it emerged, managed to patch up their differences and the striker was staying. Daniel Amokachi, too, signed a two-year contract. 'I consider Turkey as my second nation,' he enthused. 'I love this place so much. I have only kissed two shirts in my life, Nigeria's and Besiktas's. I was never as happy as this at Everton.'

Meanwhile, Toshack also hired another Nigerian, attacking midfielder Christopher Ohen from Compostela in

Spain, and another midfielder, the promising youngster Ayhan Akman. Peruvian defensive midfielder Guillermo Del Solar Alvarez, Moroccan captain Jamal Sellami, who could play in defence or midfield and goalkeeper Ekrem also headed for Istanbul. It was a massive shake-up.

Besiktas made an erratic start to the League season, though. Following a goalless draw against Gaziantepspor, Besiktas were barred from their own ground for two games due to incidents after the game, while Alpay was banned for five games for pushing the referee. Forced to play strugglers Bursaspor in Izmir, Besiktas had to come back from 3–1 down to snatch a 3–3 draw, having been 1–0 up after just three minutes through Tayfur. In his post-match interviews, Toshack complained about the injuries and suspensions, revealing that Ertugrul had started despite not being fully fit, and his replacement, Amokachi, who scored the two late goals, was also not 100 per cent.

In the first round of the Cup Winners Cup, Slovakia's Spartak Trnava were easily seen off, but as Toshack prepared his team for the second-round clash with Valerenga of Norway, trouble was brewing again.

He was unhappy over the imposition of hefty fines on two of his players by the club's directors. So unhappy, that he was threatening to resign. Oktay had missed one training session and was promptly fined £5,500, and was now threatening not to travel to Norway. Meanwhile Alpay was fined £33,000 for pushing the referee.

Toshack, the perennial disciplinarian, wasn't so much unhappy at the fines, more the way they had been announced on the eve of an important game. 'I was very angry at the announcement of these fines ahead of the Valerenga match,' stormed Toshack. 'What good is it for the team to announce these fines? While the directors carry on with this attitude, we cannot succeed as a team.'

The chairman, Suleyman Seba said ominously, 'We will settle accounts with Toshack on Monday.' The row seemed to spill on to the pitch, as Beskitas went down 1–0. The first half was goalless, but Valerenga gradually assumed control, playing on the counter with a long-ball game. Just three minutes after the restart, Fevzi cleared the ball in a duel with John Carew, but it fell to Bjorn Arild Levernes, who slotted home. Besiktas besieged the Norwegians' goal as Toshack introduced Amokachi and Ayhan from the bench, and had the chances to grab an away goal, but Valerenga held firm.

Toshack was confident his team could turn it round at home in the second leg, however. 'If we go through this round, if we reach the quarter-final, then let the European teams fear us,' he announced. 'The Cup Winners Cup is the only trophy I have not won in my career. I want to win it with Besiktas.'

And the second leg started like a dream for Besiktas, as Oktay restored parity after just seven minutes, followed by further goals just before the break from Tayfur and Oktay again. Besiktas went in at half-time leading 3–1 overall. That's when it turned into the kind of nightmare that you just can't wake from. In the space of eleven second-half minutes, Beskitas managed to concede three goals. With seventeen minutes remaining, they needed to score twice to cancel out Valerenga's away goal. It wasn't to be. The critics pointed to the fact that Toshack had chosen to take a break in Spain instead of spying on Valerenga, sending the club's general manager to Oslo instead.

In contrast, Besiktas had seemingly found their consistency in the League and, by the end of October, led the table after a 3–2 win over Fenerbahce. Alpay and Sellami were combining well at the back, boasting the League's best defensive record, Fevzi was finally living up to his promise in goal, and Oktay, Ohen and Ertugrul were creating and converting plenty of chances.

But a fifteen-match unbeaten run came to a halt against champions Galatasaray in December. Toshack shuffled his pack, selecting the ageing Mehmet and the still unfit Amokachi up front, leaving top scorers Ohen and Oktay on the bench, alongside the influential Ayhan. It was a massive mistake. Galatasaray dominated from start to finish, and their keeper Claudio Taffarel was completely unemployed. Besiktas simply didn't have a single shot on goal. Gala created a dozen chances and it was lucky for

Toshack they only managed to convert two. Besiktas were still top, but their lead had been cut to just two points. Toshack's post-match comment that 'Men played against boys, and the men beat the boys' baffled fans and journalists who could not work out why Toshack had left his biggest talents on the bench.

The club officials were starting to tire of the rows and antagonism. Toshack had managed to offend Fenerbahce when he was reported as saying that 'Fenerbahce is not a Turkish team, it's like the United Nations,' alluding to the fact that Fener had five foreigners in the squad playing under Turkish passports. On television, he made sarcastic remarks about Galatasaray after their departure from the Champions League. He also reportedly suggested that referees favoured Galatasaray and Fenerbahce, announcing that he would never work for them, because they were Besiktas's foes. He had already incensed his own board by criticising the transfer budget he had been given.

The club's board held an executive meeting, ordering Toshack to concentrate on his own team and stop criticising others. The club might have been top of the League but morale was at rock bottom, with players and coach at loggerheads. The fans were unhappy at Toshack's reluctance to select Mehmet on a regular basis. He might have been at the veteran stage, but he had the touch of genius that could win matches and keep Besiktas's championship bid on course.

But although Toshack managed to guide them into the semi-finals of the cup, the friction started to affect results and Besiktas slipped to third in the table. In the four matches since the winter break, Besiktas had won two, drawn one and lost one and now lay a distant third in the standings. The fans' anger increased and calls for Toshack's head grew louder. 'I am ashamed,' groaned chairman Suleyman Seba. 'We are fed up with the cat-and-mouse play of Toshack. Because of this string of poor results, we don't dare go out in the streets, we are ashamed to look at people's faces. The fans, I think, are right to protest.'

Events in Spain, however, meant that the situation was about to take care of itself. It was a fitting end in many ways to a turbulent time in Istanbul. Toshack had brought silverware and success to Besiktas; he had liked Turkey and the fans, but had always managed somehow to antagonise the players and officials. Not to mention the army generals.

Having left his watch at his Istanbul hotel, he phoned to tell them to give it to the Peruvian Alvarez. Toshack's time at Besiktas, he'd decided, was up.

17 History Repeating

Toshack's command of the Spanish language had always been infamously abstract. In his time at Real Sociedad, he'd even managed to introduce the concept of 'water off a duck's back' into the nation's lexicon. But now, in November 1999, his idiosyncratic take on his adopted homeland's tongue was about to earn Toshack the sack for the second time from Real Madrid.

In the midst of a dismal run of form, he had dared to criticise the precarious financial position of the club, angering president Lorenzo Sanz. But Toshack told Spanish newspaper *Marca* that he'd see *'cerdos volando sobre el Bernabeu'* – pigs flying over the Bernabeu – before he'd back down.

Summoning Toshack to his office, Sanz asked him if that was what he'd said. Toshack said yes. Unfortunately for him, Sanz had assumed that he was the pig in question. Exit Toshack once more.

'He's got this really bizarre tendency to use English colloquialisms, and he translates them,' explains Jeff King, 'but a lot of them don't translate, so the famous one was "pigs might fly" – you can translate it but it doesn't mean anything. All the Spanish journalists looked at each other aghast.'

During his first spell in San Sebastian, Toshack had been asked how it felt to be criticised after losing a UEFA Cup tie. Toshack turned to the journalist and said, *'Hombre, es agua en la espalda de un pato'* – look mate, it's water off a duck's back to me. The phrase is now enshrined in the Spanish language, endorsed by the Royal Academy in Madrid.

'He's respected in Spain, but they call him *El Phlematico*, the phlegmatic one. He never reacts the way you expect him to,' adds Phil Ball. 'You put a Spanish manager in a press conference, and they'll go, "Yeah, well, the fucking ref did this and that", and Toshack goes, "Well, what can you say, that's life . . ." He has this strangely kind of philosophical way of speaking.'

During his return to the Bernabeu, a television reporter had confronted him after a Champions League tie had left Real with a mountain to climb in the second leg. Toshack shrugged, turned to camera and replied, *'Hay muchas maneras de matar a un gato'* – there is more than one way to kill a cat. Cut back to a perplexed studio.

'He's good for Spanish football journalists because he's so quotable, he's considered to be a character,' says Jeff King. During his return to Madrid, Toshack even minted a footballing epithet to rival his old mentor Bill Shankly's ubiquitous line about life and death.

'It's a very famous quote in Spain,' explains King, 'He was at a press conference on a Monday, Real had lost the day before, and was asked whether he was going to change the team. He replied, you sit down on a Monday, you're really pissed off, you decide you're going to change the whole team. Tuesday comes along, you've cooled down a bit, you think, all right, I'll make five or six changes. On Wednesday and Thursday, you think, maybe I'll give them another chance, I'll make three or four changes. You get to Friday, now it's maybe just one or two changes, I'll give them one last chance. It comes to Saturday and you end up playing the same eleven arseholes you always pick . . .'

It had been a turbulent decade for Real Madrid since Toshack had first cleared his desk back in 1990. Ramon Mendoza was gone, stepping down as president in 1995. Real might have won five titles under his administration, but the club's finances were out of control. *Serie A* clubs had been sniffing around Butragueno, Michel and company, and that meant paying *Serie A* wages, anything up to £50,000 a week. Between 1989 and 1993, Real's annual budget doubled, and by 1995, they were making an operating loss of £10 million a year. On the pitch meanwhile, Real had been left trailing in Barcelona's slipstream.

Mendoza had been forced to surrender his power to property developer Lorenzo Sanz, and he appeared to be turning the club around. Real won the title in 1997 under Fabio Capello, but he had been lured back to Milan, to be replaced by Jupp Heynckes. And in 1998 the Dutchman succeeded where Toshack and the rest had all failed, when Real were crowned champions of Europe for the first time in 32 years. But there was no freedom of the city or lifetime contract for Heynckes. Despite landing the holy grail, he'd committed the cardinal sin of taking his eyes off the club's League form, finishing an unpardonable fourth. Just days after the Champions League triumph against Juventus, he was fired.

Heynckes was replaced by his compatriot Guus Hiddink, but despite piloting the team into the quarter-finals of the Champions League, by February 1999 Real had lost eight of their 23 League games, and just six months into his contract, Hiddink was sacked after a morale-wrecking defeat to Athletic Bilbao.

Capello, who'd just been fired by Milan, was first choice to return to the Bernabeu. But his contract was still held by the Italians until July, and Real's plight was too severe to wait. One of the reasons he had left in the first place, anyway, had been his disagreements with Sanz.

Instead, Sanz turned to another former manager, and John Toshack became the ninth manager in the four years since Sanz had taken control, with a contract until the summer of 2000, the president paying £370,000 to buy out his agreement with Besiktas. 'It was said he went back because he was big mates with the president Lorenzo Sanz, who was vice-president in his first spell there,' says Jeff King. 'He went back to Real Madrid on a massive amount of money.'

The club were sixth in *La Liga*, seven points behind Barcelona, and there was little doubt where Real's problems lay. They'd scored 44 goals in 23 matches, and only Barca had scored more. But Real had also let in 36 goals, and only basement side Salamanca had conceded more . . .

Toshack's appointment also meant subduing fans unenthusiastic about his return. Sanz turned on the PR, invoking Toshack's first stint for its 'spectacular style of football', insisting that he was 'capable of handling the dressing room'.

Many felt Hiddink had been too soft to deal with the infighting and the locker-room clique. For *la Quinta del Buitre* of 1989, read the Ferrari Brigade of 1999, comprising Davor Suker, Predrag Mijatovic, Clarence Seedorf and Christian Panucci. Seedorf had been caught on camera fighting with defender Ivan Campo during preparations for the World Club Championship in Tokyo, and had exchanged insults with Predrag Mijatovic during a heavy defeat at Depor, another incident captured by television. 'Real notoriously had lots of problems in the dressing room,' adds Jeff King, 'the main reason for getting Toshack back was they needed a tough guy in the dressing room.'

Roberto Carlos certainly seemed to know what to expect. 'He's a manager with a very strong character, he wants to win and hates indiscipline,' said the Brazilian. 'If he does want me to change I know he'll talk to me straight away. I'm not going to have any problem getting on with him.'

But not everyone would be welcoming Toshack with open arms. On the final day of his first tenure at the Bernabeu, he reportedly branded defender Manuel Sanchis 'the worst person it has ever been my misfortune to meet'. Now, eight years on, they would be coming face to face again.

Meanwhile, Toshack's short fifteen-month contract attracted knowing looks from the Spanish media pack, but he remained typically unruffled. 'I might be here five minutes. I might be here five months. I might be here five years. After 21 years now without stopping I don't really worry too much about anything like that. They talk of caretaker-manager, but we're all caretakers, there until someone else is given the job. We're friends, Sanz will get rid of me one day, and we'll still be friends.'

In his first match, Toshack got a painful reminder of the task facing him, as Real went down 3–2 at Betis. But it wasn't as though they hadn't shown any spirit. Twice Real recovered after falling behind, only to lose to an injury-time winner. Toshack had to watch from the stands, as Hiddink's contract had not yet been officially severed, conveying his instructions to the bench via phone. But the changes were there for all to see. Toshack had stepped up the intensity of Real's training sessions, and ditched Hiddink's system for his own. But the switch wasn't helped when central defender Aitor Karanka was almost immediately injured, and by the end Fernando Heirro and Manuel Sanchis had joined the walking wounded.

So with the title out of reach, Real's hope for glory lay in retaining the Champions League. Toshack's first match in charge was the quarter-final first leg against Dynamo Kiev at the Bernabeu. It was, at least, the right venue. In his first reign, Real hadn't lost in 31 matches at home.

But Dynamo Kiev would be no pushovers. In the group stages they'd dismissed Arsenal, and boasting the likes of Andriy Shevchenko and Sergei Rebrov, were among the best sides in the competition. But despite Sanz's loud proclamation that Real's entire season was on the line, Toshack's plan was to take the pressure off his players. 'Put up an umbrella, let the public throw stones at me while I give the players some confidence.'

And Real could also look forward to the return of Argentinian midfield kingpin Fernando Redondo after two months out with injury. In a 4–3–2–1 system, Toshack deployed him and Guti in front of a fragile rearguard that included the inexperienced central defenders Ivan Campo and Fernando Sanz, who just happened to be Lorenzo Sanz's son, as well as full backs Roberto Carlos and Christian Panucci, who liked to attack but were thus vulnerable on the counter. But Toshack remained phlegmatic about his flimsy defence. 'I'm not too concerned about anything. I can only hope they can get better.'

Instead of relying on them to could keep out Sheva and Rebrov, he pinned his hopes on the formidable talents of Seedorf, Mijatovic, Morientes and Raul carving out a winning lead. And they attacked flat out from start to finish.

Kiev had clearly come to defend, having been caught out by Juventus at the same stage the previous season, not long after the Russian winter break. Kiev's man-marking and deep-lying massed defence meant there was little room for Real's creative department, but they managed to generate plenty of chances. In the first half, Guti, with only the Kiev keeper to beat, scooped at a pass from Mijatovic and fired over the bar. Then Seedorf chipped in a cross from the right, only for Morientes, allowed free reign in the box, to direct his header towards the keeper.

Real's efforts were undermined when Seedorf and Hierro squabbled over who was to take a free-kick. And they looked vulnerable from the counterattack, keeper Bodo Illgner being forced to make a spectacular one-handed save on half-time from Shevchenko.

It was Kiev who took the initiative ten minutes after half-time. On the halfway line, Rebrov directed a header towards Shevchenko, who bore down relentlessly on the Real goal, before drawing out Illgner and directing the ball inches inside the right post.

Real launched a series of raids, but now without the erratic Seedorf, who'd been substituted by Toshack and jeered as he left the pitch. Then, with twenty minutes remaining, a foul by Oleg Luzhny was punished with a free-kick twenty yards out. Mijatovic curled home the perfect kick inside the left post.

But Real couldn't extend their advantage, despite a profusion of chances. However, Seedorf and Hierro decided to continue their tiff in the changing room, and there were reports that they'd come to blows and had to be pulled apart by their team-mates.

Still, the decision to take off Seedorf was applauded by Sanz. 'The coach has demonstrated that he doesn't have favourites on the field,' he said. 'When a player, whatever his name is, isn't playing well, it seems to me perfect that he is taken off.'

However, Toshack acknowledged that Kiev would be favourites to go through, pointing out that his attack had played from the heart rather than from the head. 'And it's not normal for this team to miss those four or five chances in the first half,' he added.

Real got the perfect boost ahead of the long trip to the Ukraine, recovering from going a goal down to win at Racing Santander and propel themselves into the top six. 'This was just the morale booster we wanted before,' said Toshack. 'I told the team to forget about Kiev at half-time. They did and everyone saw the result. We can get past Kiev. The team is showing improvement in every game.'

Real dominated the first half in sub-zero temperatures in the Ukraine, but couldn't break through. Fernando Hierro looked to have put them in front, heading in from Robert Jarni's corner but it was ruled out by the referee. But after half-time, Dynamo gradually took control and on 62 minutes, Shevchenko was through on goal when he was brought down in the box by Illgner, who was lucky to stay on the field. The German parried the penalty, but Shevchenko was first to the rebound. Eleven minutes from time, he hit his second. The holders were out.

Toshack was quick to praise Shevchenko. 'If you look at the scoreboard after two games you see 3–1 and he scored all three of those goals for Dynamo. He was a very important player. We dominated in the first half and we were just as good as them.'

Now, with no European Cup or *La Liga* to aim for, the only target Real had left was to finish second and earn another shot at the Champions League. But a draw at bottom side Salamanca undermined their chances. And a whole new row was about to blow up, again thanks to Toshack's personal take on the Spanish language. After the match, he had revealed he'd been thinking about making major changes, but had decided to stick with the same '*cabrones*'. Bad move.

Literally translated, *cabrone* means goat in Spanish, which in itself might have been less than diplomatic, but it also refers to a hooligan, or a man whose wife has committed adultery. Some of the Spanish media did at least point to the British sense of irony, but it was lost on the players, including Predrag Mijatovic. 'It would have been better to have used a word that does not have various interpretations. I believe the word was used as strong criticism. The coach is angry, but so are we. Everyone is to blame.'

At least Morientes was keeping his mind firmly on football when he announced, 'These *cabrones* will try to solve the problem,' and that certainly looked the case when Real beat Espanyol 2–0 the following week. Toshack was not greatly impressed, but he did at least choose his words a bit more diplomatically. 'There was an improvement but we could have won by more goals,' he said.

Toshack faced a personally difficult run-in, as Real's last five fixtures included matches against Real Sociedad and Deportivo La Coruna. And they were unlucky to go down to Sociedad 3–2. But a final day 3–1 victory over Depor secured their Champions League ticket – and Toshack's job.

But Real's assault on the following season's competition would be with a radically altered roster. Toshack decided on a wholesale clearout, in what Sanz described as Plan Renewal, after a humiliating 6–0 defeat to Valencia in the semi-finals of the *Copa del Rey*. It was a defeat described by Sanz as 'one of the worst moments in the history of Real Madrid. I couldn't take it any more, I turned off the television.'

The first import was Steve McManaman. Real had lined up the signing of Liverpool's floppy-haired winger long before Toshack's return. McManaman, now 27, had long made it clear that he wasn't willing to sign a new contract and wanted to try his hand on the continent, leaving the club for free on a Bosman transfer, signing for Real ahead of Barca, Lazio, Inter, Juventus and Arsenal, on a five-year contract believed to be worth £3 million a year. And although they had never met before arriving at Real, he emphasised the continuity the Liverpool connection he shared with his new coach would give him. 'I think he picked up a lot of ideas in the Bill Shankly days, just as Roy Evans and Ronnie Moran did. There are a lot of small-sided games.'

The major departure meanwhile was Davor Suker. The Croatian striker had lost his place the previous season after falling out with Toshack over a teddy bear. During a team jaunt to Harrods, Suker had spent £16 on the cuddly toy for his girlfriend, but was riled when Toshack suggested he could have been more generous. Toshack later apologised, but, seemingly indisposed to Suker's laid-back approach, was quick to dispose of his services when Arsenal made a £1 million bid. But while Suker was exchanging Madrid for London N5, Nicolas Anelka was heading in the opposite direction.

In two short seasons at Highbury, the Frenchman had upset just about everybody from terraces to boardroom with his surly demeanour, and now wanted out. But he was still a deadly, pacy and coveted striker, and it was no surprise that he topped Real's shopping list. And if Spanish football's ultimate disciplinarian couldn't tame him, then maybe no one could.

Toshack met Anelka and his brother Didier in Paris for talks after a match between Anelka's old club PSG and Marseille. During the summer, the deal was completed and Anelka joined Real for £22.9 million, on £55,000 a week. Despite the price-tag, Real had signed a world-class footballer. 'Major clubs in Italy wanted him,' beamed Sanz. 'But he has come to us, the most expensive player in Spanish history.'

However, Anelka was checking in at the Bernabeu with excess baggage. In all his manoeuvring, he had 'left a huge scar on the face of football', stormed Arsenal vice-chairman David Dein. 'The sad fact is that under the current legislation that exists in football, Nicolas Anelka will do exactly the same to Real Madrid.'

But on arriving at Real, Anelka insisted he'd been the innocent party throughout the negotiations, and had wanted to leave Arsenal for football reasons. 'I've come here because Real are a much bigger and more important club than Arsenal,' he said. 'Any footballer will snap at the chance to join such a club. I never had any problems with Arsenal. It was all invention by the English press.'

Toshack denied that spending a record fee on a footballer with such a notorious reputation represented a massive risk. 'No,' he said. 'I think people who have seen him here think we have something a little bit special. He has gone some time without training and he needs time to get himself together.'

Meanwhile, the Ferrari Brigade had been disbanded, with Suker, Mijatovic and Panucci departed, and fresh competition for Seedorf. It looked like Toshack was steering the club in the right direction. 'When I came here the situation was pretty desperate. Players weren't talking to the press and there was a complete divorce between supporters and players. They won the European Cup and a lot of relaxation set in and a lot of problems arose.'

Now, with £50 million spent on a total of eight new players, expectations were high. Toshack promised that his expensive attack would break the 107-goal mark his team had set in 1990. Certainly Anelka and McManaman would face intense pressure just to get in the team. In addition to the first-choice partnership of Morientes and Raul, there was right-sided midfielder Savio, Seedorf, Frenchman Christian Karembeu, Croatian Robert Jarni and Bosnian Elvir Balic, Toshack returning to Turkey to recruit him from Fenerbahce.

So with 29 first-team players, 23 of them internationals, on Real's books it was by no means certain McManaman, rated by some as just fifth choice, would get the chance to show what he could do straight away, as Seedorf coldly informed him. 'We all respect Steve, we know he has a great reputation,' said Seedorf, 'but when you move to an entirely different country you must start at zero again.'

Toshack subtly informed McManaman what was expected of him. 'We've got enough players in the club already who want a free role, because that's been the club's tradition,' he said. 'What they all have to learn is to do as they're told tactically. In England, Steve used to run down blind alleys. He lacks confidence for the moment, on his own admission, but I've told him not to let his head go down. Madrid is something different, we're so closely scrutinised every day of the week. He's got to learn the language, to get involved.

'I'm immune to the volatility of the Madrid public, I've been here before and I know where the bullets are coming from. I'll enjoy it until I get moved out one day, and I can show Steve the ropes, can relate things to Liverpool.'

Preparations for the 1999/2000 season didn't get off to an auspicious start. Real, looking short of match fitness, lost in a friendly to Celta Vigo. McManaman looked out of things on the right, while upfront Morientes and Raul were out of sorts and the defence looked as brittle as ever. Despite all the pre-season spending, Sanz had refused Toshack's request for a new central defender, no doubt unrelated to the fact that was the position in which his son Fernando played. Seedorf meanwhile had been relegated to the bench – and the fans chanted 'Seedorf yes, Toshack no!'

If he was worried though, Toshack didn't show it. 'To lose in pre-season is not such a bad thing. It will serve to wake us up a bit. Winning all the time is not necessarily good for the team.'

Real's bid to unseat Barcelona after two seasons of their dominating *La Liga* kicked off with a trip to Real Mallorca. And it almost proved a disastrous start, as Real trailed with 90 minutes on the clock, until two injury-time goals stole the three points. McManaman had started on the bench, but came on with 25 minutes left and supplied Morientes with a diagonal pass for the equaliser on 91 minutes. Two minutes later, Raul won it with a neat scooped shot.

But although the Real attack had been rigorously shackled by the Mallorca defence, many observers felt his performance proved McManaman had much to learn about the Spanish game. He was dispossessed three times, and more often than not was sent down blind alleys by his marker. Anelka, too, failed to make a lasting impression, but did at least show glimpses of his finest form, demonstrating the acceleration and turning on the ball Real had bought him for.

Real opened their Champions League campaign in Greece, and fielding a youthful team, including rookie keeper Iker Casillas, did not look like a team likely to challenge for the trophy. One down to Olympiakos after eleven minutes, they took the lead through Savio and Roberto Carlos, only to go 3–2 down in the space of four second-half minutes, and it took a Raul effort with ten minutes remaining to rescue a point for Real. 'The first goal we conceded could have been avoided and I am also not pleased we conceded two goals in four minutes.'

In the second game, at home to Norwegians Molde, Real got their campaign back on track, winning 4–1 at a virtually deserted Bernabeu. Estimates reckoned the crowd was no more than 15,000 and possibly as low as 8,000. But at least McManaman finally showed what he could do, turning in an impressive performance. But Anelka was substituted with a knee injury after a disappointing display. 'He does not look comfortable,' said Toshack, 'and after that performance he is probably lacking even more confidence. The last thing I wanted to do was substitute him but I had to think of the team.'

Real continued to stutter in the League, turning in their worst performance of the season with a 1–1 draw at Malaga ahead of a Champions League encounter with Porto. Real emerged 3–1 winners to take a big step towards the second group stage. 'My main goal now is to get the team to play the whole year as they did in the first half,' said Toshack. But bad luck continued to dog Real as McManaman had to limp off in the second half with a groin strain.

Meanwhile, Anelka had yet to score in a white shirt, and just a month into his career in Spain and dogged by a knee injury, patience was starting to run out. Sanz publicly floated the idea of loaning him to Juventus and bringing Zinedine Zidane to the Bernabeu in return. 'I hope and I trust that Anelka's signing will pay off,' said Sanz, 'he is twenty years old and I'm sure his form will eventually take off. However, if I see that Anelka doesn't deserve his place in the squad I would think about transferring him to Juve in mid-season and bringing in Zidane.'

Toshack was cool on the idea. 'I don't know what we'd do with Zidane,' he said. 'Anelka could have gone to Juve in the summer but chose to come here.' Perhaps Sanz could see in Anelka what Wenger and Dein had tired of, a player living in a hotel 300 metres from the Bernabeu, obsessed with his media image and already making dissatisfied noises. Or maybe it just summed up the insanity of the biggest football club in the world. Sanz had spent £22.9 million on a 20-year-old player who hadn't hit the net and was out through injury, and was now proposing to trade him after just a month of the season. All their spending meant Real were now said to be in the red to the tune of anything up to £170 million, although the club insisted the figure was nearer £60 million. But thanks to their unique regal status, Real were always insulated by the Spanish establishment. There was never any chance of a financial collapse at the Bernabeu.

But the club was in turmoil. There had been talk of a boardroom rebellion against Sanz, and he had to fight to survive a vote of no confidence at a stormy AGM. Still, the club had signed a £300 million deal with a cable television company. It would be a long time before the bailiffs were at the door.

On the field, the pressure continued to mount on Toshack after a 3–2 defeat at bottom of the table Valencia, a match which saw him earn a one-match ban from the touchline for some typically undiplomatic comments to the referee. It meant he would have to sit in the stands at the Nou Camp as Real took on Barcelona.

Nicolas Anelka was back from injury, and was desperate to show what he could do. 'I haven't forgotten how to play,' he insisted. 'I just need time.' He chose Real's biggest match of the season to put in a mesmerising performance in a 2–2 draw. Perhaps a pre-match show of affection from Ivan Campo had reassured him of his own ability. He worked hard and looked sharp, playing alongside Morientes and gelling with his team-mates, playing intelligent angled passes and chasing every loose ball. 'That was his first full game for us today and he tired towards the end. He just needs games. You cannot doubt the quality or potential of the player. He needs time. He signed for seven years, not seven weeks,' said Toshack, on whom the pressure seemed to lift, hailed a tactical maestro in the Madrid football press.

In the Champions League, however, Real went down 2–1 at Porto. 'We didn't have any luck but we did enough to win this match,' said Toshack after seeing his team defeated by two goals from Mario Jardel. 'There are some aspects that we have to improve, but I'm not worried about the future.'

Real clinched their passport to the next stage by beating Olympiakos 3–0 with an offensive line-up. 'I am happy with the result,' commented Toshack, 'playing with three forwards is good but I need more speed on the wings to achieve what I want.' But despite slashing ticket prices to 1,000 pesetas – about £4 – only 9,000 fans turned up. 'The cold and the rain were the determining factors,' said Sanz, 'and I think there would have been more people if conditions had been better.' Ironically, it had been Sanz, as head of the G14 grouping of Europe's biggest clubs, who had been instrumental in recalibrating the Champions League to provide more matches for the big clubs.

The pressure continued to mount on Sanz, therefore, and on Toshack too, after a 3–1 defeat in the *derbi* with Atletico, Jimmy Floyd Hasselbaink scoring twice as Real had keeper Albano Bizzarri sent off early in the second half. The defeat left Real in the bottom half of the table, with just two wins, six draws and two losses from ten games. Without a win in eight matches, it was the club's worst run in fifteen years, leaving them ten points off the lead and eight behind Barca. Ominously, the chants of 'fuera, fuera' – 'out, out' – rang around the Bernabeu as the fans waved their white hankies.

'It has never even entered my head to quit,' announced a defiant Toshack. 'I'm ready and willing to continue. However, that's not to say that they're not going to sack me. I understand the criticism. The customer is always right. I'm prepared to continue. I'm now thinking about the next game.'

He was right to do so. Although they finished top of their Champions League group following a 1–0 win at Molde, the vultures were circling. Despite heaping praise on him for the Barca result, Spain's influential football press suggested anything other than victory over shock leaders and local poor relations Rayo Vallecano would spell the end of his second term at Real.

Toshack was entitled to blame, as he did, Real's poor form on the appalling injuries that had ruled out many of his first-choice stars. But although Sanz tellingly retorted, 'That is not the reason', he still publicly backed Toshack in the face of rumours he was about to hire Christoph Daum. 'He is the only other coach that interests,' said Sanz. 'To suggest that Toshack has offered his resignation is a joke and I don't know where it came from. We were together for six hours yesterday and we spoke more than ever. I haven't spoken to anyone about the job.'

Toshack got on with preparing his team for the match and talked realistically about dealing with the team's injury crisis. 'If you have no ham for your omelette,' he said, 'then you have to make do with a plain one.' But by half-time, omelette was off the menu and the chef was heading for the sack. Rayo took the lead after 22 minutes, and six minutes later, Bizzarri fumbled a shot presenting Rayo's Manuel Canabal with a tap-in. Sanz reportedly spent half-time setting up a board meeting at his house to seal Toshack's fate.

But 30 seconds after the restart, Morientes controlled a long ball from Michel Salgado and blasted the ball past Rayo keeper Kasey Keller. Then Real had a penalty appeal turned down, and were further hard done by when Toshack was yellow-carded and Morientes red-carded for their protests. Two minutes later Real did get a penalty which Hierro converted. And five minutes from time, Raul stole it for Real, and Toshack's departure was back on ice. And promisingly, McManaman came through his first match in nearly two months after his injury. But it was clear the defensive errors which still dogged the team had not done Toshack's health any good. 'Every time the ball entered the Madrid area I closed my eyes,' he said. 'The goals that we give away break any pre-match planning. There were two individual errors to cry over. We really have to improve our goalkeeping. To play for Real Madrid you have to be good enough. Mistakes are costing us dear.'

After such a victory, Toshack's criticisms didn't play well with the team, with captain Fernando Hierro announcing, 'These sorts of problems should be sorted out within the dressing rooms, not in the newspapers.' Still, it was their first victory in nine matches, and Toshack had been generous about Real's resolve. 'The way we came back is worthy of enormous credit.'

The result had saved his job. Unfortunately, an interview with *Marca* was to lose it again. Sanz had decreed a media blackout at the Bernabeu, insisting that Toshack's criticisms of the club's administration and the constant infighting in the press could only have a negative effect on the team. It incensed Toshack, who told the media he was entitled to speak out. 'It's my right as the person in charge of the team. I'm the one that has the authority. I'm not going to allow my authority to be taken away, because after that there's nothing left. There's more chance of seeing a pig flying over the Bernabeu than of me changing.'

In a fatal echo of the 'goats' row, his old friend Sanz assumed the pig reference was directed at him. The perceived insult compounded his team's appalling start to the season, with Real still eighth in the table. After a three-hour meeting with Sanz, Toshack's second reign at the Bernabeu was over. He was the seventh manager to be fired in Sanz's four years in charge.

'The board of Real Madrid met this morning,' read a terse statement handed out at the club gates, 'and have agreed to dismiss manager John Toshack. We thank Mr Toshack for his service to the club.' The media put the boot in, with sports paper *AS* declaring, 'Toshack has proved he is nothing and that everything he touches he spoils.'

'It was well known he wasn't taking the job seriously, he was always flying off to Wales to watch rugby matches,' reckons Jeff King. 'He wasn't working hard enough and had problems with the players. By the end it almost looked as if he was trying to get the sack.'

Toshack was replaced by Vincente Del Bosque, a former Real player who had already stood in as caretaker in 1994. But if Sanz thought firing Toshack would bring an immediate end to his travails, he was wrong. Three matches into Del Bosque's reign, they were humiliated 5–1 at home to Real Zaragoza, their worst defeat in 25 years.

Fast forward six months to the Stade De France and the Champions League final, as Real thrash Valencia 3–0 with a stunning volley from McManaman, having seen off

Manchester United and, inspired by Anelka, Bayern Munich in the knockout stages. Del Bosque, somehow, had guided Real from seventeenth to second in the table. 'He is a giant,' oozed Sanz. 'He was the one who was able to make the players perform with valour. He's our coach and the players are on his side.' No doubt Toshack had a wry smile on his face as he ripped open the envelope containing a cheque for a £136,400 bonus, for his part in Real's Champions League success.

18 Don't Look Back in Anger

It was a testimony to Toshack's remarkable longevity in the managerial maelstrom that is *La Liga* that, having returned to Real Sociedad for a third time, he celebrated his 450th match as a coach in Spain, when he took his struggling team to the Bernabeu in December 2001.

In Spain's all-time rankings, only five managers have endured the pressures of the dugout longer than John Benjamin, and if he survives to the end of the 2001/02 season he will have become the fifth longest-serving manager in Spanish football history. Of foreign coaches, he is second only to Czech Fernando Daucik, who managed Barcelona during the 1950s.

But following his dismissal from Real Madrid, Toshack, now aged 50, might have been forgiven for turning his back on football management. The millennium ended in sentimental fashion, as he returned to the Vetch Field. Sadly for Swansea City's beleaguered fans, it was not as manager but as a spectator, as he watched the Swans beat Brighton 2–0 during Christmas 1999, to equal a club record of six consecutive clean sheets in the League, a feat first achieved by Toshack's side back in 1982.

Most of early 2000 was spent trying to extract hundreds of thousands of pounds in severance pay from Real Madrid. The Spanish federation turned down his bid for compensation, after he refused to sign an undertaking to stop criticising his former employers in public. He took his claim to the courts, however, and in February 2000 he won a £500,000 compensation pay-out.

Then, in October came a real blast from the past for Toshack. St Etienne were lying third from bottom of France's *Le Championnat* after ten games and, without a win in six matches, were facing the drop. Coach Robert Nouzaret, despite having led *Les Verts* to promotion and sixth place in successive seasons, had been sacked after a home defeat to Stade Rennes.

But Toshack would not be his first-choice replacement. Club president Alain Bompard first set his eyes on none other than The Beast himself, Osvaldo Piazza, now back in Argentina coaching Independiente. But talks broke down over Piazza's availability, and Bompard, infused by the spirit of '77, flew to London and offered a ten-month contract to Toshack, who, perhaps swept along by the memory of that legendary tie, signed. 'I remember how great the St Etienne crowd was,' he said. 'It was like playing against twelve men. I know there is a lot of passion at this club and the potential is fantastic.'

Conceding that his knowledge of French football was limited, he vowed that his first task had to be tightening up St Etienne's frail defence. 'I may not know a lot about the team at the moment, but I have a good idea of the style of play I want to put in place. This team has conceded twenty goals in ten League matches and that tells me plenty,' he said. 'That statistic means we need to score three times to win every game. The solution is to concede less goals.'

His first match came away to Sedan, unbeaten at home all season. 'I know one thing,' added Toshack. 'We need to win against Sedan. Then the next match, and then the next one. My overall goal is simple – to do whatever is necessary to get St Etienne back to resembling the side I played against when I was with Liverpool.'

Despite insisting that St Etienne needed a win, he was to make a losing start to his career in France, Sedan running out 2–1 winners. But gradually and inexorably, Toshack began to turn the team around, earning his first win against Metz, and slowly they began to ascend the table. It appeared the old touch was still there, as was his appetite and passion for the game, as Toshack told Basque newspaper *El Diario Vasco* during Christmas 2000. 'Whether it's with a bottle of claret, a good rioja, a glass of raki or a decent port, the attraction's still the same – come away after ninety minutes with the three points.'

But after little more than two months in St Etienne, having propelled the club to a healthier 13th in the table with a respectable 17 points from a possible 36, the lure of the Basque country was calling Toshack once more.

Real Sociedad were in an even worse state than St Etienne had been. Bottom of *La Liga* with just twelve points from sixteen matches, they had been humiliatingly eliminated from the *Copa del Rey* by Third Division neighbours Beasain. Real had already got through two coaches that season, former Spanish national coach Javier Clemente and Periko Alonso. Now president Luis Uranga was playing his cards not particularly close to his chest. 'We are working to bring in the person that everyone is talking about. We have to be respectful about pre-existing contracts, though. I can't promise that we will get this person but Tuesday should bring a definitive answer.'

It was reported that Real were ready to shell out 'whatever compensation is demanded' to hire Toshack for the third time, and naturally he simply couldn't resist the challenge – but he had been at St Etienne for less than three months and was reluctant to simply walk out. He told Real that he wouldn't break his contract at St Etienne – but if the two clubs could negotiate an agreement, he would return to the Estadio Anoeta.

Eventually Real Sociedad agreed to pay St Etienne £200,000 in compensation, and Toshack's assistant Rudy Garcia took joint control of *Les Verts* with captain Jean Guy Wallemme, although the club was now under investigation following allegations of faking the European Union passports of two players. It was, perhaps, a good time to leave.

Toshack was greeted by 1,000 Real fans as he took charge of his first training session, and outlined the size of the task facing him. 'I experienced an almost identical situation at St Etienne and so I know the recipe that has to be applied to Real,' he said. 'I am grateful to the club, because it has given me a lot and the people here have so much confidence in me that it makes my hair stand on end. I am certainly going to try and live up to their expectations. When you are scared of failing you will achieve absolutely nothing. You do not need to be brave to coach Real Sociedad because it is a privilege to do the job.'

'Toshack is a very important man for this football club,' added Uranga. 'He has already spent eight years here and is not frightened of the challenge that lies ahead.'

The players too appreciated Toshack's past achievements at Real. 'The squad has a lot of respect for him,' said defender Jose Antonio Pikabea. 'He has been in charge of big teams and is a man with a strong and demanding character just as a coach should be.'

Toshack's first game came at home against Real Zaragoza, and Real were unfortunate to earn just a point, despite having defender Sergio Corino dismissed five minutes before half-time. Sociedad might have had the best of the 1–1 draw, but having given Real the lead in the first half, Lithuanian striker Edgaras Jankauskas missed an open goal and three one on ones in a 25-minute spell in the second half, before Zaragoza equalised nine minutes from time. Toshack insisted he'd taken more positives than negatives from the game, but Real were still rock bottom.

Next up was the *derbi* with Athletic Bilbao. Real Sociedad had been unbeaten in the encounter in the last eight years, but Toshack made the fatal mistake of announcing, 'I don't want to be the idiot that loses after fifteen *derbis*.'

In a match with plenty of passion and little skill, Athletic's Joseba Exteberria, once of Real, who spent most of the match dodging flying bottles, scored both goals to keep Real pinned to the bottom of the table. But they finally got back in the winning habit with a 4–1 victory over Racing Santander, and Toshack declared that he was 'happier than I've been for a long time at Real Sociedad'.

In March, he returned to the Bernabeu for the first time since the flying pig affair. But Real Sociedad were comprehensively taken apart by a Real Madrid team that barely had to move out of first gear in a 4–0 win, Steve McManaman scoring a memorable effort near the end. *Marca* declared that 'Half the Real players didn't need to shower – they hadn't even broken sweat.'

Toshack, seeing his team trapped in *La Liga*'s basement, even went as far as proposing Real lift their self-imposed ban on signing non-Basque Spaniards, although he was quick to insist the club's heart would remain Basque. 'Eighty per cent of the team is a good figure,' he said. 'I'm going to mould this club the way I want it and if I have to piss people off who I consider my friends, so be it – Real mustn't be just any old team.'

He'd already managed to upset midfielder Stephane Collet who, under Toshack, now found himself on the margins of the team. 'Toshack is a dictator,' declared Collet. 'He does things and then gives no reason for doing them, it is not normal that he gives me no opportunity to hear reasons for his actions. This is the worst moment of my career. I was very happy under the last two coaches here and now I will just have to wait for June and then tell my agent to find me a new club. I cannot stay at Sociedad while Toshack is here. I played in some games in the early part of the season, but ever since he has taken over I have not had any opportunities.'

Toshack had remained characteristically prepared to overlook more celebrated reputations in favour of handing young players their opportunities. And once more it paid dividends as he promoted midfielder Igor Gabilondo to the first team for a home clash with Valladolid. The 22-year-old repaid Toshack's faith with two goals in a 3–1 victory. Toshack meanwhile had been forced to watch from the directors' box after receiving a red card in an earlier game at Numancia. 'It was all right,' he said afterwards. 'The only problem is that there's so many cigars up there and the smoke's really annoying.'

That win meant Real climbed above Oviedo and closer to safety, but they slipped up at home to Valencia, beaten 2–1 in a fierce match. Real were down to nine men before the break, and the referee not only had to be escorted off the pitch under armed guard, while a linesman was struck on the head by a missile, but also came under verbal barrage from Toshack. 'He's a sad man who can't even look you in the eye. He provoked us right from the start. He's refereed us twice and we've had three players sent to the street before half-time.'

The defeat left Real back in the bottom three, needing nine points from their last five games to survive, according to the back of Toshack's envelope. Three points came at Villarreal. Aitor Lopez Rekarte blasted home the opener, only for it to be cancelled out two minutes later. But a breathtaking 60-yard crossfield ball from Xabi Alonso was finished off by Turkish winger Tayfun, and Real sealed the three points with a free-kick from Inaki Idiakez. The win, and the manner in which it was achieved, amazed Toshack. 'In our position, it's not normal to play as well as we have. Even Villarreal's biggest fan would say we deserved this win.'

Real's winning streak continued as they thrashed Malaga 4–0, and by June, a 3–1 victory over Athletic Bilbao looked to have ensured Real's survival. But another passport scandal briefly threatened to pull the rug from them. Earlier in the season, Las Palmas had fielded two Brazilians playing under EU passports, then, after Christmas, re-registered them as Brazilians. Racing Santander smelled a rat, and were not entirely a disinterested party, as Las Palmas were about to finish above them and condemn them to relegation. Racing threatened not to turn up for a match against Malaga. Which is where Real Sociedad came in. If Racing didn't play, they might get kicked out of the League. And if they got kicked out of the League, the three points Real had taken off them would be annulled. And if those three points were annulled and the League table redrawn, then Real would find themselves back in the relegation zone . . .

Several nail-biting days passed for Toshack, players and fans before the matter was settled off the field and Real were declared safe, but more eyebrows were raised by the final round of matches. Real Oviedo needed to earn three points at Real Mallorca to stay up, otherwise they were relying on Zaragoza to lose to Celta Vigo or Osasuna to lose to Real Sociedad. And Osasuna believed they could rely on a quasi-Basque favour from Real Sociedad.

Publicly, however, Real insisted they were up for the game. 'We want to finish the season on 46 points,' announced Oscar de la Paula, while team-mate Javier De Pedro added, 'Everything that's been said is bollocks.'

But when Ivan Rosado gave Osasuna a first-half lead, Real's fans seemed happy to see Osasuna safe and Oviedo teetering on the brink. For their part, Oviedo were losing in Mallorca, and as Zaragoza looked good for a point, Oviedo's fate rested entirely in Real's hands. Only an equaliser in San Sebastian could rescue Oviedo, but every time Real advanced, the fans and some of the players called them back. It condemned Oviedo to the *Segunda Division*, proving once and for all that Spanish football can be a strange game at times.

Now, having escaped relegation, Real were expected to do much better as the 2001/02 campaign kicked off, boasting by no means the worst roster in *La Liga*. But the season started as badly for Real as the previous campaign did, defeated in the opening-day *derbi* at home to Athletic Bilbao 3–1, before losing 2–0 to their other Basque rivals Alaves, fresh from their run to a UEFA Cup Final defeat to Liverpool. Following the final whistle Toshack admitted he'd seen 'nothing positive' during the match.

The following week, Real had to travel to Osasuna's Estadio Sadar for their home game with leaders Celta Vigo. At the end of the previous season, they had been ordered to play one game away from the Anoeta, following the bottle-throwing incident. 'At least we've got off the mark on points,' sighed Toshack after a goalless draw.

But Real's dismal form continued as they went down 3–2 at Real Zaragoza. And it had all started so well, too. Tayfun gave Real the lead, but Marcos Vales and Yordi hauled the lead back for Zaragoza. Then Gabilondo looked to have stolen a point for Real, only for midfielder Mikel Aramburu to get himself sent off and in injury time, the ten men conceded the winner from Martin Vellisca. Sociedad were rock bottom once more.

They hauled themselves off it with a 1–0 win at Tenerife, thanks in part to a missed penalty by Tenerife's Xisco. But after a 2–1 defeat to fellow strugglers Rayo Vallecano, reports began to circulate that Toshack was about to head upstairs and confine himself to administrative duties, and be replaced on the bench by Juan Manuel Lillo, who'd had the briefest of stints in charge at Zaragoza the previous season. But many observers were not so sure, doubting whether someone who has frequently exhibited the signs of a control freak would be satisfied with a backroom role. In the event Toshack remained in charge of the team.

'Originally he rejoined Real this time to be director-general, not to be coach,' explains Jeff King. 'In Spain they have a director-general who's above the coach who's responsible for the overall package. That's what Toshack is at Real Sociedad, and for whatever reason he couldn't get the coach he wanted, so he's also still coaching, but he's made it known he doesn't want to be on the bench any more, he's been looking for another coach. You very often see snide comments in the Spanish sports press saying, "Toshack, when are you going to sack yourself?" '

The absence through injury of Xabi Alonso, one of Real's key performers, was also starting to tell on Real. 'It's not easy to walk when you've had your legs cut off,' lamented Toshack. He had recalled the nineteen-year-old from a loan spell at Eibar shortly after returning to San Sebastian, and Alonso had rapidly become an influential member of the Real engine room.

'Spanish clubs have a coach like Carles Rexach or Vincente Del Bosque,' adds King, 'but then they'll have a physical trainer, who trains the players. Toshack never has that, and one of the things he's been accused of at Real Sociedad is that the team are physically a disaster. He takes training himself, he doesn't seem prepared to modernise the structure. And they don't seem to be the most powerful of sides.'

Missing Alonso, Real drew 3–3 at home to Sevilla, taking the lead on three occasions, only to be pegged back each time. Real's real problems were at the back, with Toshack now playing a flat back four with Brazilian Luis Alberto and Norwegian Bjorn-Tore Kvarme, both brought to the Anoeta by Toshack from St Etienne, and their defensive partnership was frequently likened to a sieve.

In November, however, Real beat Valencia 2–0, thanks to Edgaras Jankauskas, who'd been singled out for criticism after a dismal performance the previous week at Deportivo La Coruna. 'When things go badly,' said Toshack, 'you have to leave.' Jankauskas responded by scoring twice.

That landmark return to the Bernabeu followed, and as Toshack walked around the pitch, he found himself applauded by the Real Madrid fans, a reaction in part to his sacking by Lorenzo Sanz, who had by now fallen from grace in the eyes of the supporters, losing in the presidential elections.

And Russian striker Dimitri Khoklov almost gave Toshack another reason to celebrate when he gave Real Sociedad the lead, only for Kvarme to hand Madrid an equaliser with an own goal. Then in the second half, Kvarme gave away a throw, and was casually strolling into the box while Morientes was releasing Raul to score the winner.

Toshack returned to Anfield the same month to sign out-of-favour Dutch goalkeeper Sander Westerveld, replacing Swede Mattias Asper, who hadn't impressed Toshack. The Dutchman made it clear why he chose to head for San Sebastian. 'Toshack is a coach with a big reputation in Europe and his presence has been very important in my transfer,' he said. 'I don't feel pressured at all because I have always wanted to play in such a good League as the Spanish one. I know I have just arrived at an historical club that is having problems in the League, but John Toshack's presence on the bench is a guarantee that we will come through. He knows me well and he has already explained to me how the club is and what his main targets and ambitions are. If you put together what he told me, that's why I just signed for Real.'

Real celebrated Christmas by thrashing Valladolid 6–0, and Toshack was clearly in festive spirit. 'Valladolid made a lot of noise but didn't get many nuts, while Real made little noise but achieved many nuts.'

The win propelled Real six points clear of bottom club Rayo. And Tayfun for one backed Toshack to steer Real out of trouble. 'I trust Toshack. He knows how to deal with pressure, just like he did last season,' he said. 'We are doing well, although there are some problems. But those problems are not so big that we will be relegated.'

Real's attack was bolstered by the return of Yugoslavian striker Darko Kovacevic in a £4 million move from Lazio. Kovacevic had previously enjoyed three successful years at Real before heading to Italy, where he'd struggled at Juventus before joining Lazio in 2000 for nearly £13 million. Toshack then returned to Besiktas to recruit Turkish striker Nihat Kavehci for £3.3 million. 'When I first saw him I saw a different player to the rest,' Toshack explained. 'He was enthusiastic about training and you also can see it during games. He's just born to be a leader. That's what convinced me he must play for my team.'

'One of the things that's always thrown at him in Spain is laziness,' says Jeff King. 'This is my opinion, but over the last three or four years at the clubs he's been in, if you look at the players he buys, he always either goes back to players he's managed before, or to clubs he's been before, like the Liverpool players at Real Sociedad. It's always the easy option, it doesn't give you the impression of a coach who's doing much work or searching for players.'

Following a controversial defeat to Athletic Bilbao in January 2002, in which Toshack was red-carded, Real lost their fourth Basque *derbi* of the season to Alaves, Westerveld making a hash of saving a late header to hand Alaves all three points. Real found themselves rock bottom once more. Once more, Toshack was left listening to calls for his head, and managed to inflame the situation when he spent three days in Mallorca looking for a team hotel for Real's forthcoming League fixture.

Despite Toshack's obvious affinity to Real, the image of John Benjamin, the Basque folk hero, was starting to tarnish as the club continued to battle relegation from *La Liga*, says Phil Ball. 'I think the novelty's worn off this time, there's a growing realism about him. The one negative thing about him is he's famously tight, he's really a hard negotiator of contracts, an absolute skinflint.'

Following the financial problems he encountered at Swansea, that's perhaps understandable. But the one thing that people in Spain wouldn't deny is Toshack's attachment to Real Sociedad. 'There's a certain emotional link to the club,' says Jeff King, 'but he's not doing a very good job. In Spain, some people think he's a bit of a chancer, living the good life. Almost the first thing anybody in Spain would say to you about Toshack is that he spends his life playing golf and eating tapas, he's seen as a kind of bon viveur. I think he walked away from Real Madrid with about £3 million for a year or so's work.

'But he's at a bit of a crossroads. He's been there, done that, as a player and a coach now, he's set up for life financially, so you ask yourself why he went back there as director-general as well as coach. In Spain coaches just coach, you'd have thought that would have suited Toshack more than director-general, which in theory entails more commitment, more hours. So I think there is an attachment to San Sebastian and the club, but I'm not sure he's the ideal man to be doing that kind of job at this stage of his career. They're struggling. History's full of teams that people spend the season saying they're too good to go down, but they keep losing.'

The received wisdom is that when Toshack finally does bring down the curtain on his career, sooner or later, he won't be returning home to Wales. John Benjamin, it seems, has found his spiritual home in San Sebastian. 'My theory has been for some time now that he wants to be president of Real Sociedad,' says Phil Ball, 'if he gets enough shares, and he doesn't have to be Basque. I think that's what he fancies doing. He's very comfortable, he's got a house in Zarautz, a coastal village near San Sebastian, next door to a Michelin-starred restaurant, and the cook's his best mate. He's happy here.'

Late on 12 March 2002, John Toshack was sacked by Real Sociedad, after a 2–0 defeat to fellow strugglers Tenerife left the club second from bottom of La Liga.

'This is down to recent results and, above all, is a way of inspiring an improvement over the last nine games,' announced president Jose Luis Astiazaran. 'The team have not been able to beat direct rivals and the remainder of the season is extremely demanding. I thank Toshack for his services.'

'We have been in a bad situation for fifteen months and other teams would have got rid of me after three months,' admitted Toshack. 'Farewells are never pleasant. I'll be encouraging the players when I say goodbye, and maybe advising some of them to concentrate a bit more.'

Toshack might have been given what's known in Britain as 'the dreaded vote of confidence' earlier in the season, but he had been given the funds to sign Westerveld, Kovacevic and Nihat. In the nine matches since that *derbi* with Athletic Bilbao, Real had actually won three, drawn two and lost four. But it was their inability to beat basement rivals like Tenerife and Rayo Vallecano that had kept Real anchored in the drop zone. Now Toshack was to be replaced by former Real goalkeeper Roberto Olabe.

'I have been in football long enough for nothing to surprise me,' added Toshack. 'If there is something that I failed in it was to not have brought in more players from the youth team. Now I am going to have a rest and consider my future. The decision to put faith in Olabe is brave, but I hope it will prove to be a good one.'

It remains to be seen whether this represents the final act of a dramatic – and nomadic – footballing career. Somehow, that seems unlikely . . .

John Toshack Factfile

TIMELINE

1949   22 March, John Benjamin Toshack born in Cardiff

1965   July, joins Cardiff City as apprentice
November, makes Football League debut aged 16

1969   March, earns first Wales cap vs West Germany

1970   November, signs for Liverpool for £110,000

1971   August, start of Keegan–Toshack striking partnership

1973   May, rainstorm earns victorious UEFA Cup final reprieve

1974   November, proposed £160,000 move to Leicester breaks down over injury

1976   May, named in PFA Division One team of the season
December, publication of poetry anthology *Gosh It's Tosh*

1977   November, final game for Liverpool vs Bristol City

1978   February, arrives at Swansea City as player-manager

1979   May, second promotion in two seasons as Swansea reach Division Two
October, final Wales cap also vs West Germany

1981   May, guides Swansea to top flight for first time in their history
October, Swansea top the league, eventually finishing sixth

1983   October, resigns as Swansea manager, briefly returning after Christmas

1985   June, joins Real Sociedad as manager for first time

1988   June, Real Sociedad finish second in *La Liga*

1990 May, guides Real Madrid to *La Liga* scoring record with 107 goals

1991 February, turns down Liverpool in favour of Real Sociedad

1994 February–March, manages Wales for one disastrous match against Norway

1997 February, resigns after unpopular stint as Deportivo La Coruna manager

June, joins Besiktas as manager, again turning down Liverpool

1999 February, returns for second spell at crisis-hit Real Madrid

2001 January, leaves St Etienne to steer Real Sociedad away from relegation

December, celebrates 450th match as sixth longest-serving coach in *La Liga*

PLAYING CAREER
Football League games and goals

1965–70	Cardiff City	162 games	75 goals
1970–78	Liverpool	172 games	74 goals
1978–83	Swansea City	58 games	24 goals

International games and goals

1969–79	Wales	40 games	13 goals

John Toshack is seventh in the list of all-time Welsh international goal-scorers

Honours
- with Cardiff City
  Welsh Cup 1968, 1969, 1970
- with Liverpool
  League championship 1973, 1976, 1977
  FA Cup 1974
  UEFA Cup 1973, 1976

MANAGERIAL CAREER

1978–84	Swansea City
1984–85	Sporting Lisbon
1985–89	Real Sociedad

1989–90	Real Madrid
1991–94	Real Sociedad
1994	Wales
1995–97	Deportivo La Coruna
1997–99	Besiktas
1999	Real Madrid
2000–01	St Etienne
2001–	Real Sociedad

Honours
- with Swansea City
  Welsh Cup winners 1981, 1982, 1983

- with Real Sociedad
  Copa Del Rey winners 1987

- with Real Madrid
  La Liga champions 1990

- with Besiktas
  Turkish Cup 1998, President's Cup 1998

Bibliography

BOOKS

Aldridge, John with Hyder Jawad, *My Story* (Hodder & Stoughton, 1999)

Ball, Phil, *Morbo* (WSC, 2001)

Barrett, Norman *The Daily Telegraph Football Chronicle* (Carlton, 1999)

Barwick, Brian and Gerald Sinstadt, *The Great Derbies Everton vs Liverpool* (BBC, 1988)

Cresswell, Peterjon and Simon Evans, *European Football: A Fan's Handbook* (Rough Guides, 1999)

Farmer, David, *Swansea City 1912–1982* (Pelham, 1982)

Grandin, Terry, *Red Dragons in Europe* (Desert Island, 1999)

Hansen, Alan, *A Matter of Opinion* (Partridge, 1999)

Heatley, Michael and Ian Welch, *The Great Derby Matches Liverpool vs Everton* (Dial House, 1996)

Hugman, Barry, *The PFA Premier and Football League Players Records* (Queen Anne Press, 1999)

Keegan, Kevin, *My Autobiography* (Warner, 1997)

Keith, John, *Liverpool, Champions of Europe: The Players' Official Story* (Duckworth/ Elmwood, 1977)

Keith, John, *Bob Paisley Manager of the Millennium* (Robson, 1999)

Kelly, Stephen F., *The Kop* (Mandarin, 1993)

Kelly, Stephen F., *It's Much More Important than That* (Virgin, 1996)

Kelly, Stephen F., *Boot Room Boys* (CollinsWillow, 1999)

Lees, Dr Andrew and Ray Kennedy,*Ray of Hope: The Ray Kennedy Story* (Pelham, 1993)

Liversedge, Stan, *Liverpool from the Inside* (Mainstream, 1995)

Nawrat, Chris and Steve Hutchings, *Sunday Times Illustrated History of Football* (Hamlyn, 1998)

Paisley, Bob, *Bob Paisley's Liverpool Scrapbook* (Souvenir Press, 1979)

Pead, Brian, *Liverpool: A Complete Record* (Breedon, 1986)

Ponting, Ivan, *Liverpool: Player by Player* (Crowood, 1990)

Richards, Huw, *We're Talking Tosh from Offside* (Andy Lyons (ed.), WSC, 1989)

Richards, Huw, 'The Gospel According to St John the Alchemist.' In Nick Hornby (ed.), *My Favourite Year* (WSC/Victor Gollancz, 1993)

Richards, Huw, and Peter Stead (ed.), *For Club and Country* (University of Wales Press, 2000)

Robson, Bobby, *My Autobiography* (Pan, 1997)

Shankly, Bill, *Shankly* (Mayflower, 1976)

Smith, Tommy, *Over the Top: My Anfield Secrets* (Breedon, 1998)

Toshack, John, *The Tosh Annual* (Duckworth, 1977)

Toshack, John, *Tosh* (Arthur Barker, 1982)

UEFA, *Champions League 1999/2000* (UEFA, 1999)

Walmsley, David, *Liverpool's Greatest Players* (Headline, 1996)

NEWSPAPERS AND MAGAZINES

Daily Telegraph
Financial Times
Four Four Two
Goal
Liverpool Echo
90 Minutes
Sunday Times
The Times
Total Football
The Western Mail
When Saturday Comes
World Soccer

WEBSITES

BBC Online
Guardian Unlimited
Onefootball
rsssf.com
Red Passion
Swansea City Mad
Swansea Till I Die

VIDEOS

Keegan on Keegan
(Watershed 1992)

Index